LATIN AMERICA
IN THE TIME OF CHOLERA

LATIN AMERICA
IN THE TIME OF
CHOLERA

ELECTORAL POLITICS, MARKET ECONOMICS, AND PERMANENT CRISIS

JAMES PETRAS
AND
MORRIS MORLEY

ROUTLEDGE
NEW YORK LONDON

Published in 1992 by

Routledge
An imprint of Routledge, Chapman and Hall, Inc.
29 West 35 Street
New York, NY 10001

Published in Great Britain by

Routledge
11 New Fetter Lane
London EC4P 4EE

Library of Congress Cataloging in Publication Data

Petras, James F., 1937–
    Latin America in the time of cholera : electoral politics, market
economics, and permanent crisis / James Petras, Morris Morley.
        p. cm.
    Includes bibliographical references and index.
    ISBN 0-415-90535-4 (hb.)—ISBN 0-415-90536-2 (pb.)
    1. Latin America—Politics and government—1980–   2. Latin
America—Social conditions. 3. Latin America—Economic
conditions—1982–   4. Latin America—Relations—United States.
5. United States—Relations—Latin America.   I. Morley, Morris H.
II. Title.
F1414.2P398   1982
320.98—dc20
                                                       92-7212
                                                          CIP

British Library Cataloguing in Publication Data

Petras, James
    Latin America in the Time of Cholera:
    Electoral Politics, Market Economics and
    Permanent Crisis
    I. Title   II. Morley, Morris H.
    980

    ISBN 0-415-90535-4 (HB)
    ISBN 0-415-90536-2 (PB)

Contents

Introduction

The essays in this book are anchored in a theoretical and analytical perspective that postulates the centrality of class as the point of departure for an analysis of the emergence and decay of Latin American electoral regimes during the 1980s and 1990s. Class analysis, located in a world-historical perspective, examines the electoral regimes in relation to the institutional and economic continuities with the previous military regimes and in relation to civic society and the sociopolitical movements derived from the electoral regimes. It studies the interrelationship between political, economic, and social processes (and structures) in Latin America and the region's relations with the United States.

Derived from this critical analysis of the civil-electoral regimes is the need to construct a democratic socialist alternative in the face of resurgent authoritarianism, growing imperial domination, and deteriorating socioeconomic conditions for the growing mass of working people. Two serious challenges confront any effort to build a democratic socialist alternative: One stems from the peculiar concentration of economic power in the hands of a domestic Latin American transnational capitalist class that invests its capital overseas, thereby blocking national regulation; the other derives from the postcapitalist experience, in which power and control are vested in a bureaucratic stratum that inhibits the development of democratic collectivism. These essays are thus analytical and prescriptive: They not only describe existing political and economic development but also provide a basis for changing it.

Several key conceptual distinctions are central to the theoretical postulates that underlie the class-analysis-in-world-historical-perspective method. The first distinction is between state and regime. The state includes the permanent political institutions of society: the military, the judiciary, the civil bureaucracy, the top officials in the central bank, etc. Moreover, these permanent political institutions are integrated with the system of class rulership; together, they form "the state." State formation is the product of historical developments that are rooted in the conflicts and growth of a particular social formation. Regimes, on the other hand, are composed of the transitory officials who occupy the executive and legislative branches and who usually devise policies within the parameters of the state and interests of the dominant classes. When regimes differ substantially from states, a crisis emerges—which is usually resolved by the overthrow of the regime by the state. This distinction between regime and state is crucial to understanding (1) the limits of Latin American political change in the 1980s, (2) the continuities of socioeconomic policy embraced by the civil-electoral regimes, and (3) the willingness of the United States to tolerate or even promote regime changes ("democratization") that preserve the (authoritarian) state that represents and defends imperial interests.

The second conceptual distinction is based on our notion of imperialism as a political/economic phenomenon and not merely as an economic mechanism for extracting surplus. Imperialism is analyzed in its two dimensions: expanding capital and the imperial state. The inclusion of the imperial state and our efforts to supply a theory of it are central to our understanding the multiple levels of U.S. penetration of Latin American society. This penetration has military and economic components. For example, the significance of U.S. intervention in Panama and Nicaragua revolves around the ability of the military power of the imperial state to defeat its Latin American adversaries. But the United States has not been able to finance economically viable client regimes—a failure of the economic component. The contradictions of imperialism can best be understood by examining the uneven development of the military/ideological and economic elements of the imperial state.

The third conceptual distinction that informs our analysis is the "internationalization" of the class structure. By this, we mean that specific segments of the Latin American ruling class occupy multiple sites—located in different social formations—from which they organize their economic and political activities. The multiple location of what we call the *Latin American transnational capitalist class* introduces a new dimension to efforts to develop Latin America. Efforts by electoral regimes to formulate reformist policies "subordinating" capital to nationalist/populist programs have led to failures and are no longer viable: The transnational capitalists touch a button and their funds are relocated in Geneva, Miami, Panama, or London. The problems of debt payments that burden Latin America's electoral regimes are not seen as merely "external" impositions of foreign bankers or the International Monetary Fund (IMF) but rather as a function of the ascendancy of this new segment of the capitalist class and of their influence within the civilian electoral regimes.

The fourth conceptual distinction involves the importance of identifying the specificity of the ideological in understanding political change. Political conflicts and their resolution are not a direct reflection of economic crisis or even of class struggle. Rather, they are mediated through political organizations and ideological programs. Thus, the blockage of radical changes is a product of structural conditions and the type and kind of ideological interventions. The essay on intellectuals (chapter 7) is based on the notion that ideological struggle is both a cause and consequence of the failure of electoral regimes.

The fifth conceptual distinction involves a critical analysis of the socialist alternative—Cuba. It focuses on the contradiction between collectivist ownership and bureaucratic control in shaping the appeals of Cuban socialism and their limitations as an alternative for Latin America. The distinction between control and ownership is central to the elaboration of a democratic socialist alternative: Collective ownership without democratic control generates the errors and abuses to which the current rectification campaign is directed.

The sixth conceptual distinction centers on the political organization and social agency for revolution or radical reforms. Dogmatic Marxists prioritized political parties and industrial workers, basing their analysis on non–Latin American experiences. Yet the two major hemispheric revolutions in the second half of the twentieth century, those of Cuba and Nicaragua, involved sociopolitical movements reflecting heterogeneous working populations. The movement/party and a broadly conceived notion of working classes are central to our analysis of the agencies of sociopolitical change in Latin America.

Our last conceptual notion focuses on the relevance of historical endogenous experiences of popular power as models for social transformation over and against imitations of external experiences: the advantages of endogenous experiences and "micromodels" of democratic collectivism are evident. The cultural traditions and political practices are much more immediate and relevant to contemporary political action than political experience extrapolated from different historical and cultural contexts. This is not to deny the heuristic value of other regions of the world; rather, given the collapse of the bureaucratic collectivist regimes in the East and rise of neoliberalism, Latin America has more to learn from its own experiences of democratic collectivism in Indian communities, from the popular assemblies of the trade unions, from the reciprocity of the urban barrios. Turning inward to recover the high points of democratic collective experience is a precondition for a reinsertion in the world economy. This is a tragic lesson that the civilian electoral regimes failed to take account of and which the new emerging democratic movements have learned.

The Crisis of Electoral Politics

1

Latin America: Poverty of Democracy and the Democracy of Poverty

Introduction

Over the past decade, liberal capitalist experiments have plunged Latin America into its deepest crisis this century—one that shows no signs of abating. Deregulated economies (free markets, "open-door" investment policies, privatization) have been synonymous with unprecedented social polarization, downward mobility and plummeting living standards for millions of people, the spectacular growth of non–wage/salaried ("casual") labor (over eighty percent of the region's work force), and multibillion-dollar fortunes obtained by "insiders" working the international financial trade circuits who have access to the public treasury. The 1980s also witnessed massive pillage of the economy (by foreign and local investors and bankers) and the state (by elected politicians and nonelected officials), leaving regimes bankrupt and providing the pretext for new and harsher forms of class-biased austerity programs.

Despite campaign promises and rhetoric, the electoral regimes that took power during this period not only failed to solve the most elementary socioeconomic needs of their populations but also failed to democratize their political systems or to even provide the minimum security necessary for the maintenance of everyday life. Instead of more democratic policy-making processes, electoral systems have become more nonrepresentative, more divorced from popular needs. Authoritarianism is on the rise everywhere and repression has become a routine feature of civilian rule.

The political response to the collapse of liberal capitalism and the deterioration of party-electoral regimes has not been uniform. Reflecting the volatility of the electorate, conventional alternatives as well as new movements and personalities have surfaced. Past political identities no longer have relevance in the wake of sharp political realignments, largely involving shifts by parties and their leaders formerly identified as center-left social democrats to the neoliberal, center-right, and beyond. At the same time, this "turncoat" phenomenon is not tantamount to a broad rightist shift among the electorate. The presidential elections in Mexico

7

(1988) and Brazil (1989) revealed massive popular support for the leftist candidates. In Brazil, Lula and the Workers' party secured an historic forty-seven percent (approximately thirty-one million) of the vote; in Mexico, Cuauhtémoc Cárdenas actually won the election only to have it stolen through Institutional Revolutionary Party (PRI) fraud. This countertrend to the continent's "right-turn" has expressed itself through both electoral and nonelectoral forms and is capable of escalating into massive confrontations if coherent and organized political movements emerge.

Except for a tiny group of overseas-funded intellectuals, the demise of Eastern Europe's collectivist regimes has created no positive groundswell in favor of liberal capitalism. The daily devastation wrought by the "free market" has had a much more decisive impact on political and economic outlooks than the pro-Western, procapitalist rhetoric emanating from Moscow and other bloc capitols. More than ever, the vast majority of Latin Americans seek to create national economies that provide secure employment, a social safety net, an equitable income system, and efficient, democratically controlled public enterprises. The market has long since lost its mystique for the urban poor in Kingston, Lima, and Caracas, the industrial working class in São Paulo, Buenos Aires, and Santiago, and for social movements throughout the region.

The failure of this latest cycle of electoralist politics and its market-driven economic programs to improve the existence of the Latin American masses was most poignantly and accurately captured in the words of a worker in the southern Brazilian state of Parana at the time of the national congressional elections in late 1990. Arriving at the ballot booth, he handed back his voting card, stating, "I hereby renounce this supposed right, which is incapable of staving off my hunger."[1]

The Failure of the Electoral Regimes to Democratize the Political System

The transition from military to civilian electoral regimes was prematurely dubbed a "redemocratization" process. Yet the political shifts in Peru, Argentina, Brazil, Guatemala, Uruguay, Chile, and elsewhere only affected a change in regimes; they were not accompanied by any diminution in the power, prerogatives, and status of the more basic state institutions such as the armed forces and secret police, the intelligence agencies, the judiciary, the civil service, and the central banks. What immediately became apparent was that while the military had surrendered formal power to the civilians, it still retained a substantial "veto" power over the "redemocratization" process. In Chile, for instance, former dictator General Augusto Pinochet enacted an amnesty law forbidding prosecution of military officials for human rights' abuses, stacked the Supreme Court with promilitary judges, and created an autonomous central bank, personally choosing its members, before handing over power to the elected politicians. Furthermore, Pinochet retains his position as head of the army, and the Aylwin government lacks the authority to remove him or any of the other top military commanders from their posts. One of the civilian regime's first acts was to "dissolve" the National Information Agency (CNI), only to have the personnel and files of this secret police organization reincorporated into the Pinochet-commanded armed forces. Likewise, in Brazil the generals retain a powerful presence within the political arena by dint of their success in getting a clause placed in the new constitution that defines the armed forces as the "defenders against foreign and domestic threats."

Perhaps the most striking illustration of democratic regimes as "hostages" to military power is the lamentable effort on the part of the newly elected officials to bring military officials to trial for crimes (killings, torture, kidnappings, etc.) against civilian populations. Fearful of the armed forces' likely reactions, they prefer to formulate and justify policies on the basis of possible responses by these nonelected authoritarians. The Argentine governments of Raul Alfonsin (1983–1989) and Carlos Menem (1989–) have probably gone furthest in this direction.

In December 1986, Alfonsin introduced a "punto final" law which sought to limit prosecutions of military officers by allowing only sixty days for new charges to be filed. After dissatisfied lower-ranking army officers staged a revolt in April 1987, an intimidated regime enacted a "due obedience" law which absolved all those under the rank of colonel from any crimes against civilians because they were only following what they believed to be lawful orders. This measure pardoned most of those directly responsible for the thousands of deaths resulting from the so-called "Dirty War" of 1976–1983. Since Carlos Menem's election, this process of accommodation and capitulation to the armed forces has continued apace. In October 1989, he pardoned 280 officers and soldiers found guilty of human rights' violations during the Dirty War. In March 1990, to combat daily strikes by workers demanding higher wages and a halt to declining living standards, and to bring to an end increasingly routine supermarket sackings by impoverished slum dwellers, Menem granted restless armed forces permission to act promptly to subdue major civil protests—i.e., he authorized police powers to repress democratic protests; that same month, he granted military officers wage increases of almost 100 percent and put into effect a $300 million increase in the military budget.[2] As his approval rate plummeted from eighty percent at the beginning of his presidency in mid-1989 to seventeen percent in March 1990, the frequency of secret meetings between Menem and the army high command increased.[3] In early October, the steady retreat from prosecution and punishment of those responsible for the Dirty War atrocities continued when Menem announced that he intended to pardon the remaining seven senior junta members, including former presidents Jorge Rafael Videla and Roberto Viola, who had been condemned to life imprisonment by the Argentine Supreme Court in 1986—despite polls showing that more than seventy percent of the population opposed such a move.[4]

The parameters of the new electoral politics are, in a profound sense, being shaped by nonelected forces largely derived from the previous authoritarian political systems. Except for the trial and conviction of the seven Argentine generals who President Menem has now promised to release, no civilian government has fulfilled its human rights' promises to the electorate: to bring the full force of the law to bear on the military mass murderers of civilian noncombatants. On the contrary, the elected rulers have attempted to ingratiate themselves with the generals and admirals, offering promotions and perks and partaking of frequent consultations, lunches, and ceremonial occasions. Symbolic gestures to the victims, such as investigations of the deaths and the uncovering of mass graves, are accompanied by insistence on "reconciliation"—amnesty for the executioners and forgetfulness for the victims. Worse still, Chile's new government not only pays homage to the Pinochet military leadership but refuses to release approximately 300 political prisoners jailed during the antidictatorial struggle.[5] The electoral regimes function with a dual legal system that punishes ordinary citizens and exonerates state officials involved in the most heinous capital crimes.

At the same time as elected regimes have elaborated policies within parameters laid down by the coercive apparatus of the "old" state they have also engaged in major efforts to dismantle, displace, co-opt, and even repress the autonomous social movements that offered the most formidable opposition to the military regimes. A continuation of autonomous popular-movement activity is frequently described by government officials as a "danger to democracy" or a destabilizing force, and is sometimes accompanied by efforts to amalgamate attempts to democratize policy-making with military conspiracies to overthrow the civilian regime—an approach described as the "theory of the double demons." Following the December 1989 presidential election in Chile, for example, the politics of movement disarticulation moved into high gear: local party functionaries pressured the leaders of the anti-Pinochet mass social movement not to engage in any activity outside of the state framework (acuerdo-marco) for fear of endangering the fledgling democracy and provoking the military to reenter politics. As party machines seek to actively neutralize movement activity and narrow political options, the scope of the political discourse, political action, and policy choices is considerably narrowed. The electoral regimes have become not the vehicle for redemocratization but essentially go-betweens transferring the political constraints from the authoritarian state to the population at large.

What the above reveals is that the only manner in which the Latin American political transitions of the 1980s can be described as a redemocratization process is by ignoring the authoritarian parameters, institutional continuities (as well as the substantive socio-economic referents of policy); and the spillover effects of generalized fear throughout the political culture, and simply focusing on the electoral procedures and short-term decision-making processes.

The failure of the electoral regimes to democratize the state and make it responsible to the interests of nationally anchored groups is directly related to another fundamental feature of the transition—the inability of the civilian rulers to stem the growing remilitarization of political life. In Peru, the García presidency (1985–1990) initially promised to reverse the Belaunde "unleashing" of the armed forces in the war against the Sendero Luminoso (Shining Path) and to investigate military human rights' abuses. Instead, after limited efforts to assert some control over the military, García sanctioned an expanded role in the war against the rural insurgents—accompanied by a declining interest in controlling abuses perpetrated against the noncombatant population. In early 1989, the government accorded sweeping powers to the military by declaring states of emergency in thirty-six provinces, including Lima, which placed almost forty percent of the population under the authority of the armed forces. The civilian death toll resulting from the Belaúnde-García military "pacification" program exceeded 15,000. In Brazil, the country's first elected president in two decades, José Sarney (1985–1990), spent more time consulting the military chiefs about public policy than the elected parliamentarians. Today, local grass-roots organisations are subject to constant repression by the armed forces, the police, and rightist paramilitary groups. In Argentina, presidents Alfonsín and Menem have allowed the military and intelligence agencies to reassume their traditional responsibility for "public security." In Chile, the Aylwin government has made no effort to curtail the autonomy of the armed forces or the police (carabineros). Not surprisingly, reports of possible military coups have resurfaced with greater frequency as civilian regimes turn to the coercive forces of the previous military dictatorships to cope with unresolved political and socioeconomic crises.

Of equal significance, the neoliberal electoral regimes have employed the armed forces as a basic policy instrument in attempts to privatize economies and enforce class-selective austerity payments to overseas bankers and local transnational capitalists. In Venezuela, President Carlos Andres Perez directed the armed forces to put down demonstrations in nine major cities in February 1989, occasioned by the signing of a $4.6 billion loan package with the IMF which obligated the government to enact a series of austerity measures including the removal of food and other basic consumer subsidies. Approximately 300 strikers were killed and more than 2,000 injured.

Without doubt, the most baleful outcome of the "redemocratization" process has been the willingness of the electoral regimes to legitimate the military and forgive and forget its past crimes against society. Ignoring the international, as well as local, condemnations of the region's generals who authorized the killings, torture, and disappearance of tens of thousands of civilians, the new "democratic" rulers undertook major efforts to refurbish the image and role of their military forces. Most have publicly praised their national, patriotic role, even as discoveries of their victims in mass graves are announced on the same day. The most recent example of this bizarre juxtaposition of official praise amid the discovery of graves occurred in Chile in July 1990 and was comprehensively reported in both the pro-Pinochet daily *El Mercurio* and the center-left *Fortín Mapocho*. The policies and practices of the electoral regimes, much more than mere pressure from the military, have once again created strategic imbalances between civilian and military power. Last, but by no means least, the resurgence of the armed forces as the major arbiter of politics has been further strengthened by agreements between Washington and Latin American civilian presidents to expand the number of U.S. military bases in the hemisphere as part of the so-called antidrug war. During 1988 and 1989, the U.S. Army's Special Forces (Green Berets), specially trained Drug Enforcement Agents, and Pentagon military-supply specialists were assigned to work with the armed forces and/or police in Bolivia, Peru, Guatemala, and Costa Rica. Following an April 1990 Bush administration decision to authorize a $35 million military assistance program for Peru (up from $1.5 million in 1989) to expand the drug war by improving the military's counterinsurgency skills in the struggle against the Sendero Luminoso, the Garcia government gave the go-ahead for a U.S. military training base to be established in the Upper Huallaga Valley—the guerrillas' stronghold, where more than fifty percent of the world's supply of coca leaf is grown.[6]

The failure of electoral regimes to consolidate democracy in Latin America is as much a structural as a policy problem insofar as it flows from a series of ideological, institutional, and socioeconomic concessions, as well as political agreements, that weakened the authority of the democratic electoral and social movements while simultaneously legitimating and institutionalizing the most authoritarian forces in society. In this setting, the neoliberal socioeconomic policies pursued by the electoral regimes were both cause and consequences of the emerging economic crisis and of the subsequent deepening social polarization and political deterioration.

The Failure of the Electoral Regimes to Arrest the Process of Economic Disintegration

If the transition from military to civilian rule was unaccompanied by changes in the structure and composition of pre-existing state institutions, it also resulted in little or no change in the neoliberal socioeconomic models constructed by the former dictatorial regimes. On the contrary, most elected governments combined a deepening of the processes of privatization and liberalization with new constraints on wage and salary earners. In Argentina, even the most extreme free-marketeer general balked at selling off or opening up to private participation virtually every enterprise in the state sector. Yet this is precisely what President Menem is currently seeking to achieve. Dramatically speeding up a process initiated by his civilian predecessor, Raul Alfonsín, Menem has signed privatization decrees affecting the oil fields, petrochemical companies, communication sectors, water supply, electricity, coal, postal and telegraphic services, and port authority. In Brazil, within a month of his inauguration as president (March 1990), Fernando Collor outlined an economic strategy that included plans to privatize 188 state-owned industries. Since then, he has been systematically placing government-owned corporations on the auction block. To facilitate his destruction of the public sector, he has already withdrawn practically all the barriers that protect the national market and the new high-technology industries. In Uruguay, the country's elected leader, Luis Alberto Lacalle, has implemented measures aimed at privatizing the fishing industry, the national airline, alcohol production, insurance sales, and port and telecommunications services. In Peru, the new civilian head of state, Alberto Fujimori, has announced a program to sell off the petroleum, mining, and metal-refining enterprises, which account for most of the country's industrial output.

During the decade of ascendant "democracy," Latin America's per-capita gross domestic product (GDP) fell by more than eight percent: Some countries (Argentina, Peru, Venezuela, Bolivia) experienced declines of around twenty-four to twenty-six percent.[7] The only notable exception to this continental downturn was socialist Cuba, whose economy (GDP) grew by 31.6 percent on a per-capita basis while gross social product (GSP) registered an impressive 44.2 percent increase.[8] Calamatous as the aggregate figures undoubtedly are, they obscure the even-more-profound income losses that occurred over the 1980s. Minimum urban salaries (earned by over half the region's labor force) fell by seventy-four percent in Peru, fifty-eight percent in Ecuador, fifty percent in Mexico, thirty percent in Brazil, and twenty-one percent in Chile.[9] Workers throughout the region now scramble to three, four, and five jobs just to be able to afford the cost of a basic-necessities' diet. In the 1980s, Brazil witnesses a steadily increasing concentration of wealth and income in the hands of the top five percent; the purchasing power of the fifty percent of the population receiving the minimum wage is currently at a historic low.[10] In Argentina, which until recently had the highest beef consumption on a per-capita basis, unemployed workers knocking on doors demanding to be fed have become a common sight. Between September 1989 and September 1990, real wages in the country's state companies plummeted by an astounding forty-nine percent—accompanied by job losses that exceeded one million in the industrial sector alone.[11] In Fujimori's Peru, real wages hover around 1972 levels.[12]

While the income gap between rich and poor has widened, social-sector spending has declined by more than fifty percent over the past decade. Simultaneously, individual sectors (especially health, education, transport, housing, and recreation) and their classes have become more and more "insulated" from one another. In Argentina today, for instance, the wealthy pay the equivalent of a schoolteacher's annual salary for three months of private health coverage while the state-run women's psychiatric hospital reports (July 1990) the death of thirty patients from malnutrition. Doctors, nurses, and medical aides simply lack sufficient drugs and equipment to cope. This is a problem throughout Latin America and affects almost half the population in some countries.

Inevitably, those least able to look after themselves have suffered most at the hands of the economic deregulators. Mortality rates, childbirth deaths, and child malnutrition have risen significantly in recent years in countries like Argentina, Brazil, Peru, and Mexico.[13] In "redemocratized" El Salvador, infant mortality rates surged during the 1980s because of deteriorating basic services—in particular, access to safe drinking water declined. By 1988, nine out of every ten peasants were being denied this fundamental right.[14] In 1990, according to the United Nations Economic Commission for Latin America (ECLA), approximately forty-four percent of the continent's population (183 million) were living below the poverty line—an increase of 112 million over 1970. Almost half of this group (eighty-eight million) were characterized as destitute or living in extreme poverty. The ECLA attributed this growing immiseration to the dramatic and regressive fall in average income, which "marked a tremendous step backwards in the material standard of living of the Latin American and Caribbean population" during the 1980s.[15]

This era of plummeting wages, chronically deteriorating living standards, and negative growth rates was directly linked to governmental policies that facilitated massive transfers of capital abroad. Between 1982 and 1989, multinational corporations and banks feasted: profit remittances and interest payments over this nine-year period totalled an astronomical $281.5 billion. Deducting new loans and investments, Latin America still remained a net exporter of capital to the tune of $200 billion.[16] The logic of the socioeconomic model pushed by the electoral regimes—freeing capital (local and foreign) and contracting the public sector—dictated this outcome (which promises to continue) because it obliged them to maintain the international circuits, meaning paying the debt; once that was decided, they had no choice but to promote the export elites at the expense of local producers and wage and salaried groups. The pillage of the economy was inextricably linked to the impoverishment and polarization of society.

The most profound subjective consequence of these economic changes has been the accelerated proletarianization of the professional and middle classes, especially those in the public sectors tied to salaried income. Equally striking has been the deproletarianization of the industrial wage-labor force: under- and unemployment are running at historically unprecedented levels (seventy percent in Lima, over fifty percent in Caracas, twenty percent in Buenos Aires, etc.); temporary and casual labor, not covered by social legislation, minimum wage rates, or safety conditions in the workplace, have become the norm. The electoral regimes of the 1980s may have granted more legal rights to trade unions but their socioeconomic policies have simultaneously emptied the unions and factories of their working members. Indeed, they have presided over the reversion of many major gains achieved through half a century of class and political struggle.

Almost as striking as the socioeconomic failures has been the absence of any public morality. Everywhere political theft of public property has reached monumental levels. In Peru, Alan García's regime has been accused of stealing at least several-hundred-million dollars—leaving the treasury with a negative balance. In Venezuela the Democratic Action regime of ex-President Jaime

Luschini (1983–1988) has at least a dozen former ministers under indictment for stealing billions in oil money—most of whom have fled the country. In Brazil the Sarney regime was universally despised for its massive appropriation of millions of dollars in state revenues for private entertainment and for depositing hundreds of millions, if not billions, in overseas accounts. In Argentina, President Menem's brother, and head of the Senate, had accumulated over a million dollars in a Uruguayan account within three months of taking office. In Chile, the Aylwin government is not expected to energetically pursue the massive fraudulent multimillion-dollar sell-off of state enterprises to cronies of Pinochet in the last days of the dictatorship. Wholesale venality (a vast scope and scale of corruption) by the neoliberal electoral regimes is their practical interpretation of unregulated capitalism—the free market. The scale of public pillage can also be explained by the drying up of private opportunities for enrichment. With the banks taking the bulk share and the established export elites untouchable, the public firms being sold off to the private sector and the public treasury remain as the two last areas for private accumulation by the electoralists. No doubt the new market ethos that encourages this behavior as the ultimate value is no small factor in easing the conscience of hesitant officials.

Privatization has taken on special meaning under the electoral regimes—in the double sense of a shift from public to private ownership and in the practice by high government officials of appropriating (directly or through family or business ties) public resources. The scope and depth of political corruption in the new era of deregulation, privatization and internationalization of capital have been well publicized in the cases of Venezuela, Brazil, Argentina and Peru—where officials literally utilized state budgets to grossly expand overseas accounts, to appropriate resources destined for public enterprises, and to run down those public properties and sell off the firms to private associates.

As a result, many of the deficits of public enterprises are not due to the inherent inefficiencies of the public firms but are in part the result of private appropriations and corrupt subcontracting. (By contrast, in Uruguay, the recently elected Socialist government of Montevideo was able to increase income from the city's casinos by 300 percent in six months, largely, it is assumed, to honest administration.) The private pillage of public enterprises become a pretext for further privatization: state corruption is linked at both ends of the privatization process fostered by the electoral regimes. The result is an economy that revolves around a kind of "primitive accumulation" in which political officials establish their initial wealth through public pillage and later convert their wealth into capital in the newly privatized sectors.

The electoral regimes have fashioned economic strategies based on the free market that have led neither to a more equitable distribution of wealth in society nor to a bridging of the income gap between the export elites and the wage and salaried groups. Moreover, they have created a highly rigid dual economy: a private sector linked to the international circuits drawing on overseas financial resources and the pillage of the state, and another sector dependent on a shrinking internal market, linked to declining wages, deteriorating state services, and a lack of job opportunities.

Electoral Regimes and the Class Structure

The peculiarity of electoral regimes and their leaders is that while often the products of class struggle, they are quick to deny its relevance once in power. In opposition, the electoralists address the class configurations of nondemocratic regimes; in office, they downplay the links between state and class in favor of a perspective that emphasizes the distinctiveness, separateness, and autonomy of each sphere. This ideological shift accompanying the political transition has been particularly acute among the Latin American intellectual classes, whose members have often been deeply involved in rationalizing, or formally participating in, the new regimes. Nonetheless, the latter have had a significant effect on class structures and, in turn, been deeply influenced by specific configurations of class power.

There are several striking patterns that are common to most of the new (and old) civilian governments of the 1980s. First is the almost total absence of populist policies and redistributive politics. Whatever coalitions of labor, middle class, and business groups exist before the presidential vote, they have no impact on subsequent policy and quickly break up in rancorous conflicts. Second, traditional ideological discourses and historical practices have less relevance in defining the policies of the new electoral regimes than have contemporary configurations of power within which the regimes are inserted. A clear example is the Peronist regime in Argentina. Menem's policies favor overseas bankers and private exporters at the expense of local producers and wage workers, directly repudiating past practices and ignoring trade union claims of "betrayal." Menem is responding to the ascendancy of Argentine transnational capitalists, overseas investors, and local exporters, the power configuration inherited from the previous Alfonsín and military regimes. Third, electoral regimes have not been oriented toward transforming the class system or even ameliorating class inequalities, but rather strengthen and consolidate the power at the top, as the only classes capable of developing the economy.

Briefly put, the electoral regimes are increasing international mobility for the twenty percent at the top while causing downward mobility for the wage and salaried groups tied to the stagnant economy. In fact, the ability of the outwardly oriented classes to appropriate surplus from the inwardly bound classes is a condition for greater international mobility. These conflicting but interrelated mobility patterns are mediated by the neoliberal state and electoral regime: while the state extracts and transfers surplus from wage/salaried classes to the local and

overseas transnationals, the electoral regime legitimizes the process by evoking the democratic liturgy.

The major class configurations and class relations are not always the result of the electoral regimes, most of which emerged during the military regime. The policies of the electoral regimes have done a great deal to reinforce the preexisting tendencies in the class structure.

Several features of the contemporary class structure require special attention. First is the predominance of a class of Latin American transnational capitalists (TNCs) as the major force throughout the continent. The TNCs are defined not by whether they are involved in production, nor by the location of their productive activity, but by their access and involvement in international markets, which ties them to international capital flows. The ascendancy of TNCs is matched by the marginalization of important sectors of the working class: the massification of unemployment and of poorly paid, underemployed, self-employed, seasonal, and temporary workers—lacking any of the traditional social-security benefits. The polarization between a cohesive self-conscious TNC class at the top and a disartic-ulated mass of workers at the bottom has had a very dramatic impact on the professional and salaried middle classes: a minority has been able to insert itself into the private networks (ideologues, accountants, lawyers, doctors), while the great majority have suffered severe downward mobility. The downwardly mobile professionals have attempted to cope by turning to multiple employment, and increasingly overseas immigration, as well as to direct action protests.

The electoral regimes, however, have also institutionalized another set of social actors who reinforce this class system—the international lending agencies, which act as representatives for overseas lenders and investors. In tandem with local TNCs and the technocratic elite of the electoral regimes, these 'external' class actors have played a major role in defining the patterns of class formation, determining which classes gain or lose income and which classes rise and fall in the class system. Hence, the electoral regimes are not merely products of internal class forces, but active agents promoting the convergence of interest between externally based, but locally involved, propertied classes.

The dynamics of this class system have been manifold—making and unmaking segments of classes and diluting the specificities of each class and unit of class. One major development is the growth of a lumpen proletariat, a spin-off from the disarticulated working class and impoverished self-employed. Throughout the region, and particularly in the large urban cities, crime rates are growing at unprecedented levels which the United Nations Economic Commission for Latin America attributes directly to "the marked deterioration in the standard of living of broad sections of the Latin American population. . . ."[17] In countries like Brazil and Argentina, security firms have become multibillion-dollar enterprises. Another development has seen the working-class household unit become the basis for a new gender realignment of political influence. As unemployment has hit male household heads the hardest, and as the negative sociopsychological effects have apparently been most strongly felt in that quarter, women and young people have become more prominent in defining class positions in social movements and in spontaneous protests in neighborhood arenas.

The dual developments of working-class disarticulation and deepening social polarization usually mean that the traditional political controls exercised by the electoral party machines and bureaucratized trade unions cease to be effective. Mass spontaneous protests, sacking of stores, street mobilizations, and unauthorized strikes begin to merge as the class identity of the electoral regimes becomes transparent. Whether the polarized class structure will find expression in polar-opposite political movements is a question of contingency and political intervention. What is clear, however, is that the electoral regimes and the dominant component parties that comprise them have not established hegemony over society. Their one-sided representation of the "externally oriented classes" and the "downward push" on the rest of the subaltern classes preclude it. Nonetheless, the distance between a deteriorating hegemonic political class and an overt political rupture is still vast and involves numerous byways. The shift from traditional parties to opposition, to protest candidates, to violent reactive protests and widespread disenchantment and a sense of betrayal reveal a volatile mass in search of new political alternatives that can confront the catastrophes induced by the pragmatists and realists of the status quo.

Electoral Politics, Class Politics, and the Crisis of the Marxist Left

Direct action by trade unions, social movements, and guerrilla forces has been a common response to the integration of the new electoral regimes into the "old" export economy. The most striking aspect of the resurgent popular challenge is the target: ostensibly "social democratic" and "populist" regimes. This reflects the fact that the old electoral elites of the self-styled democratic Left no longer have the wherewithal to capitalize on their rhetoric and evoke traditional ties. In Venezuela, tens of thousands of poor urban dwellers poured into the streets to protest the IMF-mandated austerity measures imposed by Carlos Andres Perez in June 1990; in Guatemala, urban groups, peasants, and guerrilla movements mounted an increasingly consequential challenge to the civilian Cerezo regime (1985–1990); in Argentina, Peronist public-employees' unions, whose members have been radicalized by the loss of social status and economic impoverishment, have engaged in prolonged strikes against the Menem regime; in Brazil, organized labor—bank employees, health workers, metal workers, teachers, longshoremen, migrant cane cutters, and others—have participated in strikes against the draconian economic measures implemented by the Collor regime. Apart from an estimated sixteen percent fall in real wages, the civilian government's program has led to the firing of hundreds of thousands of workers in the private sector and of a further 100,000 in the public sector since March 1990.[18]

In Peru, successful general strikes against falling living standards, wages levels and services severely undermined the government of Alan García; when his successor, Alberto Fujimori, announced an accord with the IMF which resulted in the immediate removal of subsidies on basic consumer goods and soaring overnight price increases (gasoline increased by 3,000 percent, milk and bread prices almost tripled; gas and electricity rose eight- to twelvefold) the urban slums erupted. The food price rises were subsequently followed by firings of hundreds of thousands of workers, which triggered antiregime strikes by thousands of teachers, bank employees, petroleum workers, and other segments of the labor force.[19] Even in Chile, Socialist and Christian Democratic unionists threatened to march on parliament if new labor legislation was not approved, while trade unions affiliated to the Workers' party in Brazil organized strikes against compromising municipal governments controlled by their colleagues.

The willingness of the working class and the urban poor to directly confront and challenge the traditional parties and the electoral leaders testifies to the reemergence of class struggle politics in the postauthoritarian era. However, several qualifications are in order. First, most of these movements' demands were part of the social democratic and populist programs which the civilian rulers subsequently abandoned. Second, the immediate struggles being fought are largely defensive—to prevent further losses in purchasing power, to resist new price increases, to oppose the withdrawal of food subsidies, to protest the new layoffs and firings that have accompanied the privatization programs. In Brazil, for example, where real wages fell by as much as a staggering 216 percent between January and October 1990, the San Bernardo Metal Workers Union managed to wrest a total wage increase of eighty-two percent for its São Paulo Ford Motor Company plant members after a forty-five-day stoppage which ended in late July. Meanwhile, striking national port-authority workers, facing massive layoffs, gained concessions including an agreement that the criteria for all future layoffs would be negotiated between the unions and the port management.[20] Third, there has been an ideological shift; the dominant political conceptions have moved away from specific socialist programmatic positions to vaguely democratic ones including support for amorphous "mixed economies." What is absent are any specific class configurations that can confront the entrenched, cohesive elites. Fourth, although the popular movements have challenged the hold of the electoral party regimes, they have not linked up to new political organizations. Hence, their struggles become sectoral, immediate, and reactive, rather than strategic, anticipatory, and state-centered.

In part, the defensive and fragmented structure of the popular classes reflects the post-Stalinist crisis affecting the traditional Left in Latin America as well as the repressive content of the state in most of the "redemocratized" countries. Profound divisions have emerged within the region's Communist parties stemming from the disorienting impact of the breakup of the socialist bloc governments, criticism of previous political practices (too accommodating in relations with the Argentine military dictatorship, too intransigent regarding participation in the Chilean political process), and/or disagreements over the continuing viability of centralized organizational forms (party democracy). The resultant fracturing of these parties in Chile, Argentina, Uruguay, and elsewhere has severely limited their capacity to intervene in current political struggles.

A different kind of crisis affects the other leftist parties. In Chile, for instance, the Socialist party has renounced all semblance of its reformist class politics history and become part and parcel of the neoliberal Aylwin regime—in the process disorienting thousands of party militants in the trade unions and the urban squatter settlements. In Argentina, the Peronist Justice party is openly supporting the most extreme neoliberal doctrines being promulgated by any civilian government—and forcing its trade union affiliates to do likewise (thereby undermining their working-class and nationalist beliefs) or split from the party. Mid-1990 meetings between populist trade-union and parliamentary leaders revealed the Peronist opposition at a dead end: unwilling to leave the party yet unable to solve elementary demands within the party.

In Brazil, the Workers' party is experiencing tensions between an increasingly social democratic leadership willing to sacrifice commitments to structural change in order to preserve electoral opportunities and militant rank-and-file trade unionists being increasingly pressured by Collor's neoliberal economic strategy toward more and more direct-action initiatives.

Deep divisions also affect the radical Left—the Chilean Movement of the Revolutionary Left (MIR), the Uruguayan Tupamaros, and other hemispheric revolutionary groups. Some elements want to dissolve into local movements; others are more interested in affiliating with the "successful" electoral parties; still others want to consolidate and rebuild a revolutionary party.

The crisis in the Left and the exhaustion of the historical organizations have to be counterposed to the deepening crisis of neoliberal capitalism. It is clear that the disintegration of capitalism and immiseration of the popular classes do not automatically lead to a revolutionary alternative (nor do these preclude it). The bankruptcy of a whole generation of "antiutopian," pragmatic intellectuals, many of them ex-Marxists who framed their policies in terms of managing the neoliberal state and economy, has only recently been challenged by a new generation of radical critics. The internal crisis of the political parties of the popular classes has severely weakened the political, organizational, and ideological capacities of the oppressed majorities to respond to the prolonged decay of social life: double negativity has not yet generated a positive outcome, at least at the level of state power, though, as we shall describe, the perspectives for the future are mixed.

Finally, resurgent class struggles in the new era of electoral politics still face a configuration of political power in which the military and paramilitary forces remain major actors. Guatemala, El Salvador, and Colombia offer perhaps the most striking evidence of the armed forces' continuing role in what has been aptly described as "death-squad democracy." Since early 1989, the Guatemalan military and its paramilitary allies have assassinated or kidnapped unionists, politicians, students, diplomats, business leaders, human rights' activists, church workers, peasant organizers, and other civilian opponents of the elected Cerezo regime on a scale approaching the charnel-house violence of the early 1980s. Meanwhile, the civilian president simply refused to respond to this new reign of state-authored terror, seeking instead to consolidate his alliance with the generals to ensure the government ran its full course and to increase the possibility of a Christian Democratic victory in the November 1990 presidential elections. Even the U.S. State Department's 1990 human rights report on Guatemala was forced to concede that the country's security forces had engaged in "extrajudicial killings, disappearances and other serious abuses." The more detailed and authoritative Americas Watch report presented a damning picture of a regime that "tolerated and . . . apologized for unspeakable abuses" committed by a military that "remains a law unto itself."[21]

The current situation in El Salvador is no less indicative of the persistence of military power amid the trappings of democratic politics. One of newly elected Alfredo Cristiani's first acts after assuming the presidency in June 1989 was to order the army's social-security agency to deposit its funds in the Central Bank. The generals balked and the president quickly rescinded his order. Since the March 1989 vote, between 2,500 and 3,000 civilians have been assassinated by the armed forces and their death-squad allies. The systematic targeting of union organizers, peasant leaders, and church activists in particular reveals the impotence of civilian authority—its unwillingness to reign in a military high command that opposes any institutional reforms and continues to frustrate efforts to negotiate a settlement to the country's civil war short of the unconditional surrender of the guerrilla forces.[22]

In Colombia, this same mix of elections and political murders has held sway over the past five years. Rightist paramilitary forces and death squads acting with the tacit approval, if not active participation, of the armed forces have been operating throughout the country—financed largely by the drug-trafficking cartels. In the two years prior to the 1990 presidential elections, over 2,000 members of the Communist party–led electoral coalition the Patriotic Union (UP) were assassinated; in the midst of the election campaign itself, the UP candidate Bernardo Jaramillo was publicly murdered by gunmen acting for the official and unofficial sources of terror in society. A similar fate befell Carlos Pizzaro, the presidential candidate of the former guerrilla movement MR-19, following a decision by the insurgents to turn in their arms and participate in the electoral process.[23] The chief beneficiary was the ultrarightist Liberal party candidate, Cesar Gaviria.

Electoral parties throughout Latin America, keenly aware of the undiminished power of the coercive institutions of the previous authoritarian states, have all but abandoned popular programmatic positions, while attempting to clamp down on the activities of democratic social movements, in an effort to appease and accommodate their armed forces. Electoralism, in the context of an overrepresented military presence, has not resulted in consequential structural changes or even in redistributive politics in any country where transitions from military to civilian rule have taken place. On the contrary, one could argue that electoral politics in Latin America during the 1980s increasingly revealed itself to be one more obstacle to popularly based social changes.

Electoral Politics and the Failure of the Social Democratic Left

The great paradox in Latin America today is between the spiralling downswing in the "free market" economies and the visible right turn of many of the left-wing (social democratic, populist, socialist) parties, their political leaderships, and their ideologues—the latter primarily ex-Marxist intellectuals of the 1960s. In countries such as Venezuela, Jamaica, Peru, Argentina, Chile, Guatemala, and Ecuador, this right turn is most evident at the level of the political leadership.

The current presidents of Venezuela (Carlos Andres Perez) and Jamaica (Michael Manley) are the "prototypes" of this "turncoat" phenomenon: progressive nationalists and social reformers in the 1970s who became neoliberal, quasi clients of Washington and U.S. financial and investment groups and uncritical followers of IMF austerity policies in the 1980s. Perez, the leader of the Democratic Action party, an affiliate of the Socialist International, headed a government in the 1970s that nationalized the Rockefeller-owned petroleum and iron ore holdings, supported lavish social-sector spending programs, and attempted to stimulate agriculture as the basis for creating a strong internal market. In 1991, he remains a social democrat in name only. In all other respects, he has undergone a radical change in outlook, reemerging as an active proponent of privatization of strategic industries, of economic deregulation, and of an open door for foreign investment. He is an enforcer of harsh economic adjustment programs that sharply reduce living standards through public spending cuts, wage freezing, price freedom, and job layoffs.

Michael Manley has assiduously followed the Perez pattern since regaining the Jamaican presidency in late 1988, zealously courting foreign investors while embracing the IMF, promoting the establishment of free-trade zones, and instituting a more fundamental privatization/deregulation of the economy than that undertaken by his conservative predecessor Edward Seaga. Manley's attitude toward Washington also underwent a complete turnabout. No longer the nationalist, he called George Bush "very impressive, very pragmatic, very sensible" and, among other initiatives, offered Jamaican military collaboration with the imperial state in regional antidrug campaigns.[24]

In contrast to Perez and Manley, when Alan García assumed the presidency of Peru in early 1986, he at least began by proposing a series of 1970s-type national and social reforms, including a cap on debt payments, state financial stimuli for national industries, salary and wage increases, and even a proposal to nationalize the banking system. Unable to secure the active support of the business class for his "productive revolution" or unwilling to mobilize the popular classes to move beyond moderate redistributive measures and, increasingly, under harsh financial encirclement by the international banking elite, Garcia's team eventually succumbed and reversed their policies, imposing orthodox adjustments while engaging in their private version of "income redistribution."

The elections of former guerrilla activist Jaime Paz Zamora in Bolivia, Socialist International member Rodrigo Borja in Ecuador, and human rights advocate Vinicio Cerezo in Guatemala continued the right-turn trend. Paz, who won the presidency in alliance with the rightist party of former military dictator Hugo Banzer, allowed the United States to establish new military bases in Bolivia and set about implementing economic policies that differed little from those of his rightist predecessors. Borja, lauded as the progressive alternative to the conservative, pro-Reagan Febres Cordero regime, followed in the footsteps of Perez and Manley by introducing IMF-austerity–type reforms. Of the three, the reformist Christian Democrat Cerezo's transformation was the most bizarre: apart from implementing regressive income policies he began to consistently defend (by denying their involvement) the murderous role of the armed forces and their death-squad offshoots as upholders of democracy.

Nor were Argentina and Chile exempt from this right-turn phenomenon. Carlos Menem campaigned for the Argentine presidency in 1989 as an orthodox Peronist "national populist." However, once elected, he allocated the major economic ministries in his cabinet to representatives of the most extreme right-wing big business/multinational corporate sector and then proceeded to elaborate a sweeping privatization program aimed at literally abolishing the state sector. In Chile, the political leadership of Christian Democracy underwent a major shift between the 1960s and the 1980s. Eduardo Frei's government in the latter half of the 1960s enacted a series of moderate reforms in order to modernize capitalism and promote a more equitable distribution of wealth and income. They included an agrarian reform, the "Chileanization" of the foreign-owned copper industry (including a buy out of fifty percent of the shares of the major U.S. copper firms), and a progressive tax on the upper classes. But the recently elected Christian Democratic–led coalition headed by Patricio Aylwin eschews reforms and directs the state's resources to promoting the agrobusiness export elite, opposes legislation allowing seasonal farm workers the right to strike during harvest season, increases the value-added tax (which falls mainly on wage and salaried groups) to fund social programs, and has expunged the very words "redistribution," "agrarian reform," and "nationalization"/"Chileanization" from the government's vocabulary, substituting the market rhetoric of their former Pinochet-led adversaries.

The right turn of the reformist parties over the past decade has been matched by the presidential victories of a group of rightist political figures: "traditional" conservatives like Salinas in Mexico, Gaviria in Colombia, Lacalle in Uruguay, and Cristiani in El Salvador; and others, such as Collor in Brazil and Fujimori in Peru, posing as "antipolitical" and "nontraditional" candidates, but whose political antecedents and commitments to a deregulated neoliberal capitalist agenda immediately surfaced as they began implementing "shock-treatment" economic programs devised by ministers recruited from the big-business sector—thus further perpetuating the deepening crisis of the "free-market" model. Indeed, the great irony about this continental shift to the right is how little it has had to do with socioeconomic achievements. On the contrary, it has occurred as the effects of neoliberal economic policies worsen social conditions and ensure the persistence of stagnant economies into the 1990s. Nor have the rightist or turncoat parties succeeded in creating a new hegemonic ideology: while the "free market," the "social market economy," and other such euphemisms may be currently in vogue, capitalism is still overwhelmingly viewed as an unjust system and imperialism is still commonly used to describe the financial pillage of the continent.

What accounts then for the right turn in Latin America since the early 1980s? Certainly, Washington's relative global decline has not significantly affected its position within Latin America, where it continues to exercise overdetermined influence. Economically, U.S. imperialism is still able to impose enormous burdens and pressures on dissident regimes (witness the experience of Garcia's Peru) through its ability to influence the behavior of the two major sources of the continent's external funding: the international lending agencies and the private commercial (largely U.S.) banking community. Militarily, its capacity to project its power is as great as ever. The invasions of Grenada and Panama, the use of mercenary forces in Nicaragua and El Salvador, and the recent establishment of new military bases in Bolivia and Peru are sufficient testimony to this reality. Finally, the imperial state's ideological influence has greatly increased since the 1960. Its market rhetoric and interdependency discourse circulate unhindered and are uncritically consumed by broad sectors of the political and intellectual classes. However, the problem with any explanation based on the power of U.S. imperialism is that it was equally applicable during the 1960s and early 1970s when the left political opposition was stronger and extended over a broad universe of discourse.

To understand why this continental-wide "right turn" occurred in the 1980s and what possibilities exist for its reversal it is necessary to consider a series of historical and structural changes (in both their national and global contexts) that took place in the political and ideological, as well as the socioeconomic, spheres.

First, the military-state-authored repression of the 1970s and 1980s—not least, the tens of thousands tortured, executed, and "disappeared" by the generals in Argentina, Chile, and elsewhere—had profound, long-term effects on the Left and the rest of the opposition movement: It disarticulated grass-roots' organizations through assassination of the most intelligent, active, and knowledgeable militants;

it created a political culture, during and after the bloody purges, permeated with fear and thus inhibited citizens from actively confronting public authority; it "permanently" changed the balance of power in the state, increasing the weight of the coercive instruments (armed forces, intelligence agencies, police, etc.) in the post–military-regime society. This legacy of right-wing terror and the survival and continuing power of its institutions in the new period of electoral regimes remain a reference point for the parties of the Left and the populace at large, strengthening the position of the traditional neoliberals and encouraging the turncoat leftists to accommodate these real power centers. The slow recreation of a new generation of grass-roots' leaders and their reinsertion into the trade unions and neighborhood organizations represent a challenge to this legacy and the political culture of fear, self-censorship, and internal repression.

Second, the right turn of the former reformist Christian Democrats, social democrats, populists, and socialists in particular was heavily influenced by the socioeconomic legacy of the military regime. The key components include the predominance of the export elites; reconcentrated banking, agrobusiness, and industrial power; the climate of deregulation as a basic condition for any investor cooperation; hyperdependency on the financial circuits; and high levels of overseas capital investment by local capitalists. The military's vast restructuring of the economy, society, and state in the 1970s and 1980s posed a basic problem for the former reformists: either they had to transform the structure of the economy and challenge the power of export and financial groups in order to pursue reformist policies or else they had to adapt to the existing configuration of power and pursue policies that would create "confidence" in these groups, encourage new investments, and thereby avoid a crisis of capital (overseas flight) and the resulting "chaos"—culminating in the "demise of democracy" and the return of the military to the presidential palace.

Confronting this dilemma, the old reformers chose the electoral regime and conformity—decisions they termed "pragmatic" and "realistic." Their abandonment of social reforms for the popular classes was dismissed as simply the "end of Utopia." By equating democracy with public poverty, these new rightists impoverished democracy. Integration into the new model thus engendered certain political, economic, and ideological imperatives that could not be met by any stretch of the original reformist framework. The framework itself had to be discarded, and instead of admitting to the need to submit to the new power centers, the political and ideological elites blithely proclaimed that a new "modern" world had come into being which necessitated discarding of old anachronistic nineteenth-century Marxist and socialist notions.

The alternative to conformity is confrontation and struggle. The outcome would have been uncertain, but on the alternative path there existed the possibility of a new and more equitable social and economic order, a democracy based on the social movements of the poor—not a future determined by generals and bankers.

The path of conformity has assured neither democracy, nor equity, nor development; and not even reelection—which after all is what the parties of the ex-Left have come to equate with democracy.

Third, the right turn had to do with the integration of the major research institutes into the Western capitalist foundation networks and their subsequent assimilation of liberal political and economic discourses. Several factors explain the gap between the extended crisis of market capitalism in Latin America and the intellectuals' continued support of market regimes and neoliberal economic strategies. Not only are the intellectuals integrated into the organizational matrix of Western corporate and state-funded circuits (conferences, subsidies, publications, etc.); they are no longer subject to the crisis of the local economy because their salaries, perks, and travel funding, reflecting their new class position, are in overseas currencies. Moreover, a condition for employment is agreement to jettison the language of critical Marxism—concepts such as imperialism are taboo. At the same time, the analysis of these conformist intellectuals linked to the turncoat parties is deeply influenced by their class aspirations. Looking to become managers of the current crisis, their writings are designed to catapult them into the ministries of the electoral regimes. In Argentina and Chile, for example, the major overseas-funded research centers have provided the new civilian regimes with ministerial appointees who have served to defuse popular expectations and promote incentives to investors in the private sector.

In other words, as the local economies were transformed under the military regimes into economic appendages of the foreign banks and multinationals, and as a new class of Latin American transnational capitalists emerged, so in the intellectual realm domestic research centers became in effect locally administered "branch plants" in which the managers formulated research projects within the conceptual framework devised by the "home office." The international conferences and publication outlets served to consolidate the linkages and to facilitate the transmission of the "new" market ideology and the formulas for a democracy of poverty.

Fourth, and finally, the right turn was linked to changes taking place in the world economy and the perception of those changes by left-wing political and intellectual leaders. The demise of Eastern Europe's bureaucratic collectivist regimes, the decision of the Soviet Union and China to embrace free-market economics, and the growing adherence of social democratic governments in southern Europe (e.g., Spain and Portugal) to neoliberal politics had a major ideological impact on Latin America's Communist and Socialist parties, as well as on other major leftist forces such as the Sandinistas in Nicaragua. Particularly disoriented by these events were those Communist party members who had long relied on the Soviet political/economic model and have not been able to develop another conception of socialism.

Yet, while the decline in Socialist bloc economic and military aid and the contraction of markets for Latin exports are no small matter, most of these changes subsumed in these phrases took place several years before the hemisphere's right turn. Furthermore, apart from Cuba and Nicaragua, the changes have not affected the economic patterns in most of the other regional countries. Nonetheless, the constraints on future policy are real but, at the same time, have to be put alongside the even greater constraints that the Latin American people are experiencing under the combined impact of U.S. imperialism and neoliberal market policies today and will have to contend with into the foreseeable future. Popular antagonism to perpetual reductions ("adjustments") in living standards has not diminished merely because one or other Eastern European government now proclaims the virtues of the market.

This deepening crisis of Latin American capitalism poses the obvious question: can the right turn be reversed? Is a left countertrend visible? What is clear is that since the late 1980s, the region's underlying structural class polarizations have surfaced politically in a number of countries, most dramatically in two of the "majors"—Brazil and Mexico. The 31 million votes caste for the Workers' party in the 1989 Brazilian presidential elections both exaggerated its electoral strength (member of a left-wing coalition) and underestimated its influence among the activist and movement sectors of the society. In key urban centers (industrial factories, squatter settlements, and lower-middle-class sites) the Workers' party has become the dominant hegemonic force—its influence extends outward to religious, educational, health, and public-sector institutions. It is a counterhegemonic power at the national/state level. Its strategic strength is its roots in the popular movements but its tactical weakness is the strong presence in its ranks of reformist intellectuals and municipal officials willing to "pact" with existing configurations of power.

In Mexico, the Cardenas movement, an amorphous alliance of urban and rural poor, middle-class intellectuals, and ex-PRI party loyalists, was able to win the 1988 elections but lost the electoral count: demonstrating once again the strength of the permanent state apparatus over the electoral process. Nonetheless, the continued mobilization of the Cardenas forces on the local level and the large-scale resistance to the Salinas regime in a multiplicity of municipalities, neighborhoods, and workplaces suggest that neoliberalism remains largely an elite phenomenon tied to Mexico's transnational capitalists who are strongly committed to President Bush's free trade strategy (and state support) as a counterweight to their internal political weakness.

Although the most striking, Brazil and Mexico are not exceptional cases. Progressive socialist mayors and governors have been elected for the first time in Uruguay and Venezuela; increasingly large-scale, extraparliamentary confrontations are occurring between workers and rightist electoral regimes in Argentina and Peru; the guerrilla movement in Guatemala has assumed the proportions of a national movement, now operating in 14 provinces; and in El Salvador and Nicaragua, rank-and-file militants are questioning the programs of the party intellectuals—the issues of socialism, democracy, collectivism, and capitalism are being openly debated, even as these political formations retain widespread popular support.

The left countertrend reflects the consequential insertion of left-wing political organization and ideology between the objective crisis of capitalism and the neoliberal regimes in power. In other words, the "natural polarizations" created by the application of neoliberal policy are politicized and organized through the active intervention of parties and activists. Private discontent with neoliberal electoral regimes is mobilized by a variety of political formations—from predominantly electoral parties like the Cardenas movement to electoral-movement parties like the Workers' party, to guerrilla groups and direct-action movements as in Guatemala and El Salvador. The left countertrend has the capacity to become a hegemonic force if it can avoid the pitfalls of the turncoat Left formations that preceded it.

Conclusion

The crisis of Latin American capitalism is far more severe and extended than any comparable situation in Eastern Europe, but the ruling elites do not depart, mass demonstrations do not end peacefully, opposition intellectuals in office do not purge the state of authoritarian secret-police chiefs, the dominant hegemonic power does not gracefully accept changes in the social system or write off debts. The political elites circulate from military to civilian; the economy lurches from one painful adjustment to another; and when one country, Nicaragua, ousts a U.S. client, Washington finances a prolonged war of intervention and eventually reimposes an electoral client. One priest is killed in Poland and it becomes the basis for an indictment of the entire political system; seventy thousand Christian peasants and a dozen nuns and priests are murdered in El Salvador and the leading defender of the "Free World" can speak of the "moral crisis of communism" and the "moral as well as material superiority of free market societies."

The divergent outcomes resulting from the crises in Eastern Europe and Latin America are not the result of the demise of economic systems or the superiority of one system over the other but have more to do with the willingness and capacity of the U.S. to reshuffle political regimes while retaining strategic ties to the underlying authoritarian states and economic elite structures. In contrast to the Soviet withdrawal of support for its client regimes, Washington acts quickly to prop up and buttress regional allies: military aid helps repress dissident nationalists; civilian/military pacts provide the electoral facades that perpetuate the region-wide pillage. At the same time, Latin America's coercive structures have also exhibited a capacity to hold onto power during periods of transition, thus guaranteeing the continuity of the social system in the face of democratic social movements and mass popular upheavals.

It is these continuities in international hegemonic power, authoritarian state institutions, and the concentration of economic power in the outward-looking elites that make such a mockery of proposals to learn from the "Swedish model."[25]

General and bankers are not going to negotiate the large-scale, long-term transfer of wealth from overseas accounts into social-welfare programs now or in the near future. Elite negotiations with the electoral politicians provided the political class with the freedom to try its hand at managing the existing model, pacifying the masses, securing overseas loans, and keeping up interest payments. The electoral elites have set out to prove that they can manage the existing system better than their authoritarian counterparts: that they could better renegotiate the debt—and maintain payments; that they could run popular elections that would not impair the confidence of the investor elites.

Initially they succeeded, but for a brief historical moment. By the end of the 1980s, electoral regimes were deeply mired in chronic stagnation and the electorate was rapidly losing confidence in one political option after another; in one antipolitical personality after another. The major reprieve of the system was the very severity of the crisis: the struggle for day-to-day survival was exhausting the populace and forcing them to turn inward to primary and immediate groups and networks. What new electoral "options" will appear to perpetuate the political charade? One is tempted to speak of the "end of neoliberal capitalism" much as the Western pundits associated market ascendancy in the east with the "end of socialism," but that is too easy, fundamentally wrong. The road to transcending the economic, political, and moral bankruptcy of capitalism in Latin America is long and arduous. The organizers of the death squads still command the armed forces and they have been carefully nurtured by the incumbent electoral politicians. The economies are tightly chained to the international financial networks: ruptures at one end provoke reactions at the other. Industrialists have factories in Latin America but their capital is invested abroad. When change comes, it will not be easy, nor will the initial measures restructuring the economy toward meeting popular social needs be painless: there will have to be a massive shift of resources from the upper twenty percent to the rest, and that will certainly be resisted fiercely. Elites which have exhausted economic and political options do not simply concede the game as lost and turn philosophical. Irrationality is already increasing: This is evident in the obsessive and single-minded pursuit of further austerity measures against a whole people which literally has nothing left to give; in the monomaniacal pressures to continue interest payments despite skyrocketing infant mortality rates and generalized hunger.

If socialism has a future (independently of the organizational capacities or incapacities at any given moment, or of the defection or retreat of this or the other generation of intellectuals), it is because it is the only possible way to confront the irrational tide of market madness that threatens to defend general misery with unrestrained violence.

Notes

1. Quoted in Michael Stott, "Invalid Ballots Take Lead in Brazil Election," *Philadelphia Inquirer*, October 8, 1990, p. 8A.

2. See "Argentina's Crisis Revives Military," *Washington Report on the Hemisphere*, April 4, 1990, p. 5.

3. Ibid.

4. See Jerry Knudson, "Activists Condemn Retreat from Punishing the Guilty," *Times of the Americas*, October 17, 1990, p. 1.

5. See Victor de la Fuente, "Chile Only Half Way to Democracy," *Le Monde* supplement in *Guardian Weekly*, October 14, 1990, p. 17.

6. "U.S. to Open New Base in Peru," *Washington Report on the Hemisphere*, May 16, 1990, pp. 1, 7.

7. Gert Rosenthal, "Balance Preliminar de la Economia Latinoamericana en 1989," *Commercio Exterior*, Vol. 40, No. 2, February 1990, p. 124; "How Latin America's Economies Look After a Decade's Decline," *New York Times*, February 11, 1990, p. E3.

8. Figures from the United Nations Economic Commission for Latin America and the Caribbean, reprinted in "Where Are the Real Good Performers?" *Latin American Weekly Report*, February 7, 1991, pp. 8–9.

9. Rosenthal, "Balance Preliminar de la Economia Latinoamericana en 1989," p. 124.

10. See Ken Silverstein, "Collor's 'New Brazil': Shock Treatment for the Poor," *The Nation*, November 12, 1990, p. 555.

11. See *Latin American Monitor: Southern Cone*, October 1990, p. 822; *The Nation*, November 12, 1990, p. 555; "Rich Getting Richer, the Poor Poorer," *Latin American Regional Reports: Brazil*, January 10, 1991, pp. 4–5.

12. See *Latin American Regional Reports: Andean Group*, October 11, 1990, p. 2.

13. See the *New York Times*, August 11, 1990, p. 5.

14. See Lindsey Gruson, "Salvador's Poverty is Called Worst of Century," *New York Times*, October 16, 1988, p. 14.

15. Gert Rosenthal, "Latin America and Caribbean Developments in the 1980s and the Outlook for the Future," *CEPAL Review*, No. 39, December 1989, p. 1; *El Mercurio*, July 14, 1989, p. B-1; *Latin American Weekly Report*, August 9, 1990, p. 10.

16. See "Stagnation Pummeling Regional Economies," *Times of the Americas*, January 10, 1990, p. 1.

17. Rosenthal, "Latin America and Caribbean Development in the 1980s and the Outlook for the Future," p. 10.

18. Silverstein, "Collor's 'New Brazil': Shock Treatment for the Poor," p. 555.

19. See Nicole Bonnet, " 'Fujishock' Delivers a Killer Blow to Peru's Inflation," *Le Monde* supplement in *Guardian Weekly*, October 7, 1990, p. 18; "Fujimori Under Pressure," *Washington Report on the Hemisphere*, October 17, 1990, pp. 1, 6.

20. See "Brazilian Labor Strikes Back at Collor," *Washington Report on the Hemisphere*, October 3, 1990, p. 5.

21. Quoted in Americas Watch, *Messengers of Death: Human Rights in Guatemala, November 1988–February 1990* (New York: March 1990); Wilson Ring, "Guatema-

lan Rights Performance Deteriorates Despite Promises," *Washington Post*, April 13, 1990, p. A20. Also see Lee Hockstader, " 'Climate of Terror' Again Grips Guatemala," *Washington Post*, September 29, 1989, p. A45; Lindsey Gruson, "Political Violence on the Rise Again in Guatemala, Tarnishing Civilian Rule," *New York Times*, June 28, 1990, p. 3; "Murder With Impunity Returns," *Washington Report on the Hemisphere*, October 3, 1990, pp. 1, 6.

22. See, for example, Americas Watch, *A Year of Reckoning: El Salvador a Decade After the Assassination of Archbishop Romero* (New York, March 1990); "Overlooked Abuses of Salvadoran Unions," *Washington Report on the Hemisphere,* April 18, 1990, p. 4.

23. See "Colombians Go to the Polls," *Washington Report on the Hemisphere*, May 30, 1990, p. 4.

24. Quoted in "Born-Again Ideology in Jamaica and Venezuela," *Washington Report on the Hemisphere*, August 16, 1989, p. 4. Also see Canute James, "Manley Moves to Deregulate State," *Financial Times*, October 26, 1990, p. 4.

25. See, for example, Francisco Weffert, "Sweden and Latin America," *CEPAL Review*, No. 39, December 1989, pp. 31–36.

2

Aylwin's Chile: The Nature of Latin American "Democratic" Transitions

Introduction

The transition from a military dictatorship to an electoral regime is best understood by sorting out the essential events and issues from the secondary. In order to localize the pertinent facts, however, one needs to identify the major sociopolitical forces acting in each specific context. Through an analysis of their roles, strategies, successes, and failures, the groundwork can be established for an evaluation of the nature of the transition and its consequences for the future evolution of Chilean politics.

The major sociopolitical forces acting in the transition included (1) the left-wing parties, the autonomous social movements, and the guerrilla formations; (2) the center-right to center-left political parties, trade unions, and civic associations; (3) the armed forces and the business and financial elites; and (4) the U.S. government and the international banks and financial agencies that it influences. Each of these political formations had a distinct set of interests, strategies, and visions of what the transition to electoral politics entailed. The transition is a result of the failure of one bloc's strategy and the success of another's—a success that is tempered by conditions and compromises within which it was undertaken.

The transition to the post-Pinochet regime can be dated to 1986 when major political battles were engaged and realignments and political pacts were consummated that subsequently played themselves out in the following years.[1] Several key developments came to a head in 1986 culminating in the displacement of the Left and social movements, the electoral victory of a coalition of center-right parties, and the continuity of the strategic political and economic features of the Pinochet era.[2]

The most significant of these events was the defeat of the Left, its political repression and subsequent isolation, and the reemergence of the center-right as the decisive force of the opposition.[3] The defeat took several forms: the guerrillas' failed attempt to assassinate Pinochet and the discovery of their major military arsenal, with which they had hoped to launch a national insurrection; the incapacity to sustain the mass social movements, particularly after the breakup of the Civic Assembly following the July 1986 general strike; the subsequent repression of the Left (Communist party, the MIR, fractions of the Popular Action Movement (MAPU), and the Socialist party) by the military regime and the center-right (Christian Democratic, Socialist, and Radical parties) de facto renunciation of movement politics. The defeat thus affected the guerrillas, their strategy of "popular rebellion," and the upward trajectory of the social movements, thereby undermining the growing hegemony of the Left within the opposition.

The Pinochet regime combined a dual strategy of encirclement and occupation of the rebellious popular neighborhoods (repressing the social movements) while opening up negotiations with, and opportunities for, the center-right electoral political class and its parties.[4] The guerrillas' setback, the violent state response, and a split in the social movements were compounded by the incapacity of the Left to formulate a counterstrategy to this Pinochet shift toward electoral politics. The social movements continued their activity, but the focus turned from national to local issues.[5] And, as the electoral calendar began to unfold, the movement supporters were increasingly subject to heavy pressure from the newly legalized electoral parties, while the Left parties were increasingly divided between those forces that attempted to sustain the armed struggle, those seeking to insert themselves into the electoral legal arena, and the majority—those seeking to conciliate both strategies.[6]

The Left's defeat in 1986 was in some respects as serious as 1973: it had the same extreme effect of disarticulating the mass organizations, derailing the process of reconstituting social alliances, and calling into question basic strategies. While the loss of lives was not in any way comparable, the strategic realignment of political forces was, to an extent, more significant: the Socialists definitively opted for an alliance with the Christian Democrats and redefined their policies to incorporate the neoliberal socioeconomic model already in place. While the defeat of 1973 reflected a profound and continuing split of the Chilean population, the defeat of 1986 led to a rightist shift in the entire political spectrum, a realignment which skewed politics toward the professional political class and the predominance of the permanent institutions of the state at the expense of the social movements in civil society. The *electoral transition* thus begins with the *defeat of the Left* and *on the terrain established by the Pinochet regime*.

The second essential factor shaping the transition was the negotiations and "pact" between the center-right political parties and elites and the military high command. The essential element in this process was the *preconditions* for the pact. The center-right parties affected a major shift in relation to the mass movements, directing their followers to eschew mass mobilization, social confrontation, even strikes, and in particular to reject unified activities with the Left.[7] Two factors weighed heavily in this decision. One was a growing fear that the center-right was losing hegemony over the mass movements, that the latters' demands and struggles were exceeding the political and social boundaries of their politics. The attempt on Pinochet's life was both the pretext for a political rupture with the Left and the event that precipitated it. The other factor was the increasing "appreciation" of the new socioeconomic model and the eagerness to secure political positions, even in the restricted spaced allocated by the Pinochet dictatorship.[8] Under the negotiated pact with the ruling generals, the center-right gained legality, projected a political strategy with an immediate target (defeat the dictator), and had access to the mass media in a fashion that completely marginalized the Left. Thus, *what the center-right gave away in terms of institutional power to the Pinochet right, it gained in electoral organizational influence at the expense of the Left.*

The pact legitimated the 1980 military constitution, the armed forces as a political interlocuter, and the rules of the political transition laid down by Pinochet. By circumscribing the activities in civil society and increasing the role of the professional political elites, the issues of the transition were largely redefined into problems of "governability": the capacity of the new political elites to sustain the confidence of the established economic investors, maintain the allegiance of the military, and contain the pent-up social demands of the popular classes.[9]

The politics of the "negotiated transition" prefigured the political style and socioeconomic substance of the resulting electoral regime. A premium was placed on demobilizing social movements, refocusing political debate on a narrow set of legal/political changes, and centralizing politics in the hands of a professional political elite willing to compromise with the established institutional powers of the state.

The emergence of the center-right military pact was accompanied by a new political discourse which eliminated the politics of structural change and rationalized the new accommodationist and conformist politics of the opposition parties with a rhetoric of "realism" and "pragmatism."[10] The transition presented a paradox in which greater electoral freedom was accompanied by a shrinking of the acceptable political/economic spectrum of views and policies. More important, the negotiating process, involving mutual recognition on the institutional and constitutional terrain of the military regime, provided the model for the construction of the reformed political system: the cohabitation of the electoral regime and the authoritarian state. The success of the center-right in wresting temporary hegemonic influence over the mass movement from the Left was secured by paying a steep price to the military: conceding strategic positions in the state, economy, and constitutional framework.

The third factor influencing the transition was the role played by the U.S. government and the "international banks." Washington's policy in the Third World has been based on a willingness to sacrifice dictators to save the state.[11] It has consistently distinguished between defending permanent and transitory U.S. interests and has always sought to adapt to social challenges through political changes. For American policy-makers, the defense of the capitalist system, international alignments, and integration with U.S.-centered military/economic regional organization are permanent interests defended by strategic institutions in the state. Rigidity in support of state institutions defending strategic interests has been accompanied by flexibility toward regime changes affecting transitory interests.

In the Chilean context, Washington supported the Pinochet military coup that overthrew Allende and the free-market, export-oriented economic model the generals implemented (providing aid and promoting trade). However, with the emergence of the mass social movements from 1983 onward and the radicalization of the forms of struggle and leadership in 1985/1986, the Reagan White House moved increasingly toward advocacy of a regime change based on a negotiated transition which would divide the opposition and preserve the state. The goal was to facilitate the ascendancy of the center-right "antiregime" forces over and against the left "antisystem" movements, while minimizing the changes in the socioeconomic model and state institutions. Financial and political support from the U.S. and its NATO allies to the center-right was conditioned on breaking ties with the Left and participating in the electoral calendar outlined by the dictatorship.[12] In turn, Washington agreed to pressure Pinochet to comply with his electoral timetable and accept the outcome. The result was the best possible outcome from the point of view of U.S. permanent interests in Chile: a regime change which disarticulated the social movements challenging strategic state allies and the legitimation and (temporary) stabilization of state institutions and the socio-economic model by the new electoral regime. While the movements forced the issue of regime change, it was Washington that "brokered" the negotiation process that produced the hybrid political system—a popularly elected regime inserted in military-constructed state institutions. The Reagan-Bush White House sacrificed the Pinochet regime to save the neoliberal state and, in the process, took credit for promoting democracy.

The fourth character of the transition follows from above: the defeat of the Left, the primacy of the military/civil negotiations, and the crucial role of the United States as political broker led to a transformation in the relation of forces between the regime-centered political-party machines and professional politicians and the social movements in civil society. The rise to prominence of "political society" (the exiled politicians, lawyers, institutional intellectuals, economic consultants, etc.) was accompanied by the displacement of the militant grassroots leaders. The transition reflected the circulation of elites. Electoral party elites replaced the technocratic/military elites. The transitional process thus was marked by an intensification of the politics of elite pacts and maneuvers oriented toward political reconciliation at the top and the displacement of movement leaders involved in mass confrontations and popular mobilizations from below. At the ideological/cultural level, the new ascending elites developed a double discourse: that directed toward the electorate privileged the issues of popular representation; that directed toward the institutions of the state, the economic elite, and Washington spoke the language of accommodation with the armed forces, investors, and overseas bankers. This double discourse captured the ambiguity of the political change—the limited transfer of power and the strategic strength vested in the powers of nonelected officials.

In summary, the essential features of the transition were marked by the defeat of the Left and the social movements, and by the organization of an electoral process on the terrain of the authoritarian Right. The victory of the center-right in December 1989 and the new civilian regime was thus situated within the authoritarian parameters and rules of the game established by the Pinochet military dictatorship.

Institutional Continuities and Their Consequences

The most striking feature of the post-Pinochet electoral regime is the vast range of institutional continuities in the political, legal, and socioeconomic spheres. Once the electoral campaigns ended and the euphoria generated by the electoral parties and their leaders subsided, it was clear that the armed forces and the investor classes backing them had secured the better part of the political bargain. At the theoretical level, these continuities call into question the notion of a "transition to democracy" and even raise serious doubts about whether one can even speak of a "democratization" process, except in a very partial, one-sided manner.

The most important structures of the political system, the institutions of the state, have to an extraordinary degree remained intact from the previous authoritarian period. An examination of five institutions of crucial importance to any concept of a transition to democracy is illustrative. The armed forces and police, the courts, the civil bureaucracy, the central bank, and the universities all retain the same personnel, in many cases with the same top officials and under the same ideological/political rules, as under the previous regime.

The armed forces is the most striking example: the commander-in-chief is Pinochet and the commanders of all the military branches are holdovers from the dictatorship.[13] The military also retains control over all policies regarding training, recruitment, and indoctrination, leaving them in a position to reproduce themselves in their current mold, retain cohesion, and withstand any civilian/democratic influences in the future. Meanwhile, the secret political police (CNI), although formally dissolved by the civilian president, have been absorbed and reconstituted within the intelligence branches of the military.

Equally important, the armed forces have marked out narrow boundaries for the emerging political class: limiting its capacity to apply the law of the land to past human rights' violations by military officials and imposing a constitution which skews congressional representation toward the right, including a minority of nonelected senators capable of blocking any constitutional amendment that trespasses on the power and prerogatives of the military and propertied classes. In addition, military officials frequently project their views into the political system and are perceived as an important branch of the government by both legislators and the executive who hasten to court their support.[14]

As a result, in the post-Pinochet period, the military has far greater political weight in the state (and in the political system) than in the period preceding the dictatorship. The military swiftly put the newly elected politicians on notice that their status is conditioned on maintaining stability and order, sending a clear message that social disorder would result in a self-invitation to take back the reins of government.[15] This directive from the armed forces has clearly negative implications concerning the capacity of the electoral regime to carry out consequential socioeconomic reforms, which inevitably provoke the ire of the upper classes and require the mobilization of the popular classes.

Just prior to leaving office, the dictatorship offered handsome pensions for early retirement of Supreme Court justices and, subsequently, replaced them with even more subservient, unconditional loyalists.[16] The immobility agreements signed by the electoral politicians and Pinochet freeze the judicial system in the mold left by the authoritarian system. Moreover, given the composition of the legislature, the power of the military, and the discretionary power of the incumbent judges, there is the narrowest of margins for utilizing the legal system to modify the existing concentration of political and economic power. The continuity of the judicial and legal system, reflective of the compromises between the military and electoral politicians in the transition, thus reinforces the immobility of the new electoral regime.

Similar constraints to political and social change exist in the civil bureaucracy. The military/civilian electoral pact included guarantees securing the jobs of the dictatorship's civil appointees, who, in most cases, were recruited because of their loyalty to the generals rather than their competence.[17] They are now entrusted to implement policies which in many cases they are opposed to. Using their discretionary powers, they are capable of delaying, distorting, or undermining policies proposed by the new Aylwin administration. Moreover, the civilian government has been obliged to add to the bureaucracy to circumvent existing administrative units and/or to supply a minimum number of jobs as political patronage. In all the ministries, from Foreign Affairs to Economics, the opposition is in a strategic position to influence policy, secure internal information and documentation as to regime strategy—and plan countermeasures. In many ways, the Cabinet heads and other senior officials appointed by President Aylwin are captives of Pinochet's bureaucratic functionaries. And with the immobility agreements there are few prospects for any democratic renovation of the civil service or even the reinsertion of officials arbitrarily fired by the dictatorship. It is not surprising that the military and right-wing defense of "legality" overlooks the violent crimes on which the current legal norms were constructed. It is a tragedy that the civilian electoral politicians accept the legitimacy of those claims as the basis for the new political order.

Before leaving office, Pinochet decreed that the director of the Central Bank would possess powers independent from the elected officials, extended his tenure for the greater part of the following decade, and increased his decision-making authority over the economy. By appointing a staunch neoliberal, Andres Bianchi (with the approval of the Christian Democrats and the Socialists), Pinochet ensured that the main contours of the military's economic model and its leading beneficiaries, the export-oriented elites, would have a strategic ally in the state. The electoral regime's submission to this appointment and restructuring of state economic decision-making reflected both its conversion to Pinochet-style economics and its impotence in posing alternatives in the negotiating process.

The extremely narrow political bounds within which the center-right chose to consumate its agreements with the dictatorship are particularly evident in the area of higher education. Here, as in other spheres of civil society, the ruling generals engaged in a savage purge of progressive university professors and dissidents, replacing them with political toadies, time servers, and neoliberal ideologues. One would have expected, with the advent of the electoral regime, a sustained effort to reinstate the professors purged by the dictatorship or at least an effort to open all positions to public competition. Nothing of the sort happened. A proposal to that effect presented by the head of the Chilean Sociological Association was rejected by the Socialist party as too risky "for the stability of democracy."[18]

What is striking about the new regime is not merely the continuities with the past but the rigidity and tenacity with which it upholds the existing legal and institutional order. It is apparent that the electoral-political class is not merely reflecting external pressures but represents a new political orientation, a long-term conversion to neoliberal strategies. The political forms and organizational structures (the "Socialist" and "Christian Democratic" parties) within which this new political class operates bear no resemblance to the parties of the past. The rupture is total and enduring, involving a basic shift in ideology, programs, development strategy, international orientation and relationship to the class structure. The terms "reformist" or "populist" no longer apply in the context of supply-side economics, export-oriented strategies, and the embrace of Washington's free-market program. In present-day Chile, no leader of the two major governmental parties speaks of agrarian reform: "that is the dead language of the past" declares one "renovating socialist," echoing the editorial pages of the conservative daily, *El Mercurio*.[19] In the economic ministries, "modernity" and "realism" speak to the same technocratic productionist discourse as Pinochet's economic advisors.[20] The electoral regime shares with the Pinochet Right the need to maintain and promote "efficient farmers" with the proviso that they improve housing conditions and wages for "their" workers.[21]

The electoral regime has entered into the logic of the new pattern of accumulation as they seek to convince investors that their rulership is more likely to avoid large-scale conflict and provide better crisis management than a rightist regime. It does not propose any socioeconomic changes that in the least way hinder the consolidation of the military pattern of export growth. To the armed forces, the electoralists argue that political legitimacy and a better international image are more effective in extending access to markets, credit, and military aid.[22]

The clearest expression of the continuity of the Pinochetist agromineral export model is found in Finance Minister Alejandro Foxley's assertion that his main job is to "manage the macroeconomic" indicators.[23] The new economic team of Christian Democrat Foxley and the Socialist party's Carlos Ominami have set themselves the task of deepening and extending the free-market model set in place by the former minister of finance, Hernán Buchi. Hence, Foxley's immediate embrace of Bush's proposal for a Latin American free market and Economy Minister Ominami's boasts about the increased level of foreign investment during his first six months in office.[24] The efforts by the Christian Democrats and Socialists to outflank the Right through ultraliberal policies reveal the distance which separates these parties from their roots in the pre-Pinochet period.[25]

The new electoral regime's policies are firmly directed toward extending and deepening the export and financial sector in the Chilean economy and sustaining the leading economic groups that control the international circuits; the regime is opposed to any changes—even at the margins—in the rules of the game under which the multinationals plunder Chilean natural resources and labor.[26] On the contrary, global corporations and their Chilean counterparts are described as crucial actors by the managers of the "macroeconomic indicators." Of all the top capitalist class players, the financial and banking sector (domestic and foreign) have been accorded a particularly decisive role in economic decision-making, reflected in the civilian government's overriding preoccupation with controlling inflation and fiscal balances.[27]

The parameters of the Pinochet political, economic, social, and ideological system shape the policies of the Aylwin electoral regime and, in turn, are reinforced by the regime's insertion within that system. These parameters provide the substantive power framework within which policy debates, electoral campaigns, and ideological and cultural production of the electoral parties take place.

Discontinuities: The Electoral Regime

The basic changes in Chilean politics have taken place at the level of the political regime: A new political base for the regime has emerged; political space for public expression, political organization, and electoral competition has been substantially enlarged; and new forms of political legitimation have been elaborated.

The Aylwin government has expanded the basis of its political appeal beyond the limited electorate that characterized the previous regime.[28] At least formally, it is obligated to appeal to, and cajole, a broad array of classes to vote for their candidates. Furthermore, the electoral parties seek to legitimate their policies in terms of the interests of the "electorate." Nevertheless, there is a growing gap between the formal freedom of the electorate to choose and the diminishing choice of alternative development strategies. Since both the center-right regime and the right-wing opposition favor the current neoliberal model and have agreed to work within constraints of the Pinochet constitution and political structures, the freedom to choose is sharply restricted by the informal mechanisms of political control over the media and the monopoly of party finances enjoyed by the major electoral actors.

While the electoral regime has expanded the possibilities for the various forms of public expression, the military courts still punish critics of the dictatorship, and a number of government officials have indicated a desire to restrict speech that "destabilizes" democracy.[29] Mass-media access is for all intents and purposes controlled by the supporters of the neo-liberal model and the civil/military agreement (*convivencia*), thus restricting alternative critical perspectives to marginal access to the larger public. Opinions critical of the current regime are branded "ultraleftist" and their exponents are disqualified as "extremist ideologues." Moreover, the carabineros, the paramilitary forces, and the military still exercise their power when they feel that democratic expression conflicts with their conceptions of law and order.[30] Likewise, armed forces' generals have pronounced on a whole range of political issues—from human rights to foreign policy—that are theoretically the prerogative of the civilian government.[31]

The electoral regime has been most willing to subordinate the interests of popular democratic development to those of the armed forces over the issue of human rights. Throughout 1990 scores of skeletons and mutilated corpses of trade-union and peasant activists, elected local and state officials, political-party leaders, managers of public enterprises, professionals, and students were discovered in mass graves—the victims of execution, frequently after torture, by military officials of the Pinochet state after the terrorist generals violently seized power from the democratically elected socialist government of Salvador Allende in September 1973.[32] Those responsible for many of these mass executions are known and have been identified by witnesses and human rights groups —yet they remain at large, charged with no crime.[33]

The "unofficial" position of the elected Aylwin government and the Christian Democratic and Socialist parties has been to uncover the victims of the terror, exhume the bodies, identify the cause of death, and pay an indemnification to the families.[34] This is described as "truth and reconciliation," and is the name of an official commission also established to investigate the political murders of the Pinochet period. The rationale for absolving military commanders of the terrorism is put in terms of "consolidating democracy" or "closing the wounds of society."[35] Stability and political democracy, in this view, can be achieved only by avoiding confrontation with the armed forces and their political backers. Hence it is deemed necessary to ignore demands for justice from the families of the victims. These demands are described as "retribution," a phrase used by the Pinochetist press, some electoral politicians, and overseas journalists.[36] Justice is seen as a monetary payoff rather than as equity before the law.

But neither stability nor democracy nor justice is served by "reconciliation." First, absolving the military of capital crimes places it above the law; its members are exempted from punishment for what would be crimes if committed by civil-

ians. This double standard in law enforcement cripples the basic principle underlying democracy: equality before the law. Second, the exoneration of the military for past crimes creates a precedent for the commission of future crimes: impunity encourages recidivism. The "pragmatic" argument made by some government spokesmen—that the application of law against the military could endanger democracy —is an argument against democracy. It presumes that a nonelected, authoritarian institution and not the popularly elected government has the final say in applying the law of the land. Insofar as the armed forces continue to determine when and where and against whom laws will apply, Chile does not measure up to any internationally accepted standard of democracy.

The stability of a democracy is not built by granting concessions to the military on issues pertaining to its violent intrusion into democratic politics. Moreover, the exoneration of the armed forces perpetuates the culture of fear and intimidation that prevailed during the period of military rule. As one Chilean human rights leader observed, "The Truth and Reconciliation Commission encourages some to speak up, but others fear that truth without justice puts the witnesses in danger." Fear of military retribution is real; the military and police courts are still prosecuting their critics in the press, while their paramilitary counterparts have been active in threatening potential witnesses to the crimes committed by the Pinochet armed forces.[37]

In the human rights' sphere, as in the socioeconomic, the major concern of the regime is to accommodate the military/civilian Right and gain their confidence in order to manage the system more smoothly. The historical amnesia of the electoral political class is a convenient recourse in pursuing their incremental politics: they want to forget and forgive the crimes of the military in order to bargain for greater acceptability; they want to denigrate the successful structural reforms and popular power experiments of the late 1960s and early 1970s in order to forge alliances with the investor classes of the 1990s.

While the transition from the dictatorship to an electoral regime represents a substantial qualitative shift in political opportunities for the intellectual and political class, the shift in political forms has not led to a similar increase in political participation, power, and independent organization for rural labor and the urban poor, and has led to only marginal increases for urban labor. The contradiction between the expansion of formal political space and the continuing constraints imposed by existing state structures and the neoliberal model are already beginning to manifest themselves. The reemerging struggle between the social movements and the regime is precisely over the former's efforts to provide a substantial popular content to the elite-controlled political forms.

Conclusion

In extenso, this discussion of political change in Chile applies to other contemporary Latin American experiences. The basic issue that is raised concerns the essential difference between "regime" and "state" change. Our basic argument is that electoral regimes are not always democratic. In a democracy, there exists a civic culture in which decisions are freely made without fear of state terror; in Chile, there is a pervasive culture of fear cultivated by the political parties and elites who control the legitimate demands of the electorate through constant references to the danger of "provoking a return of the military." A culture of fear is incompatible with democratic practice. In a democracy, elected national officials decide major issues. Today in Chile, nonelected officials, foreign and national, shape the basic trade, investment, and debt payment issues. Military officials define the parameters of government action and pronounce on vital issues of human rights, violating the notion of "equal protection under the law." Pinochet-appointed judicial and banking officials define crucial legal and economic issues.

Finally, democracy involves an active, organized, and independent civil society based on social movements responsive to popular needs. In Chile, as elsewhere, electoral machines attempt to subordinate and disarticulate the social movements, to atomize the electorate, and to shrink political vision. The electoral regime has in the best of cases only taken the first tentative legal steps toward opening up the Chilean political system. Substantive democracy requires a different political alignment with a different relationship to the state and civil society.

Notes

1. For a detailed discussion, see James Petras and Fernando Ignacio Leiva, "Chile: The Authoritarian Transition to Electoral Politics," *Latin American Perspectives*, Vol. 15, No. 3, Summer 1988, pp. 97–114. See also Fernando Paulsen, "La Política Despues de Los Arsenales," *Revista Análisis*, No. 157, 1986.

2. The decisive organizational change was the decision of the Alianza Democrática (the coalition of seven opposition parties from center-right to social democrat) to break with the left-wing coalition, the Movimiento Democrático Popular, and to engage in a "fruitful dialogue."

3. Interview with Augusto Samanieo, one of the early proponents of the Communist strategy of "popular rebellion," July 24, 1990. Also see Manual Fernando Contreras, "La Actual Situación Política Sus Proyecciónes," *Critica y Socialismo* (Santiago: Ediciónes CISPO, 1989), pp. 116–122.

4. During 1986–1987, over 100,000 people between fourteen and sixty years old were arrested (most temporarily) in operations against forty shantytowns (poblaciónes). See Fernando Leiva and James Petras, "Chile: New Urban Movements and the Transition to Democracy," *Monthly Review*, Vol. 39, No. 3, July/August 1987, p. 122.

5. See "The New Class Basis of Chilean Politics," in James Petras and Morris Morley, *U.S. Hegemony Under Siege* (London: Verso, 1990), pp. 241–242.

6. Interview with Communist party leaders, March 1987.

7. See the interview with Josef J. Brunner in *La Segunda*, September 26, 1986. Brunner is the chief ideologue of the Nuñez faction of the Socialist party. For the Christian Democrats, see the interview in *La Segunda*, September 8, 1986. Nuñez's explicit acceptance of the Pinochet constitution is found in *La Tercera*, October 5, 1986.

8. Eugenio Tironi, "Crisis, Disintegraction y Modernizaction," in *Proposiciónes* (Santiago), No. 18, pp. 16–42.

9. The main architect of the "governability" thesis was Manuel Antonio Garrelson. See his *The Chilean Political Process* (Boston: Unwin Hyman, 1989).

10. This rhetoric pervades the publications of all the self-styled renovated Socialists and their political mentors in the leadership of the Socialist party.

11. U.S. Under Secretary of State for Inter-American Affairs Robert Gelbard flew to Chile after the July 2–3, 1986, general strike and bluntly told the renovated Socialists and Christian Democrats that the Reagan administration opposed the tactics of "social mobilization" and alliances with the Left. Immediately thereafter, the alliances broke apart and the center alliance rejected mobilization politics. See Petras and Leiva, "Chile: The Authoritarian Transition to Electoral Politics," pp. 99–100.

12. The National Endowment for Democracy, the Reaganite political interventionary arm, provided hundreds of thousands of dollars for several Chilean research institutions run by right-wing Social Democrats and Christian Democrats, many of them ex-leftists from the 1960s, who were eager recipients of these funds for "political education" in conformity.

13. On the continuities of military privilege, see "Militares Gastan Mucho y Quieren Mas," *Página Abierta* July 23–August 5, 1990, pp. 18–19.

14. See interview with Admiral Jorge Martinex Busch, *El Mercurio*, July 22, 1990, pp. D-1, D-3.

15. This threat from the military, in turn, has been transmitted by the regime to its electoral supporters, thus inhibiting the free expression of popular demands and creating a culture of fear.

16. It was believed that Pinochet spent several million dollars to secure the "early retirement" of several judges to facilitate his packing the court.

17. Pinochet's pact with Aylwin closely resembles the pact that the Christian Democrats imposed on Allende as a condition for allowing him to take office in 1970.

18. Interview with Manuel Barrera, July 19, 1990.

19. *El Mercurio* gave prominent coverage to right-wing Social Democrat Jose J. Brunner's messianic promarket message. He described the market as "one of the most powerful mechanisms of coordination [*sic*] of the economy and society that civilization has perfected over the length of its history. . . ." Quoted in *El Mercurio*, July 20, 1990, p. C-5.

20. See the special issue of *Proposiciónes*, No. 18.

21. "Policies, Mechanisms and Organization of International Cooperation," "Concertación de los Partidos para la Democracia," October 1989. Even this minimalist preelectoral reform program has since been abandoned.

22. During 1990, President Aylwin's regime began pressuring the U.S. Congress to resume military aid to Chile in the hopes of demonstrating to the Chilean military the utility of better working relations.

23. Quoted in "Los Cien Días de Aylwin," *Análisis*, July 16–22, 1990. Also see A.

Diaz, "Interrogates Sobre el Rumbo Economico del Gobierno," *Análisis y Perspectivas*, No. 2, May 1990.

24. *El Mercurio*, July 13, 1990, p. B-1, and July 12, 1990, p. B-1. On Foxley's support of the Bush plan, see *Fortin Mapocho*, July 26, 1990, p. 9.

25. On the pre-1973 Socialist and Christian Democratic parties, see James Petras, *Politics and Social Forces in Chilean Development* (Berkeley: University of California Press, 1968).

26. President Aylwin defended the existing Pinochet-established rules for foreign investment by citing the needs of foreign capital for "stable norms"—thus rejecting trade union demands for tax reforms affecting the mining multinationals. See *El Mercurio*, July 19, 1990, p. A-1.

27. See *El Mercurio*, July 21, 1990 p. B-1.

28. The mass appeal of the Aylwin presidential campaign was evident in its sweep of almost all of the urban centers except for two in Santiago. Aylwin won in districts covering the range of social classes from affluent professionals to the marginal.

29. See, for example, the pronouncement by the general secretary of the government, Enrique Correa, against "excess liberty" of the press. Quoted in *Fortin Mapocho*, July 16, 1990, p. 2.

30. On police repression, see *Fortín Mapocho*, July 21, 1990.

31. On Aylwin consulting with the armed forces, see *El Mercurio*, July 20, 1990, p. 1. In September 1990, Pinochet accused the armed forces of the German Federal Republic of betraying their traditions and being a collection of "homosexuals" and "misfits." The Aylwin government merely apologized to the Germans and took no action against Pinochet.

32. *Analisis,* July 25, 1990, lists several of the mass graves throughout the country.

33. See Patricia Verdugo, *Los Zarpazos del Puma* (Santiago: Ediciónes Chile America, 1989); *Fortín Mapocho*, July 14, 1990, p. 14. Extensive documentation is present in the archives of the Agrupación de Familiares de Ejecutados Políticos. Also see *Fortín Mapocho,* July 20, 1990, pp. 12, 8; and the special issue of *El Siglo,* July 8–14, 1990.

34. The regime's "forgive-and-forget" position on military assassinations was most clearly stated by the president of the congress, Jose Antonio Viera-Gallo: "We should end polemics about past facts." Quoted in *El Mercurio*, July 20, 1990, p. C-3. Also see *El Mercurio*, July 22, 1990, p. D-8.

35. Viera-Gallo, quoted ibid. He argued that it was much more important to "develop common tasks with the military which are prejudiced by polemics." Mass murder and torture have become "polemics"; the demands for equal justice before the law are obstacles to pursuing the common neoliberal economic project.

36. *El Mercurio*, long-time apologist for Pinochet and the military dictatorship, is the primary exponent of this position in Chile. Anthony Lewis and Shirley Christian of *The New York Times* have followed suit.

37. Interviews with Ross Silva and Berta Ugarte of the Agrupacion de Familiares de Ejecutados Políticos de Chile, July 25, 1990. See also *Presos Político del Régimen Militar: Nominas y Guadros Estadísticos al 30 de Junio* (Santiago: FASIC, 1990).

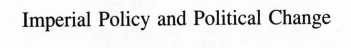

Imperial Policy and Political Change

3

U.S. Policy Toward Latin America: Military Intervention, Client Regimes, and Economic Pillage in the 1990s

Introduction

The end of the Cold War has if anything *strengthened* the drive in Washington to *consolidate* its informal empire in Latin America. Moreover, the relative decline in the U.S. global position, particularly its displacement by Germany in Europe and Japan in Asia, has *intensified* Washington's efforts to hold onto its favored dominion of exploitation, profits, and interest payments—Latin America.

Through trial and effort, improvisation and deliberate intervention, the United States has come to fashion a complex and coherent regional strategy that operates on three mutually reinforcing and interrelated levels: First, through the imposition of an *economic policy* ("freeing markets") designed to dismantle a half-century of state regulations, diminish the role of domestic producers and markets, privatize public enterprises, and lower the costs of labor. These policies facilitate the takeover by U.S. corporations of local productive and extractive enterprises, sustain the payment of foreign debts, and decrease U.S. corporate wage and tax payments. The doctrine of "free markets" is a euphemism for private foreign pillage through monopoly profits. The crucial theoretical point is that the U.S. strategy does not expand or create new sites of production but takes over and drains the investable surplus to the imperial mainland. Unlike earlier periods when large-scale industrial expansion combined investments in new facilities, expansion of domestic markets, *and* the appropriation of surplus, in the present context the political economy of financial pillage and debt-swap takeovers reigns supreme. Whereas the Alliance for Progress combined state, public, and private investment for exploitation through the development of productive forces, the Bush administration's "Enterprise of the Americas Initiative" facilitates foreign takeovers of existing markets and firms. This fundamental shift in imperial relations is intimately linked to changes in the U.S. economy, the shift from industrial to finance capital, as well as to a dramatic transformation in the role and structural components of the U.S. imperial state: in the 1990s the military/ideological dimensions have clearly eclipsed the economic/political.

Second, the United States has designed a *military strategy* that is integrally related to the "free-market" doctrine. Its overall goal is to install and sustain in power regimes promoting free-market policies and to undermine national movements and governments advocating alternative development models. The military strategy operates on multiple levels, taking account of different political contexts, but all converge toward the same objective: (a) *narco-intervention*, basically covert counterinsurgency activities in order to establish a continuing military presence in South America (Bolivia, Peru, Colombia) so as to gain direct access to command structures and to promote a more repressive solution to the "problems" of guerrilla movements, peasant organizations, and other organized forces challenging the client regimes; (b) "*low-intensity warfare*" in Central America, a euphemism for an expanded and intensified military offensive by the armed forces and their paramilitary death-squad allies against the region's social and political movements—funded by the White House with senior Pentagon officials directly controlling the military/political decisions regarding the prosecution of these wars; (c) *direct, large-scale military intervention*, involving U.S. armed forces (Grenada, Panama) or contra surrogates (Nicaragua) for the purpose of destroying the target regime, its state institutions and socioeconomic structures, and installing a compliant puppet government; and (d) *routinized bureaucratic and ideological convergence* (the rest of Latin America) to prevent popular upheavals. Each of these military strategies is designed to strengthen regimes promoting free-market policies (e.g., Peru, Bolivia), destroy indigenous movements challenging this model (e.g., El Salvador), or to undermine regimes directly or indirectly in conflict with it (e.g., Nicaragua). The economic inability of the United States to compensate for the disastrous socioeconomic consequences accompanying the continent-wide "free-market" pillage requires the elaboration of such a comprehensive military strategy.

Third, Washington has elaborated a *political strategy* which involves the promotion of electoral regimes in the interstices of its economic policy and military framework. The electoral regimes serve to provide pseudolegitimacy to the authoritarian and exploitative systems while pursuing programs compatible with the imperial state's hegemonic interests. The pivotal cohabitation of civil regime and military power serves to facilitate domestic public support for imperial policies while retaining the armed forces as political insurance if the electoral regimes lose control or the disintegration of "free-market" economies provokes popular uprisings. The existence of these tightly restricted civilian governments, and the parliaments, parties, and political processes that accompany them, also serves (or attempts) to demobilize opposition social movements ("they endanger democracy"), to co-opt "progressive intellectuals" ("we have to ensure democratic 'governability'"), and to restrict political agendas ("there are no alternatives to neoliberalism") in a way that U.S. policy-makers could not accomplish directly. The new collaborator electoral regimes are a key ingredient in Washington's larger strategy, even as they are subject to continuing stresses and tensions in their relations with the military and the "free market." Therefore, the imperial state assumes the role of manager of such conflicts in order to ensure the continued success of its hemispheric policy.

Since the late 1970s and early 1980s, the United States has employed its formidable military and ideological power to oust "hostile" Latin American governments and establish the groundwork for their replacement by civilian clients. Subsequently, it has endeavored to influence and shape the economic direction of these elected regimes. Products of U.S.-brokered "transitions," these regimes are highly receptive to the "free-market"–trade liberalization doctrine promoted by Washington. But despite success in the short-run, a fundamental contradiction confronts White House and State Department officials: the imperial state has demonstrated an increasing inability to provide sufficient infusions of capital, expertise, and technology to transform these political clients into viable capitalist associates. The decline in U.S. global economic power (exacerbated by the dominance of parasitical-speculator overproductive capitalist-class forces through the 1980s) undermines efforts to construct and consolidate a cluster of dynamic electoralist allies. The rhetoric of "growth through free trade and free markets" has provided an effective cover for a policy of pillage, not financial support and economic reciprocity. The appropriation of Latin America's dwindling economic resources (debt payments, market takeovers, etc.) has substituted for long-term, large-scale productive investments. Paralleling this latter-day "sacking" of regional economies by U.S. public and private institutions, the Reagan-Bush administrations have systematically increased Washington's ties with the hemisphere's armed forces—an insurance policy in case the electoralist experiments falter and collapse.

Washington Promotes the "Free-Market" Doctrine

Since the early 1980s, Latin American governments have followed the economic directives of the United States, international banking institutions (multilateral and private), and local transnational capitalist interests by deregulating economies, privatizing state sectors, abolishing tariffs, and permitting the "free flow" of capital profits. In return, the "free-market" ideologues in Washington and elsewhere promised that the region would attract sufficient large-scale capital investments to sustain long-term development and growth, bring hyperinflation under control, and increase national income levels. To attract foreign investment, increase exports, and eliminate chronic trade deficits, Reagan-Bush policy-makers and international bankers stressed how important it was for Latin economies to make "adjustments" to lower government spending, wage levels, and the like.

The spread of "free-market"–export strategy programs across the region has produced the exact opposite effect of that predicted by its advocates. Instead of large-scale inflows of foreign capital, the "free-market" experiments have been accompanied by a net decline in new overseas investment, rising principal and debt interest payments abroad, and accelerated capital flight—thus undermining any rational basis for creating stable economies and promoting long-term development and growth. The application and deepening of "free-market" policies devastated Latin America's investment capacity, which fell by twenty-five percent between 1980 and 1989. During the same period, aggregate figures on per-capita gross national product (GNP) reveal a cumulative decline of −9.6 percent, a trend which shows no signs of abating (−2.6 percent in 1990). Over the decade, the region's terms of trade deteriorated by twenty-one percent, its foreign debt skyrocketed to $434 billion (end 1989), and it was transformed into a massive net exporter of capital (approximately $225 billion between 1982 and 1990). Finally, recent capital trends do not bode well for Latin America's future: new foreign commercial bank lending plunged from $5.5 billion in 1988 to $2.3 billion in 1989; and U.S. economic support funds declined from $545 million in 1988 to $350 million in 1990 (a fall of thirty-six percent).[1] Not without justification was the 1980s termed a "lost [economic] decade" for the region.

The massive transfer of profits, interest and principal payments, and capital from Latin America to the United States and other advanced industrialized countries during the 1980s was the fundamental purpose (and overriding achievement) of the "free-market" strategy. Washington's proposed solutions to the region's decapitalization "problem" were the "Baker plan" (1985) and the "Brady plan" (1989). The former involved the commercial and international banks providing $29 billion in new loans ($20 billion and $9 billion, respectively) to seventeen (mostly Latin American) debtor countries between 1986 and 1988. But the failure of the scheme was virtually preordained given that the average annual negative transfers of financial resources from the proposed seventeen recipients was $40 billion. Subsequently, the scheme was further undermined by the decision of the commercial banks to commit only slightly in excess of fifty percent of the amount requested by U.S. officials. The Brady plan took a different tack, announcing that it would seek to ease the transfer burden by promoting debt write-offs and other reduction programs such as debt swaps for local assets. This approach has been no more successful than its predecessor. Write-offs have been plagued by insufficient financial commitments from the commercial and international banks; debt reduction typically has done little more than shift the source of overseas transfers from interest payments to profits from newly acquired local productive enterprises.[2] Ultimately, the failures of national development throughout the hemisphere were merely by-products of the private successes of international and Latin American transnational capital—the real constituency of Washington policy-makers.

The Reagan-Bush policies eschewed reciprocity (long-term large-scale investments) in favor of short-term profit-taking (pillage). Calls for new economic adjustments in response to the failure of old economic adjustments were all directed toward the same interrelated goals: the seizure of regional resources and breakdown of barriers to U.S. commerce and investment expansion. During his

December 1990 tour of Latin America to sell Washington's economic prescriptions, President Bush spoke glowingly of the newly elected civilian rulers who were "stripping away state controls. . . ."[3] For the great majority of the populations of these countries, however, the results have been disastrous: falling real wage levels; massive increases in unemployment; growing concentrations of wealth and income; and unprecedented declines in overall living standards.

Non-Reciprocity in U.S. Policy: Case Studies

The "free-market" doctrine propounded by Washington was supposed to be based on the notion of reciprocity: in return for opening up its economies and markets, Latin America could expect equivalent U.S. concessions in the form of new market openings and capital funding. In practice, however, the Bush White House, like its predecessor, has applied the doctrine in an extremely one-sided manner—taking advantage of large-scale deregulation of Latin economies without providing much in the way of capital resources or market opportunities for its client regimes. In this section, we examine a series of "case studies" illustrating the principle of nonreciprocity.

Both Central America and, to a lesser extent, the Caribbean have been affected by Washington's lack of economic reciprocity. Jamaica offers one of the more striking instances of this U.S. behavior. Soon after his electoral victory in February 1989, Michael Manley began implementing a number of "free-market" reforms—those particularly favored by the International Monetary Fund (IMF)—in an attempt to resolve the deep-seated problems that confronted the Jamaican economy: Millions of dollars in public subsidies were slashed when the government mandated price increases on a number of basic food staples; a ceiling was imposed on wage increases; and publicly owned real estate was auctioned off to private investors. Manley's reward was a $65 million standby loan negotiated with the IMF in May. Ten months later, his government received a further fund "seal of approval"—a $107 million loan in return for Manley's commitment to maintain the clampdown on wages, begin a new round of price increases, and impose a new set of taxes. In mid-November 1990, reflecting his total capitulation to the IMF (and U.S.) economic panaceas, Manley announced a major privatization offensive. The nationalist policies that marked his first presidential term (1972–1976) had now been completely supplanted by his embrace of "free-market" doctrines; his earlier independent foreign policy had now given way to a determined effort to accommodate U.S. regional interests. But, according to a Jamaican official, the Bush administration still "hardly has the time of day for him."[4] This stony Washington response to Manley's pro-imperial shift was reflected in the last-minute decision to provide Jamaica with a miserly $13.7 million in economic aid for 1990. Bush and the U.S. Congress had initially decided to reprogram Jamaica's proposed 1990 aid allocation (originally $20 million) to Poland.[5]

In Central America, the Bush administration has systematically contracted markets and cut aid programs. Under new U.S. tariff quotas on sugar imports announced in September 1990, for instance, the total subregional quota has been cut by 58.4 percent between 1989–1990 and 1990–1991.[6] In the area of economic aid, the trend has been in the same direction: combined U.S. aid to El Salvador, Guatemala, Costa Rica, and Honduras fell by twenty percent between 1989 and 1990; the White House 1991 request for those four countries, together with Nicaragua, Panama, and Belize, is thirty percent below the level of funding provided in 1985.[7]

The application of "free-market"–open-economy doctrines in South America have provoked similar economic debacles and a similar lack of U.S. reciprocity. Colombian President Virgilio Barco, currently presiding over a five-year program to open up the country's economy to foreign competition, blamed Washington for the collapse of the international coffee agreement in July 1989 which saw the world price for Colombia's biggest legal export plummet by fifty percent. According to Barco, the coffee price supports were not extended "due to a lack of political willingness on the part of the United States."[8] But those economies most negatively affected by "free-market" doctrines have been Brazil, Peru, and Argentina, where per-capita GNP declined by 5.9 percent, 7.3 percent, and 3.2 percent, respectively, in 1990—the worst in the entire continent.[9]

In March 1990, Brazil's newly elected President Fernando Collor, a self-styled free marketeer, announced an IMF-type antiinflation (stabilization) program which included an end to price controls, the elimination of producer subsidies, and a major reduction in the size of the public sector. After ten months, "Plan Collor" proved a spectacular failure, creating the worst recession in over a decade: industrial activity in the country's industrial belt fell by eleven percent; gross domestic profit (GDP) contracted by four percent; the agricultural harvest decreased by over twenty-one percent; the value of the stockmarket plummeted by sixty-eight percent; real wage levels declined by an estimated sixteen percent; hundreds of thousands of public- and private-sector workers lost their jobs; and the annual inflation rate reached 1,800 percent—an all-time high.[10]

Not only did "Plan Collor" devastate Brazilian workers and industrialists; U.S. investors and bankers reaped minimal benefits, at least in the short term. Only $1 billion in new foreign investment entered Brazil during the first nine months of 1990, compared with $2 billion in 1988, which led all Latin American countries. Using a broad definition of applications of foreign capital in the region, Brazil's 1990 effort lagged behind Mexico, Venezuela, Chile, and even Argentina.[11] This disappointing result was partly attributable to the reluctance of investors, especially American, to become involved in a country that had a continuing unresolved problem with its foreign commercial (mostly U.S.) bank creditors. Interest owing to these commercial banks since the central government stopped payments in July 1989 had risen to $8 billion. Collor's programs seem to have served only to satisfy the "free-market" ideologues.

Undeterred by the failure of Plan Collor, the Brazilian president, with Washington's enthusiastic support, implemented "Plan Collor II" in February 1991, which calls for a new round of adjustment/austerity measures (wage freezes, increases in public utility rates, etc.) and will effectively end all forms of wage indexation linked to the consumer price index and/or past inflation levels.[12] The government also declared its intention to accelerate the privatization process by auctioning off ten state-owned enterprises in the hope of raising between $6 billion and $7 billion. In other words, the "free-market" doctrine as applied to Brazil, by promoting industrial recession and widespread bankruptcies instead of U.S. investment, banking, and trade interests, was actually undermining Brazil's capacity to import and even pay its foreign debt. Thus, the contradiction between the imperial ideology of pillage ("free market") and the incapacity to realize private imperial economic interests.

In the interim, the effects of Plan Collor directly contributed to major defeats for government-backed candidates in the November 1990 gubernatorial run-off elections. In the first round of voting in October, Collor associates won ten of the eleven state governorships that were decided. This time around, a discontented industrial working class, whose wages had been eroded by inflation and were no longer adjusted for higher living costs, ensured the defeat of regime supporters in the politically powerful states of Sao Paolo, Minas Gerias, and Perana. Hence, the contradiction in imperial policy: by following IMF-Bush free-enterprise ideology, the U.S. mass-media–style president was at the same time eroding his capacity to serve as an effective political collaborator to legitimate American policy. Such contradictions between the different components of White House strategy are being replicated throughout the hemisphere.

The Fujimori government's economic program in Peru, similarly praised by imperial state officials, has had no more success than the "adjustments" imposed by Collor. Between his election in June 1990 and his inauguration in late July, Fujimori reached a tentative agreement with the international banks (World Bank, IMF, Inter-American Development Bank) to implement a series of austerity measures to supposedly counter hyperinflation in return for new loans from these institutions. But the measures taken (withdrawal of basic consumer subsidies, selling off public companies, eliminating protectionist barriers, etc.) produced results contrary to what the bankers forecast. Instead of economic stabilization, they triggered economic destabilization: massive demonstrations and rioting in Lima's impoverished "new towns"; rising unemployment and business bankruptcies; lowered living standards; and a worsening inflation rate. According to official government calculations, the latter increased from 3,000 percent to 7,650 percent during Fujimori's first six months as president; according to a local private consulting firm, Cuanto, the figure was well over 10,300 percent at the end of 1990—more than triple the rate at the time of Fujimori's inauguration. [13]

Entering 1991, almost seventy percent of the population was living below the poverty line while more than fifty percent lacked access to adequate drinking water and sanitation services. In late January, the "free-market" doctrine brought Peru its first cholera epidemic in more than 100 years. Within less than three months, the disease had claimed over 1,000 lives and infected more than 150,000 others. The head of the Pan-American Health Organization, Dr. Carlyle Macedo, stressed the need for an international emergency plan to check the epidemic, which had spread to Colombia, Brazil, Chile, and Ecuador. He warned a regional health ministers' conference in April that hopes of controlling the disease were receding: "It is almost inevitable that we will have an epidemic of a monstrous nature in Latin America which will be nearly impossible to contain."[14] Accompanying the cholera outbreak in Peru were reports of an upsurge in the incidence of malaria, also linked to poor sanitation and health facilities. Neither the Peruvian population nor U.S. interests have benefited from the government's policies. But the "free-market" ideologues in the Lima, Washington, and the international banks have waxed enthusiastic over Fujimori's economic approach, as have foreign investors since Fujimori announced the most liberal profit remittance rules in four decades.[15]

Of all the electoral regimes in South America, perhaps the most extreme case of following U.S.-IMF economic directives is the neoliberal Menem government in Argentina. In mid-1989, Menem embarked on what some critics aptly called the "liquidation of Argentina," together with a harsh austerity program to supposedly get inflation under control and renovate the economy. But the recovery plan centered around a sweeping privatization offensive: the only sectors off-limits were health, education, justice, security, and foreign relations. Topping the agenda were communications and transport, including the enormous state-run telephone company. In late 1990, the government sold sixty percent of the company to two consortiums of American and European multinationals. Meanwhile, the austerity measures served to decimate the industrial work force. Between October 1989 and October 1990, a reported one million out of 2.3 million workers lost their jobs. At the same time, real wage levels slumped to all-time lows, rates for basic public services increased by 50 percent, and the government shut down 18,000 miles of railroad to save on maintenance costs, thereby isolating whole areas of the interior.[16]

Buffeted by the demands of international creditors and massive capital flight (an estimated $4 billion in 1989) on the one side and hyperinflation on the other, the regime implemented those adjustments demanded by Washington and the foreign bankers but received little or no financial assistance from the Bush White House. This despite Menem's unprecedented decision (alone among Latin American governments) to send two warships to participate in the U.S.-orchestrated naval blockade of Iraq following discussions with U.S. Vice President Dan Quayle and a personal letter from George Bush.[17]

The cases of Peru, Brazil, and Argentina highlight the principal features of the U.S. "free-trade" doctrine: (1) its nonreciprocal character, opening up Latin America to pillage without compensatory concessions from Washington; (2) its devastating effects on the region's growth and income levels; (3) the contradictions that it provokes within the U.S. imperialist strategy—undermining collaborator political regimes and even some U.S. economic interests; and (4) privileging the role of ideological and political conformity over and against economic rationality.

The U.S. strategy emphasis on nonreciprocal "free trade," and unregulated appropriation of interest payments, and Latin "flight" capital is directly linked to the reduction of U.S. official lending to Latin America. Given the region's position as a source of economic surplus to buttress U.S. balance-of-payments deficits with its global competitors, the decline in foreign aid is a logical outcome. Washington's economic assistance strategy and its application are clearly evidenced in the Caribbean Basin Initiative (CBI).

In 1990, the White House rationalized the decline in U.S. economic aid to the Caribbean (a miniscule $20 million compared with $82 million in 1987) on the grounds that what the region needed most was not foreign assistance but multinational investments—which would only be forthcoming if governments deregulated their economies and offered new investment concessions and guarantees. Bush officials admiringly referred to the Reagan administration's CBI program of trade benefits and investment incentives as the most appropriate strategy for generating economic development. But the history of the CBI during the 1980s provided no basis for believing that such an approach was likely to revive the depressed Caribbean economies.

The CBI was basically undermined by the power of U.S. national corporate interests to maintain protectionist barriers against some of the subregion's strongest exports. Although a number of export commodities received a twelve-year exemption from duties in 1983, products such as textiles, petroleum, tuna, clothing apparel, leather goods, and watches were deemed ineligible for tariff relief. The effectiveness of the measures taken to benefit Caribbean exporters was further undermined by a provision authorizing the president to revoke the duty-free status of any specific import if it was deemed to be hurting the domestic industry—which the White House did on a number of occasions. Some of the supposed tax benefits offered the subregional clients were also rendered useless by complex or inconsistent U.S. Food and Drug Administration and Customs Service regulations. In several instances, pesticides approved for use on Caribbean produce imported into the United States were banned during production or shipment, leaving the produce to rot on the Florida docks. Finally, Caribbean sugar exporters were subject to substantial quota cuts by the U.S. Farm Act of 1985, which sought to safeguard the interest of American producers. The value of Dominican Republic sales to the United States, for example, declined by seventy-five percent between 1985 and 1988.

Overall, the CBI experiment was a windfall for U.S. manufacturers able to take advantage of low-cost labor, not a boon to Caribbean traders. Between 1983 and 1989, the value of their exports to the United States plummeted by one-third due to the collapse in sugar sales (down by seventy percent) and a $4 billion fall in the value of the subregion's oil exports. As a result, a $3 billion positive trade balance was transformed into a $2.5 billion trade deficit.[18] The intended beneficiaries of the CBI were powerless in the face of American domestic producers and their congressional allies, who placed so many restrictions on the program that the rhetoric of the stated objectives never came close to being achieved. In 1989, the new Bush administration introduced CBI II, ostensibly to remedy the failings of the original bill. But domestic industry lobbyists once again used their influence with lawmakers to gut most of the proposals to increase access to the U.S. market for Central American exports. Representative Sam Gibbons, chairman of the House Trade Subcommittee and author of the legislation,called the final result "a hollow, tinkling bill. . . ."[19]

However, the centerpiece of the Bush White House strategy for further pillage of Latin America's deteriorating economies was not the CBI but a plan announced in June 1990 and dubbed the "Enterprise of the Americas Initiative." Like the CBI, it was based on the proposition that trade, not aid, was the key to hemispheric prosperity. The initiative was basically an extension and deepening of the IMF–World Bank economic model of the 1980s, now repackaged in the form of an imperial state policy. It involved "free-trade" pacts, new concessions to foreign private capital, and debt reduction. The latter centered around an administration offer to assist the most heavily debt-burdened Latin regimes by reducing $7 billion of the amount ($12 billion) owed to American government agencies, conditional on the recipients adopting the requisite "free-market" reforms designed to provide U.S. traders and investors with greater access to regional economies. Indeed, one of the prime goals of the initiative was to revive U.S. exports to Latin America, which had declined in value by as much as $130 billion between 1982 and 1988.[20] Washington also generously offered to "encourage" the foreign commercial banks that were owed the vast bulk of the hemisphere's debt to also provide some relief in return for an accelerated deregulation of markets. The prospects on this latter score were limited, given that a number of creditor banks had already taken losses on Latin portfolios and were steadily cutting back on their overall exposure in the area.

The "trade not aid" formula is peculiarly suited to the pillage of Latin America—the takeover of local markets and enterprises. In the past, U.S. economic policy was based on trade *and* aid: state assistance involved large-scale, low-interest public loans to finance infrastructure, energy projects, and education to provide the "shell" for long-term, large-scale U.S. and local investments; and short-term loans for social programs and the growth of small businesses to cushion the adverse impacts of the market. The new formula of trade not aid that informs the Bush initiative scheme is designed for short-term speculative investments without concern for the socially negative consequences.

This latest White House program compares most unfavorably with the previous major U.S. effort to stimulate development in Latin America—the ten-year, $20 billion Alliance for Progress. While failing to achieve a number of its stated objectives, it nonetheless constituted a serious attempt at capitalist modernization based on large-scale assistance to rising industrialists and other dynamic entrepreneurial groups in the region. The alliance reflected America's position as an expanding global economic power; the initiative and its miniscule financial commitment testify to America's declining economic position in the capitalist world of the 1990s. The limited scope of the Bush offer was reinforced by "[the] business as usual [policy] with respect to U.S. import controls. On August 14 [less than three weeks after the initiative was made public], the U.S. International Trade Commission ruled that imports of Mexican cement were injuring U.S. cement producers, clearing the way for stiff antidumping penalties against Mexican exporters."[21]

Bush's "free-trade" plan for Latin America particularly targeted Mexico because the Salinas regime was excessively hospitable to the project and Mexico offered U.S. speculators, investors, and bankers the most lucrative labor product and natural-resource market in Latin America—as well as the largest number of public enterprises for pillage. The Salinas government has become the cutting edge of the entire U.S. strategy of consolidating its domination of the hemisphere and projecting its power abroad.

Entering the presidency in December 1988, Salinas moved quickly to open up the economy to foreign investors. In May 1989, laws were revised to allow for majority foreign ownership in selected enterprises and to encourage the entry of overseas capital into industrial sectors previously off-limits or largely the domain of national capitalists. Tariffs on imports were also slashed or removed, exposing such highly protected industries as computers and pharmaceuticals to increased overseas competition. A supporter of the IMF–World Bank–Washington development model, Salinas also announced his intention during 1990 to promote a wholesale privatization of the state sector, beginning with the country's largest insurance company, Aseguradora Mexicana (Asemex).[22]

That June, Salinas and Bush began informal discussions regarding the establishment of a U.S.-Mexico "free-trade" agreement. It soon became obvious that while Washington approved of the direction in which Salinas was taking the economy, more was required to satisfy the White House. The United States wanted increased, and more reliable, access to the country's oil and gas, greater access to its market, and additional concessions to American investors. A prime U.S. objective was to get Salinas to loosen the state monopoly on the petroleum and natural gas industry and provide for at least minority foreign ownership.

In late November, the two presidents agreed to pursue the goal of eliminating nearly all tariffs and other barriers to unrestricted commerce. Salinas signalled his intention to abolish not only tariffs but also requirements for import licenses and to further ease restrictions on foreign investment. At the same time, the Mexican government began preparations to sell off the huge state-owned telecommunications conglomerate, Teléfonos de Mexico (Telmex), the eighteen biggest state-run banks, and a number of other publicly owned companies (copper mines, steel mills, food distribution, etc.)—predicting a combined revenue from these auctions in excess of $20 billion.[23]

Since 1986, the labor-exploitative border assembly plants (maquiladoras) have absorbed the great bulk of new American investments in the Mexican economy. As *Business Week* noted in November 1990 "Thousands of American producers . . . are suddenly pouring into Mexico for low-cost labor. . . . In the past four years, U.S. trade with Mexico has tripled . . . and growth in the maquiladora plants along the border is exploding." But the "spillover" impact of these plants, which expanded at an average annual rate of twenty-three percent between 1986 and 1989 and now employ 500,000 workers at an average daily wage of five dollars, has been almost nonexistent. *Business Week* described them as "little more than foreign enclaves on Mexican soil. The plants buy 97% of their parts from the U.S. and sell next to nothing inside Mexico." Additionally, some American multinationals (Ford Motor Company, Bayer, etc.) have established subsidiaries to take advantage of the economy's low wage structure, training workers to operate the most sophisticated machinery and paying them a miniscule percentage of the salary paid to equivalent trained workers in the United States. In other words, the perfect combination for maximizing profits: "high-productivity" employees paid "rock-bottom wages."[24] The proposed agreement on the dismantling of most existing obstacles to free trade will give American corporations even greater access to Mexico's market and cheap labor—and make them doubly attractive in the absence of strong environmental controls and workplace regulations. Also likely to benefit disproportionately are those American companies that facilitate or finance U.S. overseas trade.

Free trade and economic deregulation have already significantly benefited U.S. investors, who accounted for the bulk of the $6.62 billion in new foreign direct investment that flowed into the Mexican economy during 1989 and 1990.[25] Furthermore, the contract for privatizing Telmex was finally awarded to a consortium of American, French, and local companies led by Southwestern Bell. But notwithstanding Salinas's concessions to U.S. capital, a successful renegotiation of Mexico's massive foreign debt (owed largely to U.S. banks), and the promise to sell off the state-controlled banks and television industry and to allow private financing of specific oil industry projects up to 100 percent, the benefits accruing to Mexico are hard to identify. Per-capita GDP is still fourteen percent below the 1981 level and the economy remains hostage to the ups and downs of the U.S. economy. The latter's downturn during 1990 led to a precipitious fall in the rate of growth of new maquiladora plants (only six percent compared with twenty-three percent in 1989), and its effects on the Mexican economy were only cushioned by fortuitous circumstances: a $3 billion windfall from higher oil prices.[26] Given the central importance of Mexico within the larger U.S. regional hegemonic strategy of pillage and domination, however, it is not surprising that the U.S. government, corporations, and foundations have poured millions of dollars into research centers and institutions promoting the notion of "integration," "free markets," and the implementation of Bush's Enterprise of the Americas Initiative—in the process co-opting Mexico's nationalist and socialist intelligensia into the imperial project.

The economic basis of U.S. involvement in Latin America today is defined by the underlying structures of debt and pillage (wealth appropriation). Washington's contention that "free markets" and open economies are the key to economic development in the region has not been borne out by the results. Instead of creating a climate conducive to large-scale, long-term investments, expanding industrial development, declining debt, downward inflation trends, and rising living standards, this strategy has accelerated disinvestment; contracted industrial development; and produced worsening hyperinflation, rising indebtedness, and growing marginalization and immiseration of the Latin American masses. While the region has contributed to record foreign bank profits, levels of new investment, finance, and public capital inflows, especially from U.S. public and private sources, have plummeted.

Narco-Intervention: The Military Component of U.S. Strategy

The second major component of U.S. strategy revolves around the extension and deepening of military influence throughout the continent. The approach varies with geopolitical location: in Latin America, the intrusion of U.S. military force disguised as part of the antinarcotics campaign; in Central America, the resort to low-intensity warfare to consolidate clients and overthrow regimes deemed hostile to U.S. interests; throughout the hemisphere, routine ideological/technical training programs, arms supplies, and high-level bureaucratic interaction to expand and consolidate Washington's leverage over regimes and state institutions. While the context and the scope, depth, and intensity of U.S. influence vary, this military strategy is integrally related to the goals of promoting "free markets" and protecting electoral clients from popular/nationalist movements.

Washington's war against narcotrafficking has been a key component of its Latin American policy. Official U.S. pronouncements on the need to eliminate cocaine production, however, have consistently been accompanied by efforts to get the client electoral regimes to sanction an increased American military presence—often in areas of major guerrilla concentrations. These attempts to bolster the Pentagon's policing capabilities in the region raise serious questions about the underlying objectives of the entire program. At the same time, imperial state policy-makers have been forced to deal with clients' ambivalent attitudes toward their narco-interventionist proposals. Until quite recently, the involved Andean regimes have exhibited limited interest in a military response to what they perceive to be a fundamentally economic problem. And they are aware that if the cocaine market were to disappear overnight, their fragile civilian governments would face the certain prospect of a socioeconomic upheaval—and the likely direct intervention of the armed forces into the political arena.

In mid-1989, President Bush signed a National Security Decision Directive (NSDD) authorizing an expanded role for U.S. military personnel in the antidrug war in Latin America, including new "rules of engagement" allowing Special Forces troops to participate in narcotics patrols. In particular, the NSDD would permit the deployment of American military officials in areas of Peru's Upper Huallaga Valley, the coca-growing region that U.S. officials acknowledged was "effectively controlled" by the Sendero Luminoso guerrillas. One administration official predicted that as many as "several hundred" trainers, advisors, and support personnel might be assigned to Peru, Bolivia, and Colombia.[27] Although Special Forces members had been sent to Bolivia and Drug Enforcement Administration (DEA) agents have been based in Peru since 1987, this announcement promised a major escalation of Washington's military involvement in the hemisphere's drug-producing nations.

At a February 1990 "drug summit," Bush publicly announced a five-year, $2.2 billion program of economic and military aid to Peru, Colombia, and Bolivia. Over two-thirds of the funding of this so-called "Andean initiative" was earmarked for the armed forces, police, and intelligence agencies—constituting a dramatic increase in military aid compared with the token U.S. contributions provided during the 1980s. Under the plan, Bolivia would receive military assistance amounting to $41 million annually between 1990 and 1994 (a sevenfold increase over 1989); Colombia would benefit to the extent of $60 million (also a sevenfold increase over the previous year); Peru's share would jump a mammoth fifteenfold from $2.6 million in 1989 to $40 million over each of the next five years. In addition, each country would receive $15 to $20 million to equip and train their police forces. In a more ominous vein, the Latin governments were told, according to diplomatic and U.S. congressional sources, that the economic aid packages would be withheld if they balked at accepting the military funding.[28]

Only the Colombian government of Virgilio Barco had no reservations about signing the military agreement, enabling the Bush White House to deepen its relationship with one of the more brutal and corrupt officer corps in the hemisphere which, in alliance with the police and rightist death squads, had worked closely with the Medellín cartel for more than a decade. This link between senior military officials, paramilitary groups, and the notorious drug traffickers was the subject of a revealing analysis by the human rights organization Americas Watch in October 1990: " 'the so-called Medellín Cartel,' while being pursued for its drug trafficking, has at the same time entered into an unholy alliance with certain military and security chiefs conducting the anti-trafficking campaign, whose primary goal remains the defeat of the Left at any cost."[29]

The May 1990 presidential victory of the ruling Liberal party candidate César Gaviria, while welcomed by the White House, produced a major setback for U.S. drug-policy objectives. In his August 7 inaugural speech, Gaviria announced that the extradition of drug traffickers—long a top Washington priority—would no longer be used as an instrument in the conflict. Henceforth, deportation of traffickers to the United States or elsewhere would be at the discretion of the government—and would not be invoked against cartel members who turned themselves in for legal prosecution in Colombia.

Apart from the extradition announcement, Gaviria has criticized the U.S. military aid program, the Bush administration's failure to provide greater access to American markets for Colombian exports, and Washington's seeming disinterest in responding to his requests for financial compensation to help offset the estimated $1 billion cost of fighting the drug war.

But if the client is no longer willing to extradite the narcodealers and downplays Pentagon assistance, the determination of Gaviria and the armed forces to continue waging an aggressive counterinsurgency war against those guerrilla movements still operating outside of the electoral system remains undiminished. According to a U.S. congressional report, the army high command planned to use almost all of the Andean initiative military aid package promised Colombia in fiscal year 1990 (just over $40 million) to fund activities in a part of the country not known for narcotics production or trafficking.[30] At the time of the December 1990 elections for a Constituent Assembly to rewrite the constitution, which saw the disbanded M–19 guerrilla movement's slate win twenty-seven percent of the vote and nineteen out of seventy assembly seats, the government authorized the military to launch a massive ground-and-air attack against the headquarters of the Revolutionary Armed Forces (FARC), the nation's largest insurgent force.[31] In February 1991, the FARC finally agreed to demobilize and return to civilian life—preconditions established by Gaviria for dialogue and negotiations.

Direct American involvement in the war against drug trafficking in Peru began in the late 1980s. DEA and other U.S. officials participated in Operation Snowcap at the behest of the García government and within weeks of the February 1990 "drug summit" Washington announced plans to build a military training base in heart of the country's coca growing region—the Upper Huallaga Valley—to train and equip the Pervian armed forces fighting the Sendero Luminoso guerrillas.[32] However, in September 1990, the newly elected president, Alberto Fujimori, took a more critical view of U.S. drug-war activities, subsequently rejecting the first installment ($36 million) of the military aid part of Bush's Andean initiative. In its place, he proposed Washington fund an extensive crop-substitution program.[33]

Like Gaviria in Colombia, though, Fujimori's attitude toward U.S. involvement in the battle against the narcotraffickers was not accompanied by any weakening in the government's resolve to prosecute the counterinsurgency war against the Sendero guerrillas. He continued to renew the thirty-day "states of emergency" in the affected provinces while the area under military control (now estimated at sixty percent of the country, where more than half the population live) kept increasing. Toward the end of 1990, Fujimori proposed new measures to give the military even more freedom in waging the antiguerrilla struggle. These included granting the military authorities legal jurisdiction over alleged human rights' abuses by members of the armed forces and giving military courts the power to try "suspected subversives."[34]

In late January 1991, an even more dramatic policy shift seemed imminent when the Fujimori government presented a new plan to U.S. officials for a joint antidrug strategy: "In a break with previous Peruvian policy, the plan calls for the United States to help 'feed, equip, train, outfit and adequately renumerate the police and armed forces who will be fighting drug trafficking and *those who support*' the traffickers."[35] If the proposal was agreed to, Washington, for the first time, would be granted Peruvian government authority to play a direct military role in the war against the Sendero.

Bolivian President Jaime Paz Zamora initially expressed limited enthusiasm for the Andean initiative and challenged the U.S. over its seeming lack of interest in, and support for, drug-substitution economic programs. During a 1990 state of the union address, Paz Zamora observed that the Bush administration's fiscal year 1991 budget authorized the grand total of $175 million to "cushion the macroeconomic effect on Peru, Bolivia and Colombia of reduced foreign exchange inflows, finance alternative development activities in the rural areas, and increase jobs, income and foreign exchange earnings throughout the economy."[36] The Bolivian leader conservatively estimated that it would take $300 million annually to implement an effective substitute economic program in his country alone, where coca-trade earnings ($660 million in 1987) exceeded the combined income derived from legal exports. Nor was the proposed U.S. economic package likely to have any more positive impact on Peru (coca-production earnings estimated at $800 million annually) insofar as funding the costs of a realistic program to enable the nation's 200,000 producers to shift to other crops was concerned.[37]

Since mid-1990, however, the Bolivian government has bowed to relentless U.S. pressure to militarize the struggle against the narcotraffickers, including a greater direct Pentagon involvement. The head of the Bolivian Labor Confederation, Julio Arce, revealed a proposal to construct a number of "military garrisons" in the coca-growing Chapare region. Meanwhile, access roads into Chapare were destroyed by DEA officials without authorization, and antidrug raids by teams of American and Bolivian officials in Chapare, Santa Cruz, and elsewhere started becoming routine.[38] In April 1991, the Bush administration achieved a major breakthrough when the Paz Zamora government capitulated to U.S. economic pressures and agreed to allow the Bolivian military to join the police in combating the cocaine traffic—and to host 36 U.S. military instructors to train the army troops.[39]

During the 1980s, Central America was the cockpit of Washington's prosecution of its so-called low-intensity conflict (LIC) strategy in the Third World against popular movements threatening to displace local clients from power and established regimes pursuing policies deemed antagonistic to U.S. permanent interests. Through the application of a flexible mix of aid blockades, trade sanctions, economic sabotage, political and psychological pressures, civic action "pacification" programs, military warfare, and electoral intervention, Reagan-Bush policy has attempted to consolidate or install in power in Central America elected governments willing to accommodate White House objectives—not least in the economic sphere.[40] In the case of Panama, LIC actually culminated in direct military intervention to oust General Manuel Noriega from office and replace him with a civilian president (Guillermo Endara) committed to implementing U.S.–IMF–World Bank economic formulas. But the most sustained targets of Washington's LIC strategy during the decade were located in El Salvador and Nicaragua.

In El Salvador, the United States spent almost $4 billion in pursuit of two interrelated objectives: the defeat of a guerrilla-led national insurgency and the creation of a client regime willing to cohabit with a military-terrorist state and implement a "free-market" economic program. To establish the requisite political and social context for "redemocratization," the Reagan administration funded and orchestrated a counterinsurgency war against the Farabundo Martí National Liberation Front (FMLN) guerrillas, in the process turning a blind eye to the widespread and continuing violence by the armed forces and their paramilitary (death squad) allies against all centers of civilian opposition (trade unions, popular movements, peasant organizations, the church, the mass media, etc.).

Having laid the groundwork for a return to civilian rule, based on a limited electorate, Washington then proceeded to pump millions of dollars into the coffers of its preferred presidential candidate, the conservative Christian Democrat Jose Duarte. These "demonstration elections" were designed to establish, and maintain, the facade of civilian rule while obscuring the reality of the continuing hegemony of the armed forces. By the end of the decade, however, Washington's faith in Duarte had not been realized. His IMF-type austerity programs led the economy to the brink of collapse: per-capita income and industrial and agricultural production plummeted while unemployment and living costs increased significantly. The state of the economy and the government's inability to bring the counterinsurgency war to a successful conclusion all but ensured the Christian Democratic party's demise in the 1989 presidential election, which was won, much to the White House's initial dismay, by the candidate of the extreme right-wing National Republican Alliance (ARENA) party, Alfredo Cristiani. But Cristiani, a U.S.-trained businessman and local oligarch, was soon taken on board by the Bush administration when he signalled his intention to implement even more comprehensive "free-market" policies than his predecessor. During his first year in office, the new president lifted price controls on basic foodstuffs, increased public utility costs, laid off thousands of public-sector workers, moved to reverse the limited agrarian reforms enacted by the Christian Democrats in the early 1980s, and embarked on a far-reaching privatization program.[41]

The other fundamental strategic goal of U.S. low-intensity warfare in Central America during the 1980s was the destabilization and overthrow of the Sandinista government in Nicaragua. The Reagan administration mounted a coordinated and sustained strategy involving political, economic, covert, psychological, and military warfare. It imposed bilateral economic and trade sanctions; blocked the revolutionary regime's access to multilateral development bank loans; pressured Western allies to curtail trade with Nicaragua; funded, armed, and trained an exile mercenary army to wage a protracted campaign of military confrontation and economic sabotage; and established a semipermanent U.S. military presence in neighboring countries (especially Honduras) hostile to the Nicaraguan regime.

The combined impact of these measures was a devastated economy: the U.S. economic blockade denied the revolutionary regime hundreds of millions of dollars in aid and trade, complementing direct infrastructure and production losses resulting from the contra war which ran into the billions of dollars. The imperial-backed mercenaries wrecked the critical agricultural, transport, and communication sectors, while the social sector (especially health and educational institutions) bore the brunt of their terror campaign against the civilian population. At the height of the conflict, the Sandinistas were being forced to spend between fifty and sixty percent of the national budget to guarantee the survival of the revolution. In the process, scarce resources were diverted from the social and development programs.

The U.S.-contra war precipitated a major shift in Sandinista economic policy. The initial programs, funded by a mixture of public, private, and foreign capital, featured a consequential socioeconomic redistribution including a major land reform program. Washington's relentless hostility produced the hoped-for economic crisis, forcing the government to subordinate its regulated mixed-economy approach to IMF-style stabilization programs. The new austerity measures brought within them rising unemployment, spiralling inflation, scarcities of basic consumer goods, etc. The impact on workers, peasants, and the urban poor—the Sandinistas major social base of support—was profound, eroding political support for the regime.

Meanwhile, the U.S. signalled its determination to continue the terrorist war in the absence of a Sandinista commitment to institute a "redemocratization" timetable—the electoral strategy—deemed acceptable by the imperial state. The Sandinistas capitulated and national elections were scheduled for February 1990. In the run-up to the election, the Bush administration directly, and successfully, intervened in the process on the side of the conservative-rightist National Organized Union (UNO) coalition, ploughing millions of dollars into the campaign of its presidential candidate, Violetta Chamorro.

To date, however, the economic counterrevolution envisaged by Washington and the contra forces within the new governing coalition has not taken place. Continuing Sandinista power in the state and civil society has forced President Chamorro to slow down the process of "free-market" changes or risk the possibility of civil war. However, in February 1991, Chamorro signalled a renewed determination to push ahead with the privatization process in order to obtain IMF and World Bank stabilization loans. An IMF mission to Nicaragua in January gave its "seal of approval" to the government's plan to sell off about 200 state enterprises, create "free-trade" zones, offer private property guarantees, and provide incentives for nontraditional exports.[42]

Electoral Regimes and U.S. Strategy

The third component of U.S. strategy has been to promote civilian electoral regimes inserted between the "free-market" socioeconomic forces on the one hand and the military on the other. As in the past, Washington has alternated between support for electoral and military regimes depending on political circumstances: U.S. policy-makers have supported military coups against progressive civilian regimes and shifted support from the armed forces to compliant electoral regimes when popular movements threatened to overthrow the military rulers and American interests vested in the state apparatuses. The U.S. strategy of promoting "free markets" and increased military penetration needs political legitimacy for its otherwise obvious imperial pretensions—and the electoral regimes have served that purpose reasonably well. They have loyally echoed Washington's "free-market" doctrine, implementing its policies and defending it against popular protest, frequently at the cost of numerous civilian lives. The electoralists have also legitimated the role of the military, largely through laws granting impunity and amnesty for massive human rights' violations. Finally, and most importantly, these regimes have provided a legal cover for the increasing U.S. military presence in their societies—whether in the guise of fighting the antidrug war or subversion or for the "common defense."

Today, pro-U.S. civilian presidents hold power throughout the hemisphere—often due in no small measure to Washington's interventionist behavior (military, financial, electoral) over the past decade. But these electoral transitions, brokered in part by American policy-makers, have nowhere attempted to challenge the power of the armed forces or the preexisting configuration of socioeconomic power. The notion of the civilian regimes as instruments of U.S. strategy has been most evident in Central America.

In Guatemala and El Salvador, to take the most obvious examples, the electoral processes of the 1980s were accompanied by an increase in the power of the generals and a deepening role and influence of the U.S. military. Washington promoted a political strategy based on support for electoral regimes to secure external legitimation, entice foreign aid, co-opt the intellectuals, and demobilize the social movements; and to increase the size and scope of the military (which is beholden to the United States for financial aid, weaponry, and Pentagon advisors) as an instrument for beheading and decimating popular social movements that stand in opposition to imperial-state strategic interests.

The armed forces in both Guatemala and El Salvador remain "a state within a state," the decisive arbiters of political, and even economic, life: killing and "disappearing" perceived opponents with near impunity; establishing parameters that elected presidents crossed at their peril; controlling banks, agricultural enterprises, private companies, and lucrative government agencies.[43] For their part, the new civilian regimes accepted the constraints on their ability to rule and been complicit in the ongoing violence perpetrated by the armed forces, the police, and the death squads against the political and guerrilla Left. These elected presidents accepted the reality of political subordination and revealed themselves willing to countenance a high level of military brutality and abuse of human rights as the price they must pay for survival in office.

The current situation in Guatemala has its roots in the U.S.-orchestrated overthrow of the moderate reformist Arbenz government in 1954. For the next thirty years, Guatemala was ruled either directly or indirectly by a military that was tightly integrated with U.S. policy interests. It was showered with U.S. aid precisely because its extreme violence and ruthlessness served U.S. political, military, and economic interests. The return of civilian rule in 1985 was preceded by a five-year counterinsurgency war, visibly supported by the Reagan administration, which decimated the guerrilla movements but also resulted in the deaths of approximately 75,000 civilians.

Under the terms of the electoral transition, promoted by Washington as a means of securing public support and financing for the "free market," the armed forces retained a major role in the political arena. The Cerezo government was subject to an effective military veto over political and social expression, organization, and action. With more than eighty-five percent of Guatemalans living in poverty, the promise of political freedom ensured a revival of labor militancy and political agitation—and military repression. By the end of the 1980s, the killings and disappearances were on a scale approaching the Ríos Montt-Mejía charnel house in the years preceding the election. Yet the electoralists blithely defended the military actions and denied their responsibility for the terror. Washington continued to praise Cerezo's presidency and its commitment to human rights, even as it legitimated mass killings—because both Cerezo and the armed forces promoted U.S. strategic interests and hegemonic status throughout the subregion as well as the "free-market" development model.

At the end of Cerezo's five-year term, Americas Watch presented the most comprehensive, and devastating, assessment of this Washington client's performance:

> The military remains a law unto itself and human rights violations have risen sharply. Instead of bringing the perpetrators to justice, the Cerezo administration has constantly tolerated and worse still, apologized for, unspeakable abuses committed by the men the President supposedly commands. Human rights has essentially been viewed as a public relations problem. . . . Instead of taking forceful action to end the political killings, disappearances, and torture which besmirch its image abroad, the Cerezo government has hired three lobbyists in Washington to convince U.S. lawmakers it is deserving of ever-increasing amounts of aid.[44]

During Cerezo's final year in office (1989–1990), Guatemala was generally acknowledged to be the worst violator of human rights in Latin America, with estimates of extrajudicial killings and disappearances by the military, the national police, and their rightist death-squad allies ranging from more than 2,100 to over 10,000.[45]

This marked increase in electoral-regime-authored violence proceeded from the "free-market" policies promoted by the Reagan–Bush White House. Washington exculpated the government from responsibility for the crimes and expanded its links with the Guatemalan military. American officials continued to insist that they were only working with "moderate" officers who had "clean" human rights records in order to combat drug trafficking. But even the State Department's 1989 report on Guatemala conceded that the armed forces were immune from prosecution for human rights abuses committed in the course of the antiguerrilla war and continuing to the present day.

In 1988, the State Department signalled a major shift in U.S.-Guatemalan military relations when it approved the first "lethal" assistance since the military-aid program was renewed in 1985: a $13.8 million commercial sale of 16,000 M–16 rifles for the Guatemalan army. During 1989, American troops participated in military exercises and training programs, some of which took place in areas of heavy guerrilla activity. According to local residents, U.S. army engineers and Guatemalan soldiers constructed a road around one such area—Lake Atitlan—to give the military forces "easier access to combat and greater control of the population."[46]

Washington's promotion of the civilian/military formula in pursuit of its strategic interests also explains its essential indifference to military-sponsored human rights' abuses in El Salvador. The critical issue was the defeat and destruction of the popular movement and the guerrillas, even at the cost of civilian noncombatant deaths: strategic supremacy entailed death-squad democracy. During the 1980s, U.S. military aid to the Duarte and Cristiani governments totalled just under $900 million and played a pivotal role in sustaining the power and authority of the armed forces, reinforcing their position as the ultimate arbiter of the electoralist experiment in El Salvador. Far from promoting reforms within the institution, these funds were simply "absorbed into a network of corruption and patronage [that] has made the Salvadoran military an empire unto itself," wrote Joel Millman after a year-long investigation of the "empire," including interviews with senior members of the officer corp. "A picture emerges of an already powerful institution grown virtually untouchable on the spoils of a lucrative war."[47]

Since Cristiani came into office in 1989, state terror against the civilian population has approached levels reminiscent of the early 1980s, involving not only the armed forces but also the three branches of the security forces (National Police, Treasury Police, National Guard) who operate under the authority of the generals. However, this marked deterioration in the human rights situation has had little or no impact on the Bush administration, which continues its large-scale funding of the perpetrators of the violence ($172 million in military aid during 1989 and 1990).[48]

The United States has acted in other ways to reinforce the dominant position of the armed forces within Salvadoran society. Following Cristiani's election, Air Force officers indicated a strong desire to see their commander appointed as the new defense minister. The president's reluctance to do so almost provoked a coup. Ultimately Cristiani compromised and chose a senior military official, General Rafael Larios, who had no institutional backing whatsoever. Washington played a major role in getting Cristiani to "accommodate" the generals on this issue or risk a major confrontation between the electoral client and the armed forces, thereby undermining U.S. strategy in El Salvador: "In the showdown over the Defense Minister appointment, the United States encouraged Cristiani to bow to Army pressure, avoiding a challenge to the powerful officers and thus reaffirming the military's role as an untouchable institution."[49]

Washington's strategy of combining "free markets," military power, and electoral clients to secure its hegemony occasionally creates tensions and even conflicts—over such issues as key cabinet appointments. In these situations, the United States must adjudicate between the competing forces, protecting its civilian collaborator regimes from being deposed (to retain the facade of legitimacy) while pressuring them to be more accommodating to the military.

Carter and Reagan policy-makers consistently sought to disassociate the Duarte regime from the violent and criminal behavior of its armed forces, blaming extremists of the Right and Left. Bush officials have done their best to absolve the Cristiani government of any and all military atrocities against unarmed civilians. In a familiar refrain, State Department officials attributed the rise in human rights' abuses since 1989 to right- or left-wing extremists over whom the regime and the armed forces have no control. Consider the administration's initial response to the November 1989 murder of six Jesuit priests by military personnel. President Bush attempted to implicate the leftist guerrillas while other U.S. officials repeatedly asserted that "anyone could have done the deed." But, as Americas Watch pointed out, the evidence against the military was overwhelming. The massacre of the Jesuits was "a military operation conducted by troops at the direct order of their commander."[50]

Bush not only sought to indict the guerrillas for the Jesuit murders; he simultaneously told Congress that the White House had no intention of cutting aid to El Salvador. To the military, the message was unmistakable: Their behavior was a secondary concern beside their role as a strategic imperial-state ally. It was only President Cristiani's subsequent acknowledgment of military responsibility for the killings and growing popular revulsion in the United States that forced the White House to at least be seen to be reconsidering the assistance program. But the administration was unfazed by a U.S. congressional study issued in May 1990 which showed a steady increase in military–security forces–death-squad killings and disappearances during 1989 and 1990. This persistent and systematic repression of trade-union organizers, church activists, leaders of popular organizations, displaced persons, and other regime opponents merely testified to the continuing impotence of civilian authority.[51]

Following the large-scale FMLN guerrilla offensive in November 1990, with unconditional backing from Washington, President Cristiani instituted a state of seige, suspending constitutional and legal freedoms, and gave the military expanded powers to crush this latest challenge to the existing political order. Not surprisingly, the troops did not discriminate between the armed and unarmed opposition. As a result, "opposition politicians once again left the country in fear of their lives. Prominent labor and human rights activists went into hiding, and the offices of most popular organizations were closed."[52] Determined to frustrate a negotiated settlement of the civil war, Washington, Cristiani, and the armed forces ruled out any substantial military reforms and insisted on a virtual unconditional surrender by the guerrillas as a precondition for resolving the conflict.

American strategy for retaining hegemony in Latin America is heavily dependent on preserving the image of its political clients and the military as legitimate actors. Otherwise, the White House would have a difficult time mobilizing domestic and alliance support and financial resources for its hemispheric objectives. In the absence of external support, the civilian and military clients might collapse, forcing the United States to intervene directly or engage in prolonged surrogate wars. Hence, through direct funding and private foundations and grants to propagandists and academics, the United States has systematically promoted the myth that Latin America has gone, or is going, through a "democratization process."

Throughout South and Central America and the Caribbean, as the United States makes deep inroads in taking over and pillaging economies via its "free-market" doctrine, it increasingly depends upon extending its direct and indirect military presence to contain sociopolitical resistance and guarantee the survival of malleable and compliant electoral regimes in order to validate the overall project. The collaborator electoral regimes, discredited as they have become (witness the increase in massive popular demonstrations against their policies, not to speak of their limited electoral mandate anyway, as evidenced by high rates of abstentionism on voting day), are assigned a vital propagandistic/ideological role in legitimating U.S. hegemonic interests. But while such governments retain Washington's military and ideological support, their socioeconomic base remains very fragile, precisely because they willingly implement the very U.S. "free-trade" doctrines that facilitate the pillage of their economies.

Washington and New "Collaborator" Regimes

The most striking contradiction in the U.S. position as a global power entering the 1990s is its continued ideological and military power and its steadily declining economic strength—the latter fed during the 1980s by the rise of the speculator capitalist, the dominance of fictitious overproductive industrial capital, and a record number of Savings and Loans and other bank failures. This eroding capacity of the domestic economy has had profound consequences for U.S.

relations with Latin America. Whereas in the 1950s and 1960s Washington provided large-scale economic aid to allied regimes pursuing 'appropriate' development models, today it demands massive changes to benefit U.S. capital and commerce in return for historically low levels of funding support. Whereas in the earlier period, Washington flexed its military power to overthrow nationalist governments and followed up by major economic commitments to bolster and consolidate the new dictatorial clients, the Reagan-Bush approach has been distinguished by its inability to finance the newly installed collaborator regimes in rebuilding and revitalizing their economies, even in a class-exploitative fashion. Having allocated billions of dollars in military spending to oust adversary regimes in Grenada, Nicaragua, and Panama, the imperial state has made little or no effort to resuscitate their economies. The current levels of activity are below those that existed under the previous "unacceptable" governments. This contradiction between U.S. military/ideological power and economic weakness in consolidating hegemony is best revealed by examining the three cases noted above.

The U.S. military invasion of Grenada in October 1983 and the ouster of Maurice Bishop's New Jewel Movement (NJM) government were not followed by large-scale economic aid to the State Department-sponsored conservative regime of Herbert Blaize's New National Party (1984–1989). American financial largesse amounted to approximately $125 million—a yearly average of less than $14 million. Meanwhile, under the auspices of State's Agency for International Development (AID), the Reagan administration proceeded to impose its own development model on Grenada, based on "freeing" the market, privatizing the state sector, opening the economy to foreign investors, and upwardly redistributing wealth and income (eliminating income tax, weakening foreign exchange controls, implementing new indirect taxes). The socioeconomic consequences of almost a decade of client rule in Grenada have been disastrous: dramatic falls in purchasing power and living standards for the bulk of the population, deteriorating social-sector facilities (health, education, housing), a massive rise in unemployment, and a record high foreign debt.[53] Even the private sector began to express discontent with the so-called economic reforms and to compare them unfavorably with the period of nationalist rule. Prior to the 1990 presidential election, the head of Grenada's Chamber of Commerce spoke wistfully about relations between local business and the NJM government: "[It] was much more aggressive in support of economic programs . . . [and was] much more motivated. Since the [invasion], AID has not created a very palatable situation for the private sector." Another local entrepreneur spoke of the U.S. contribution to Grenada's economic development since 1983 in even more scathing terms: "What the United States brought to Grenada is window-dressing, not real development."[54]

Following a decade of sustained military, covert, and electoral intervention in Nicaragua, Washington achieved its fundamental strategic objective: the end of revolutionary rule and its replacement by an electoral client committed to "freeing" markets, dismantling the revolutionary state, and transferring power back to the old elites. But having poured hundreds of millions of dollars into the anti-Sandinista campaign, the White House not only offered very limited economic assistance to the new client but also demanded financial concessions before releasing the bulk of these funds. This despite the herculean task that confronted the Chamorro government of rebuilding an economy and society that suffered billions of dollars in physical damage resulting from the U.S.-orchestrated contra war, and additional billions forfeited due to trade losses, military expenditures, and so on, also a direct consequence of Reagan-Bush destabilization policies.

In early 1990, the Bush administration submitted a $300 million aid package to Congress, urging immediate approval of the funds on the grounds that "with democracy at stake, there is simply no time to delay."[55] Six months later, less than one-third of these funds approved by the legislative branch had been disbursed by the White House. The sticking point was an administration demand that Nicaragua waive its right to a $17 billion International Court of Justice decision against the United States to compensate for the mining of Nicaragua's harbors and other acts of U.S. economic sabotage stemming from the contra war. Washington refused to recognize the court's jurisdiction in this matter. In meetings with State Department officials during September 1990, President Chamorro's chief of staff, Antonio Lacayo, was left in no doubt that the United States was unwilling to contemplate a settlement forcing it to pay any fraction of the award.[56] Nor did the Bush 1991 foreign-aid submission to Congress signal any significant funding policy shift in the immediate future: a 5.6 percent increase over the modest 1991 request (from $193 million to $204 million).[57] Meanwhile, the client regime confronted an economic crisis of major proportions (steadily declining agricultural and industrial production, forty-percent unemployment rate, spiralling inflation, etc.) that weakens its capacity to govern and makes it more vulnerable with each passing day.

In December 1989, after two years of severe financial sanctions, culminating in a military invasion, the United States achieved its objective of ousting the Panamanian dictator General Manuel Noriega from office. In the process, Panama's economy suffered losses totaling approximately $4 billion. Yet the Bush administration has refused to accept liability for the damage or to discuss claims for compensation, insisting that it is not responsible for losses resulting from armed actions. This despite precedents already established following the Dominican Republic (1965) and Grenada (1983) interventions. Worse still, the imperial state proceeded to block the release of millions of dollars in reconstruction aid to force the new client regime of Guillermo Endara—ensconced in power courtesy of the Pentagon—to accept sweeping changes in Panama's banking laws.

In May 1990, the administration designated $420 million in emergency assistance for Panama, supplementing U.S. congressional authorizations of $42 million in aid for fiscal year 1990, the equivalent of $500 million in bilateral credit and increased access to American markets. By year's end, however, less than one-third of the pledged funds had been disbursed, including the withholding of $84 million until the Panamanian legislature passed a mutual legal assistance treaty to halt tax evasion by U.S. companies and money laundering by drug traffickers. Despite relentless pressure from Washington throughout 1990, the Endara government opposed the demand, accusing the Bush White House of seeking carte blanche to investigate any type of economic crime—which would simply kill off Panama as a thriving international banking center.[58]

Compounding Panama's economic woes, the United States conditioned the release of an additional $130 million on the country paying the $540 million in debt-interest arrears owed to the multilateral development bank (World Bank, International Monetary Fund, Inter-American Development Bank). In turn, these American-influenced financial institutions informed the Endara government it would receive no debt relief under the Brady plan in lieu of these payments and until it had implemented a "satisfactory" economic program based on "freeing" markets and large-scale privatization of the state sector. Neither Bush officials nor the international bankers expressed much sympathy for Panamanian pleas that they were too strapped for capital resources to make payments to any of their debtors (total arrears at end–1990 was $800 million on a $3.5 billion debt).[59]

As Washington demonstrated first in its relations with Grenada and more recently toward regimes it helped to, or did, install in Nicaragua and Panama, its determination to destroy Latin regimes considered unacceptable is matched neither by a will nor, increasingly, by a capacity to participate in putting the pieces back together again. What these studies reveal is that U.S. imperial power is based on projecting military force, destroying nationalist and progressive regimes or movements, and then attempting to promote and consolidate client electoral governments. The absence of consequential economic aid to these new "collaborators" is a reflection of the changing nature of U.S. capitalism: its role as a debtor nation to its wealthy industrialized competitors. The United States cannot finance development abroad when it is unable to do so at home. Thus, through military and ideological power and client regimes, Washington hopes to extract and pillage Latin America's existing wealth to finance its own debts and improve its own negative balance-of-payments situation. The decline of the United States and the militarization of its hemispheric policy accompanying extractive imperialism push the region's economies and societies further downward and backward as they enter the 1990s.

Conclusion

The U.S. strategy of promoting "free markets"; deepening and extending its military reach through drug, counterinsurgency, and bureaucratic strategems; and consolidating client electoral regimes reached its high point of success at the end of the 1980s: Mexico was signed on for the "free market," opening the door for unprecedented levels of pillage and exploitation; Panama was occupied and the contras were in power in Nicaragua; the continent was blanketed with electoral regimes pursuing "free-market" policies, exonerating human rights' violators, and increasing their role in policing society. Nonetheless, cracks and divisions were appearing at the top, and challenges were appearing from below. Most dramatically, the "free-market" economic programs were killing the goose (industries) that laid the golden egg (interest and profits transferred abroad and imports purchased from U.S. exporters).

As the levels of pillage ravaged Latin America, as debt payments and capital transfers drove living standards lower, and as public services went bankrupt, nineteenth-century diseases (cholera, maleria, yellow fever epidemics) returned: The adoption of the past century's economic doctrines reproduced that century's disastrous health conditions. Declining living standards and decaying infrastructure, products of the "economic adjustments" promulgated by the free marketeers, drove out potential investors and attracted only short-term speculator capital. American politicomilitary domination in Central America was accompanied by its economic incapacity to revive these economies, thus discrediting its ideological claims and delegitimizing its political clients even among the traditionally pro-U.S. "middle classes."

The strategy of projecting military/ideological power and pillaging the economy is delegitimizing the loyal client electoral regimes: Political abstentionism is growing; violent direct action (collective and individual) to redistribute wealth is increasing. In the 1990s, this process of disintegration will either revive the Marxist view of democratic collectivism or create a Hobbesian world of war of all against all.

Nowhere have the "free-market" policies promoted economic recovery or growth; nowhere have the social polarizations lessened; nowhere has unemployment or inflation diminished. The U.S. strategy has destroyed the status quo in a radical, reactionary way. It has uprooted Indian communities with counterrevolutionary wars, undermined public/private relations through doctrinaire privatizations, increased the role of the state in civil society by increasing its military capability, and privatized long-standing social services at the expense of employees and consumers. Washington is hollowing out Latin American economy and society, returning the majority to a more backward, primitive form of individual existence. Paradoxically, the depth of the crisis has provoked its strongest defense: the systematic disaggregation and atomization of long-standing collectivities weakens the opposition and reduces the victims to strategies of absolute survival.

The fundamental weakness of Washington's strategy is the growing gap between its military/ideological power and its political/economic effects: the exhaustion of neoliberal ideology; the inability of the United States to finance and sustain its electoral or military clients. The most striking example is Panama where majority support for the December 1989 invasion has since turned against the United States and its imposed political client, whose policies, or lack of them, have provoked rising large-scale opposition.

The United States is attempting to *intensify* its pillage of Latin America to counterbalance its trade deficits with dynamic imperial competitors Japan and Germany as well as its declining access to markets in their regional blocs. The heightened U.S. imperial presence in Latin America in the post–Cold War period belies the arguments that imperialism is a function of "superpower conflict": Imperial expansion is a product of the demands of U.S. domestic economic, political, and military institutions.

In the 1990s, U.S.–Latin American relations revolve around conflicts engendered by the three levels of U.S. strategy: cleavages between proponents of "free-market" pillage (the local neocompradors and self-styled advocates of interdependency) and the neonationalists who seek to develop a national industrial policy grounded in the producer classes as a precondition for insertion in the international market; cleavages between the proponents of state-to-state militarization strategies and social movements and revolutionary formations in civil society; cleavages between co-opted electoral political classes and their intellectuals, and the institution of mass popular assemblies and their organic intellectuals.

The current decade will see sustained efforts by Washington to follow the path of military influence, client regimes, and economic extraction. To counter this strategy requires a radical rethinking of the prevailing notions about democracy and mixed economies: Without dismantling the state, the electoral regimes and processes remain hostages to imperial military strategies; without uprooting the neocomprador "free-market" classes and technocrats, revitalization of the national market and producer classes is impossible; without replacing the elected class with the direct representation of the popular movements, international political clientelism will continue.

Notes

1. See *El Día Latino Americano*, January 7, 1991, p. 19; *La Jornada* January 7, 1991, p. 23; "Latin Debt Arrears Jump to $18 Billion," *Journal of Commerce*, September 5, 1990; "Adjusting to US$25,000mn in Foreign Debts," *Central America Report*, July 20, 1990, p. 210; "1990s Could be Decade of Opportunity," *Latin American Monitor: Southern Cone*, November 1990, p. 839; Andres Oppenheimer, "Latin Nations Bemoan Loss of U.S. Aid," *Miami Herald*, February 18, 1990; "Stagflation Pummeling Regional Economies," *The Times of the Americas*, January 10, 1990, p. 1.

2. For a discussion of both plans, see David Felix, "Latin America's Debt Crisis," *World Policy Journal*, Vol. II, No. 4, Fall 1990, pp. 740–745.

3. Quoted in James Gerstenzang, "Bush Ends Trip With Praise for Reduced State Role in South American Economies," *Los Angeles Times*, December 9, 1990, p. A14.

4. Quoted in Lee Hockstader, "Caribbean Leaders Seek to Counter U.S. Aid Cuts," *Washington Post* June 18, 1990, p. A16.

5. See John M.Goshko, "Overhauling Assistance Plans: Different Philosophies Emerge," *Washington Post*, May 18, 1990, p. A11.

6. "US Slashes Sugar Quota," *Latin American Monitor: Mexico*, November 1990, p.832.

7. Lee Hockstader, "Baker Offers Central America Help in Finding Aid Elsewhere," *Washington Post*, June 19, 1990, pp. A12, A16; Al Kamen, "Reagan-Era Zeal for Central America Fades," *Washington Post*, October 16, 1990, p. A18; Hockstader, "Caribbean Leaders Seek to Counter U.S. Aid Cuts," p. A15.

8. Quoted in Council on Hemispheric Affairs, *News and Analysis*, September 14, 1989.

9. *El Dia Latino Americano*, January 7, 1991, p. 19; *La Jornada*, January 7, 1991, p. 23.

10. Christina Lamb, "Collor's Inflation Crusade Wins Few Converts," *Financial Times*, January 15, 1991, p. 7; Michael Kepp, "More Austerity," *Times of the Americas*, February 20, 1991, pp. 1–2.

11. See "Mexico Takes Lead, Brazil Falls Behind," *Latin American Weekly Report*, January 24, 1991, p. 4.

12. See "Brazil Faces Deteriorating Economic Situation," *Washington Report on the Hemisphere*, March 20, 1991, p. 4.

13. Nicole Bonnet, " 'Fujishock' Delivers a Killer Blow to Peru's Inflation," Le Monde supplement in *Guardian Weekly*, October 7, 1990, p. 18; "Inflation in Peru Soars to New High," *Sydney Morning Herald* January 2, 1991, p. 8.

14. Quoted in "Cholera Epidemic Will be 'Almost Impossible to Contain,' " *The Australian*, April 24, 1991, p. 8. Also see Eugene Robinson, "Peru Facing Long, Dirty Fight Against Cholera," *Washington Post*, February 17, 1991, p. A24; "On Top of Cholera, an Outbreak of Malaria is Spreading in Peru," *Latin American Weekly Report*, March 7, 1991, p. 1; William R. Long, "Cholera Racing Through South America," *Los Angeles Times*, April 21, 1991, pp. A1, A4, A5; "Cholera Epidemic Goes on Spreading," *Latin American Weekly Report*, May 9, 1991, p. 2.

15. See James Brooke, "Peru Struggles to Digest Free-Market Reforms," *New York Times*, April 30, 1991, p. D5.

16. "Menem Administration Seeks International Aid," *Washington Report on the Hemisphere*, June 13, 1990, p. 4.

17. See Luis Barbieri, "Argentine Troops Participate in Blockade," *Latinamerica Press*, October 11, 1990, p. 3.

18. See "Caribbean Basin Escapes Crushing Blow," *Washington Report on the Hemisphere*, January 23, 1991, p. 3.

19. Quoted in Nancy Dunne, "Caribbean Moves Closer to US Trade Fold," *Financial Times*, August 16, 1990, p. 5.

20. See Nina Serafino and Betsy Cody, *The Enterprise for the Americas Initiative: Issues for Congress* (Washington, D.C.: Library of Congress: Congressional Research Service, September 13, 1990), p. 3.

21. Felix, "Latin America's Debt Crisis," p. 764.

22. See Stuart Auerbach, "Mexico Opens Door to Foreign Investment," *Washington Post*, August 6, 1989, pp. H1, H5; Richard W. Stevenson, "Selling a Free-Trade Pact With Mexico," *New York Times*, November 11, 1990, p. 12F; "New Wave of Liberalization," *Latin American Monitor: Mexico*, March 1990, p. 752.

23. See "Salinas Plans Major Sell-Off," *Washington Report on the Hemisphere*, November 14, 1990, p. 1; Michael Lederman, "Mexico: Full Steam Ahead," *Times of the Americas*, November 14, 1990, p. 8; "Mexico Looks to Private Capital," *Latin American Monitor: Mexico*, May 1991, p. 895.

24. "Mexico: A New Economic Era," *Business Week*, November 12, 1990, pp. 103, 104, 105, 108.

25. "Mexico Takes Lead, Brazil Falls Behind," p. 4.

26. See Mat Moffett, "Along Its U.S. Border, Mexico Experiences North's Economic Ills," *Wall Street Journal*, January 14, 1991, pp. 1, 10.

27. U.S. officials quoted in Michael Isikoff, "Drug Plan Allows Use of Military," *Washington Post*, September 10, 1989, p. A1.

28. See Christopher Marquis, "Coca-Growing Nations Shun U.S. Military Aid," *Miami Herald*, August 11, 1990.

29. Quoted in "US Aid's Link to Violence in Colombia," *Latin America Regional Reports: Andean Group*, November 15, 1990, p. 4.

30. "The Andean Initiative: One Year Later," *Latin America Update* (Washington Office on Latin America), September–October 1990, p. 4.

31. See, for example, James Brooke, "Colombia Presses Drive on Rebels, Smashing Base," *The New York Times*, December 14, 1990, p. 16.

32. See James Brooke, "U.S. Will Arm Peru to Fight Leftists in New Drug Push," *New York Times*, April 22, 1990, pp. 1, 18.

33. See Sam Dillon, "Peru Rejects U.S. Drug Aid, Pokes Holes in Bush Plan," *Miami Herald*, September 27, 1990, p. 13A.

34. "The Killing Fields of Peru," *Latin America Update*, November–December 1990, p. 5.

35. Quoted in James Brooke, "Peru Develops Plan to Work With U.S. to Combat Drugs," *New York Times*, January 25, 1991, p. 2.

36. Quoted in Council on Hemispheric Affairs, *News and Analysis*, September 28, 1990.

37. "The Economics of Cocaine in South America," *Washington Report on the Hemisphere*, September 13, 1989, p. 5.

38. "Washington's Last Stand," *Washington Report on the Hemisphere*, December 12, 1990, pp. 1,7.

39. See Doug Farah, "GIs Train Bolivian Army in Anti-Drug Fight, Drawing Opposition," *Washington Post*, April 23, 1991, p. A10.

40. For discussions of the concept of low-intensity warfare and its application to Central America, see Sara Miles, "The Real War: Low Intensity Conflict in Central America," *NACLA Report on the Americas*, Vol. XX, No. 2, April/May 1986, pp. 18–48; Michael T. Klare and Peter Kornbluh, eds., *Low Intensity Warfare:*

Counterinsurgency, Proinsurgency, and Antiterrorism in the Eighties (New York: Pantheon Books, 1988).

41. On U.S. policy toward El Salvador, see Daniel Siegel and Joy Hackel, "El Salvador: Counterinsurgency Revisited," in Klare and Kornbluh, eds., *Low Intensity Warfare*, pp. 112–135; *NACLA Report on the Americas*, Vol. XX, No. 1, January/March 1986, pp. 15–39; *NACLA Report on the Americas*, Vol. XXIII, No. 2, July 1989, pp. 15–38.

42. See "Privatizations Pave Way for IMF Deal," *Latin American Monitor: Central America*, March 1991, p. 876. On U.S. policy toward Nicaragua, see Morris H. Morley and James F. Petras, "The Reagan Administration and Nicaragua: Washington Constructs its Case for Counterrevolution in Central America," in Morris H. Morley, ed., *Confrontation and Crisis: Ronald Reagan's Foreign Policy* (Totowa, N.J.: Rowman and Littlefield, 1989), pp. 158–213; Thomas W. Walker, ed., *Reagan Versus the Sandinistas* (Boulder: Westview Press, 1987); Peter Kornbluh, "Nicaragua: U.S. Proinsurgency Warfare Against the Sandinistas," in Klare and Kornbluh, eds., *Low Intensity Warfare*, pp. 136–157.

43. See Richard Boudreau, "Trying to Tame the Latin 'Tiger'," *Los Angeles Times*, September 2, 1990, pp. A1, A28.

44. Americas Watch, *Messengers of Death: Human Rights in Guatemala, November 1988–February 1990* (New York: March 1990), p. 1.

45. See "Guatemala is Worst Hemispheric Violator," *Washington Report on the Hemisphere*, January 23, 1991, p. 5.

46. Americas Watch, *Messengers of Death*, pp. 80, 81; Inter-American Committee on Human Rights in Latin America (Canada), *ICCHRLA Newsletter*, Nos. 1,2, and 3, 1990, pp. 55, 56.

47. Joel Millman, "A Force Unto Itself," *New York Times Magazine*, December 10, 1989, p. 95.

48. See Americas Watch, *A Year of Reckoning: El Salvador Decade After the Assassination of Archbishop Romero* (New York: March 1990), pp. 93, 143.

49. Millman, "A Force Unto Itself," p. 97.

50. Americas Watch, *A Year of Reckoning*, pp. 149, 151.

51. See Ibid, p. 147, and passim; Inter-American Committee on Human Rights in Latin America, *ICCHRLA Newsletter*, pp. 44–50.

52. Americas Watch, *A Year of Reckoning*, p. 116.

53. See Council on Hemispheric Affairs, *News and Analysis*, March 27, 1990; James Ferguson, *Grenada: Revolution in Reverse* (London: Latin American Bureau, 1990), pp. 66–90.

54. Both quotes in Council on Hemispheric Affairs, *News and Analysis*, March 27, 1990.

55. Quoted in Lee Hockstader, "U.S. Aid Funds, Urgent Last Spring, Delayed in Delivery to Nicaragua," *Washington Post*, December 13, 1990, p. A38.

56. See Mark A. Uhlig, "U.S. Urges Nicaragua to Forgive Legal Claims," *New York*

Times, September 3, 1990, p. 18. In September 1991, the Nicaraguan government finally agreed to drop the pursuit of its multi-billion claim.

57. See "Drugs Take Lead in 1992 Aid Package," *Latin American Weekly Report*, March 14, 1991, p. 5.

58. See Mark A. Uhlig, "Panama Resisting Move to Clean Up Banking System," *New York Times*, October 22, 1990, pp. 1,8.

59. "Lending Agencies Demanding Payment," *Latin American Monitor: Mexico*, November 1990, p. 841.

4

Washington's Invasion of Panama:
Myths and Realities

The December 1989 invasion of Panama by a 26,000-strong U.S. military force caused an estimated $2 billion worth of damage and cost some 2,500 lives.[1] The ouster of General Manuel Noriega and the subsequent American occupation were not merely the culmination of an extended bilateral conflict; nor did they have much to do with the Bush administration's articulated positions on drugs and democracy. Washington's policy toward Panama through most of the 1980s was dictated primarily by its hegemonic aspirations in Central America and the pursuit of objectives to that end—in particular, the isolation, destabilization, and overthrow of the Sandinista regime in Nicaragua. "America's major listening post in the region was in Panama," writes Frederick Kempe, "and the U.S. regional defense—including CIA secret operations, anti-terrorist activity, and even support of the contra war—were waged from Panama."[2] To establish the primacy of the White House agenda, it is necessary to examine the myths promulgated by U.S. policy-makers to justify the direct, forcible ouster of the Noriega regime.

According to President Bush, the invasion was launched, first and foremost, to protect the lives of American citizens; more specifically, in response to the killing of a marine, the interrogation of a Navy lieutenant and his wife, and Noriega's declaration of a "state of war." Yet, there is ample evidence that the invasion was at least contemplated as a possible option seven or eight months earlier and that it moved into the concrete planning stage following an abortive coup by dissident Panamanian army officers in October. As far back as May 10, 1989, following Noriega's annulment of the national election results, President Bush signed a National Security Directive "laying out an action plan to force Noriega's overthrow."[3] Soon after, the chairman of the Joint Chiefs of Staff (JCS), Admiral William Crowe, instructed the new commander of American military forces in Panama, General Maxwell Thurman, "to review existing invasion plans 'top to bottom,' and start getting us ready."[4] On the day of the invasion itself, Richard Cheney acknowledged that the military scenario "has been in existence for some time. It was one of the first items I was briefed on when I became Secretary of Defense last spring [March 1990]."[5]

The White House refused to militarily support the October 1990 coup plotters not least because it considered them "politically unreliable, proclaiming their opposition to Noriega in the name of Torrijos and calling for new elections rather than backing the [May 1989] Endara victory, as the United States advocated."[6] This position was reinforced by a belief that the coup attempt was premature and doomed to failure. "Getting rid of Noriega," declared Crowe's successor as JCS chairman, General Colin Powell, "was something to do on a U.S. timetable."[7] The failure of the October coup effectively terminated American covert efforts to promote a "made in Panama" overthrow of Noriega. The Bush administration now decided to "reactivate plans for a massive military intervention." Between October and December, tanks, helicopters, and other "heavy offensive military equipment" were secretly transported to Panama.[8] In other words, large-scale military supply and troop movements were put in place for an invasion well before the alleged threat to American lives or property.

Bush's references to the marine's death and Noriega's declaration of a state of war were similarly flawed. American military and civilian officials in Panama rejected the White House portrayal of the former as an unprovoked act of aggression: "Instead it was a step in a pattern of aggressive behavior by a small group of U.S. troops who called themselves 'the Hard Chargers' and who frequently tested the patience and reaction of Panamanian forces."[9] Regarding Noriega's statement, it was no more than a description of a de facto situation initiated by Washington—not a "threat" to American interests as White House officials contended.

The second administration justification for its resort to the direct military option was that Noriega was a "narcotics kingpin" whose arrest and extradition to stand trial in the United States were critical to the success of Washington's "war on drugs." This ignored the fact that most of the General's wealth derived from official corruption ("spoils of office"). Insofar as it resulted from drug-trafficking activities, "the evidence suggests that Noriega participated in major drug activity for only a two-to-three-year period in the early 1980s and then became a trusted and overly zealous DEA [U.S. Drug Enforcement Administration] collaborator."[10] Moreover, his narcodealings never complicated his close working relationship with the DEA or the CIA during the 1970s and the first half of the 1980s. The Carter White House preferred to ignore the matter in its single-minded determination to ensure passage of the Panama Canal treaties,[11] while the Reaganites attached an equivalent importance to Noriega's anti-Sandinista stance. A memorandum prepared by CIA Director William Casey following a meeting with Noriega in November 1985, for instance, "made clear that Casey let Noriega off the hook regarding drugs . . . Noriega knew if he kept us happy regarding Nicaragua, he could do what he pleased."[12] Finally, the Bush administration provided no evidence at the time of the invasion demonstrating that the general's arrest would contract the flow of drugs through Panama—a flow which has actually increased in volume under the client Endara regime.

The third myth invoked by Washington was that the invasion targeted a politically isolated and repressive dictator—and would be welcomed by all Panamanians. But the U.S. marines met surprisingly strong resistance precisely because Noriega retained a modicum of popular support in the poorer neighborhoods around Panama City—which were the communities where the invading force concentrated its firepower. Significant resistance was confirmed after several days of fighting when President Bush dispatched 2,000 more troops to reinforce the original 24,000 because of "the slow pace of efforts to establish control in the Panamanian capital."[13] Twenty-four hours later, American military commanders "conceded growing alarm over the unexpectedly stiff resistance by forces loyal to . . . Noriega."[14] General Maxwell Thurman, directing the U.S. operation from Panama City, called them an "organized force" and criticized the preinvasion intelligence as too optimistic: "The target population of the Dignity Battalions were [sic] considerably larger than we had estimated."[15]

American aircraft systematically bombed working-class communities that were strongholds of nationalist opposition. On December 24, the Associated Press described one such attack: "In the latest attempt to rout Noriega backers, an Air Force plane repeatedly bombed a hilltop . . . in the working-class district of San Miguelito. . . . Later yesterday, dozens of U.S. troops descended on the neighborhood, which has been the site of strong resistance."[16] Bombing attacks on the densely populated community of El Chorrillo, located near the Comandancia, Noriega's headquarters, accounted for hundreds of civilian deaths. The JCS's General Colin Powell referred to "heavy fighting in the vicinity of the Comandancia" where U.S. ground forces were supported by Army and Air Force helicopter gunships and fighter aircraft.[17]

Instead of ending Noriega's "reign of terror," the U.S. substituted one kind of lawlessness for another—attested to by the thousands of civilians killed, arrested, or left homeless and by the massive destruction of property and economic infrastructure caused by the invasion. And, contrary to Washington assertions, there was substantial popular opposition which was crushed only through the application of what Defense Secretary Cheney termed "maximum force." By terrorizing the population and bolstering the newly installed Endara regime, the United States hoped to secure an additional client who would wholeheartedly support its Central American policy. Overthrowing Noriega was merely a means to that end.

The fourth myth, and one vociferously promoted by the imperial state, was the notion that the invasion was undertaken in response to a request from the democratically elected government of Guillermo Endara. The chronology of events, however, suggests otherwise. Neither Endara nor any of his closest associates were consulted about the invasion. One reason may have been Endara's initially ambiguous comments suggesting he might have opposed it. Interviewed after the marine landing, he spoke of hearing the news as "like a kick in the head.

It was not the best thing I would have thought. We were not really consulted. . . . I would have been happier without an intervention."[18]

According to Endara, Bush informed him of the plans only two or three hours before the invasion. After momentary agonizing, he agreed to go along with the use of external military force to get rid of Noriega: "The gringos have their defects, but I am used to . . . them," he told the *Philadelphia Inquirer*.[19] Appropriately enough, Endara was installed as president at a U.S. military base and his first orders were sent out on U.S. fax machines. His subordination to Washington was vividly evidenced by the matter-of-fact way in which the United States simply flew Noriega to the mainland despite the absence of an extradition treaty between the two countries. The fact that Endara accepted U.S. control and the trappings of power, and rejected Noriega's rule, did not make the process or the structure any more democratic.

The fifth, and final myth, was Washington's claim that the world enthusiastically supported Noriega's demise and that the invasion contributed to the global democratic trend, especially in Latin America. But the hemisphere overwhelmingly condemned the use of force against Panama. In an unprecedented twenty-to-one vote, the Organization of American States (OAS), which had traditionally functioned as a rubber stamp for past U.S. interventions, expressed its opposition in no uncertain terms. Regimes across the political spectrum, from Chile's right-wing government to the Sandinistas in Nicaragua, joined in repudiating the invasion.[20] Predictably, only the U.S. clients in Central America followed Washington's lead: El Salvador supported the action while Honduras and Costa Rica abstained in the voting. In the United Nations, the outcome was equally lopsided; only the West European bloc, together with Israel, sided with the White House. The puppet nature of the Endara regime was so transparent that the international organization at first refused to seat it.

The high diplomatic cost that accompanied the military victory in Panama was, however, far less important to the Bush administration than the capacity to successfully project U.S. military power, to incorporate another Central American regime into its regional, basically anti-Sandinista, strategy, and to build a bipartisan domestic consensus for the politics of military intervention. Yet, even though the White House achieved its primary objective, in the process it tore a considerable hold in the still fresh notion of an East/West thaw leading to a more peaceful world, one in which big-power restraint would encourage greater pluralism around the globe and the breakup of the Cold War-bloc politics.

Critical to any explanation of the U.S. decision to oust Noriega from political power were the timing and the context. Prior to 1987, Washington readily accommodated the drug-dealing general's business and political relations with a broad array of conflicting forces: He provided covert military aid and a base for the contras while allowing the Sandinista government to deposit most of its funds in local banks and set up import houses to gain access to vital spare parts and other commodities, thereby evading the U.S. trade/financial blockade; he provided banking facilities for U.S. multinationals and Colombia's Medellin drug cartel, and allowed the Cubans to establish "front companies" (to acquire American-origin goods) and, like Nicaragua, to also circumvent U.S. economic sanctions; he supplied the CIA with valuable intelligence information on Cuba and Nicaragua while simultaneously performing an identical function for the revolutionary government in Havana; he dealt with Israeli arms merchants and Libyan weapons purchasers; and he turned over drug traffickers and information to the DEA at the same time as he allowed the Medellin cartel to use Panama as a "pass through" for cocaine shipments to the United States.[21]

Noriega benefited politically from his balancing act and economically by skimming payoffs from all involved. In 1985, however, he incurred the Reagan administration's displeasure as a result of his central role in the ouster of pro-U.S. President Nicolas Ardito Barletta, which initiated what became an ongoing debate within the foreign-policy bureaucracy—particularly between the State and Defense departments—over relations with the general. Nonetheless, anger over the Barletta dismissal and other irritants in the bilateral relationship continued to be accommodated given Noriega's support for U.S. regional policy, including his offers to CIA Director William Casey and the NSC's Oliver North to become more actively involved in the anti-Sandinista war. Through 1986, the dominant feeling among senior U.S. policy-makers was that "tactical differences and differences of perception"[22] notwithstanding, "Noriega should be put on the shelf until Nicaragua was taken care of."[23]

During 1987, a consensus emerged within the administration on the need to get Noriega to relinquish power. Although the White House decided to suspend military and economic assistance, the disagreements over how best to achieve the strategic goal were not easily resolved, with State pushing for a forceful approach (not excluding consideration of kidnapping Noriega or fomenting a coup by dissident Panamanian military officers) in contrast to the Pentagon, which argued for a more "congenial" strategy.[24] Noriega's removal of President Eric Arturo Devalle (whom he had installed in office in place of Barletta) in February 1988 further increased Washington's resolve to do something about the general, which was compounded by the latter's refusal to abandon his balancing act (particularly his unwillingness to tighten the economic blockade against Nicaragua and his lack of enthusiasm for activating the direct intervention option) and follow the lead of the other Central American clients in their unqualified support for the counterrevolutionary war against the Sandinistas. Following the collapse of White House-authorized secret negotiations in May 1988 to pressure Noriega to leave Panama in return for the dropping of U.S. drug-trafficking indictments and the general's abrogation of the May 1989 election results, the Bush administration began in earnest to demonize the Panamanian dictator—all the while increasing economic pressures, giving encouragement to dissident officers to lead a coup, and making its own plans to forcibly remove Noriega from power. This process culminated in the December 1989 invasion.

With the U.S. military in direct control of Panama, and the obedient Endara regime in place, the White House was not only poised to refashion the country's political system and state institutions into unconditional supporters of U.S. regional policies; it was finally in a position to close off the last significant loophole in its economic blockade of Nicaragua (and to clamp down on Cuba's use of Panama to obtain access to U.S. technology and other goods)—thus further strengthening its hegemonic status in the area. The imperial state's eventual determination to overthrow Noriega, and the ends to which it went to achieve that goal, testified to the importance it attached to gaining these broader, principally anti-Nicaragua, regional objectives.

Imperial Occupation: Pursuing Hegemonic Ambitions

The Endara regime inherited an economy in a deep recession that was exacerbated by the invasion: Largely as a result of U.S. sanctions, the country's gross domestic product declined by twenty-eight percent during 1988–1989 while offshore bank deposits plummeted from $29 billion in 1986 to $3.6 billion in 1989.[25] In the hope of attracting large-scale reconstruction aid from Washington and the multilateral development banks (MDBs), the free marketeers who dominated the new government—described by one U.S. official as "gung-ho advocates of the private sector and the marketplace"[26]—signalled their intention to preside over an export-based World Bank–IMF development strategy. High on the agenda was the privatization of state firms, major public spending cutbacks, the deregulation of labor laws, the rebuilding of the banking system, and support for the "free trade" zone. In October 1990, the pace of the austerity program quickened with wage freezes, the first sell-offs of public enterprises, and the firing of tens of thousands of state-sector workers—the latter triggering mass demonstrations by an increasingly hostile populace. Seven months later, the government announced plans to privatize the telephone industry, ports, airlines, sugar mills, and cement and banana factories as part of an effort to satisfy the demands of its international creditors (one of the conditions for new inflow of U.S. and MDB funds) and declared its intention to eliminate import quotas and reduce existing tariffs by up to ninety percent.[27]

The economy grew by six percent in 1990 due primarily to the replacement of inventories (totalling $500 million) lost during the invasion, the completion of a number of building projects, the lifting of U.S. trade sanctions, and a slight improvement (up to $5 billion) in off-shore bank deposits—in the absence of significant U.S. or other foreign economic assistance. Washington conditioned large-scale reconstruction aid to its new, financially strapped, client not only on the repayment of outstanding debt interest owed to the MDBs but also on the signing of a mutual legal assistance agreement easing bank secrecy laws and permitting U.S. investigators access to financial records in search of drug launderers and tax evaders. Endara, his economics ministers, and the local financial sector resisted such an accord on the grounds that it would undermine the recovery of the critical banking industry which, prior to the imposition of U.S. sanctions, had employed approximately 9,000 people and pumped $200 million annually into the country's economy.[28]

Nonetheless, the Bush administration was determined to lift the veil of secrecy on Panama's banking transactions and continued to target the economic pressure point until the regime finally relented, signing the agreement in April 1991.[29] But, contrary to the latter's expectations, neither this capitulation nor Endara's commitment to a "free-market" economic program appears to have induced Washington to fulfill its side of the bargain. The aid spigots were barely opened. The *Los Angeles Times* reported that the White House was planning to limit Panama's 1992 economic assistance package to a miserly $27 million.[30]

Contrary to Bush White House assertions, the U.S. marine invasion and occupation did not bring a rapid end to the cocaine smuggling that the Noriega regime tolerated and promoted. Illegal drug trafficking is more open and abundant than ever, due largely to the activities of the Colombian cartels and some of the general's former associates.[31] The Colombian government's crackdown on the Medellin traffickers during 1990, combined with Panama's lax enforcement procedures and its shared borders, made Panama a natural refuge for the cartels. In early 1991, the number of cocaine production plants in Darien province, which borders Colombia, was estimated by Panamanian police to be as high as twenty.[32] Under Noriega, the Colombians' activities had been confined to moving drug shipments across Panamanian territory to third countries and laundering the profits in local banks.

According to U.S. and Panamanian officials, "a lack of government resources, experience and any effective program have allowed the level of narcotics trading, nearly all of it controlled by the [Medellin cartel] to equal—and in some cases to exceed—what went on in the year before Noriega was arrested in December 1989."[33] Endara's 1990 budget, for instance, allocated a miniscule $5 million to the Customs Service, barely sufficient to enable it to keep up with the routine work of collecting duties and enforcing tariffs, let alone searching for narcosmugglers.

Washington has given the problem no greater attention than its client. Of the $12 million in reconstruction aid officially designated for law-enforcement activities during the first fifteen months of Endara's rule, the entire amount was specified for judicial reform purposes only.[34] This marginalization of the "war against drugs" merely confirms its irrelevance as a justification for the U.S. military invasion.

If the White House has offered limited support for economic reconstruction and growth, it has shown a much greater commitment to remaking the Panamanian state—establishing new coercive, judicial, and bureaucratic institutions and refurbishing existing government agencies responsive to American long-term political, economic, and strategic interests. Within days of the December 1989 coup, the Pentagon dispatched hundreds of special operations troops, including a civil-affairs unit responsible for "stamp[ing] American influence on virtually every phase of the new government from rebuilding damaged roadways to assembling a bureaucracy."[35]

The highest priority was given to substituting a new collaborator military institution—the Public Force (PF)—for Noriega's corrupt Panamanian Defense Forces (PDF). Despite assertions that it would function more as a police than a military force, the PF not only retained a military-style command structure but was composed almost entirely of decommissioned—albeit "acceptable"—PDF officers and troops, many of whom had histories of drug trafficking and were involved in the torture and repression of Noriega political opponents.[36] The inaugural PF leader, Colonel Roberto Armiji, was a Noriega loyalist; his successor, Colonel Eduardo Herrera Hassan, was in charge of the general's special-forces unit responsible (under his leadership) for the July 1987 "Black Friday" massacre of civilians demonstrating against the dictator's rule. "Nothing has changed," said PF commander Captain Luis Donadio (previously a senior PDF officer), referring to the troops he commanded at the beginning of 1990: "Same units, same ranks, same men. Only the name has changed from Defense Forces to Public Forces."[37] Twelve months later, on the anniversary of the invasion, the PF membership was still dominated (more than eighty percent) by former PDF troops.[38]

True to its shadowy past, the PF has also been implicated in the crime and corruption that still plague Panama. The most commonly heard explanation for the unprecedented increase in burgularies and robberies during 1990 was that the PF and the lawbreakers were usually one and the same. As one prominent regime critic put it: "These are the same guys doing exactly the same as before the U.S. took out Ali Baba [Noriega] and left us the 40 thieves."[39]

Washington instituted comprehensive training programs for the PF, largely under the direct supervision of U.S. Department of Justice officials based in the newly established national police academy. Although joint U.S.-Panamanian patrols were terminated in November 1990 on the grounds that the PF were now sufficiently capable of maintaining "law and order," senior PF officers continued to maintain daily contact with American military advisors.[40] Indeed, the Endara regime was no less dependent for its survival on the presence of thousands of U.S. troops on Panamanian soil at the end of the year than it had been at the beginning. This was vividly demonstrated in December when Endara was forced to turn to the U.S. Southern Command to quell an antigovernment rebellion led by the former head of the PF, Colonel Eduardo Herrera. The attempted *golpe* collapsed following the intervention of 500 American marines.[41]

The CIA, assisted by the Justice Department's police training mission, has been as active as the Pentagon in rebuilding the military/security apparatus of the Panamanian state. Under a program authorized by presidential decree in February 1990, the CIA provided funds, personal training, and technical assistance to establish a top-secret intelligence office, the euphemistically named Council of

Public Safety and National Defense. Installed in the Office of the Presidency (the CIA opposed locating it in the PF), and headed by a former Noriega associate and treasury minister, Menalco Solis, the council began operating in July. Its objectives were twofold: to exchange information with the CIA and, in the words of one Endara official, to target domestic "troublemakers."[42] Ensuring long-term control over the Panamanian state and regime, rather than promoting economic recovery, has been the major preoccupation of the Bush administration.

By late 1990, the Endara government was in crisis. Opposition to the president's economic policies was compounded by growing political instability as the fragile anti-Noriega ruling coalition began to disintegrate into self-serving factions. Deep rifts developed between the supporters of Endara and his ambitious vice presidents, Christian Democrat Ricardo Arias Calderón and Molinera leader Guillermo Ford, over policy goals, the allocation of government jobs, and personality conflicts. The "partial" legislative elections of January 1991 exposed the government's narrowing political base. Approximately half of the 200,000 eligible voters were so disillusioned that they did not even bother to vote; and pro-Noriega candidates won five of the nine seats that were contested. In mid-April, the coalition finally collapsed when Endara replaced five Christian Democratic appointees in his twelve-member cabinet, including Vice President Calderón, after months of disagreement over economic policy.

The fragmentation of the regime was accompanied by an even more dramatic slump in Endara's personal popularity. Not surprisingly, the attempts to restructure and "adjust" the Panamanian economy, under U.S. tutelage, had proved extremely unpopular with all classes—workers who lost their jobs, small-business-people bankrupted by the loss of tariff protection and access to state credits, and members of the capitalist class who viewed the "free-market" strategy as reducing Panama to a service economy benefiting only a narrow elite in the financial sector. Entering 1991, an estimated thirty percent of the labor force were unemployed, another twenty percent underemployed, over forty percent of the population lived below the poverty line, and more than half of these lived in conditions of extreme poverty.[43] Endara's failure to arrest declining living standards was largely responsible for his collapse in the public-opinion polls from a positive rating of eighty-four percent at the time of the invasion to less than two percent some sixteen months later.[44]

Conclusion

The U.S. invasion of Panama was motivated not by any profound democratic impulse but by a determination on the part of the White House to reassert America's military and ideological hegemony in the Third World. It reaffirmed the centrality of imperial power politics: It was the culmination of almost a decade of promoting contra "surrogate" wars and the forerunner of future military interventions dictated by hegemonic interests. The message to the Third World was sharp and clear: The Bush administration was willing and prepared to use overwhelming military force to resolve conflicts with regimes deemed hostile to fundamental U.S. economic, strategic, and/or political interests.

Washington's rhetoric about toppling the Noriega dictatorship and replacing it with a popularly elected government has been powerfully contradicted by the subsequent decision to maintain a large military/administrative presence in the country with the primary objective of recreating the Panamanian state, regime, and economy in the image of U.S. permanent interests. But the application of maximum force to overwhelm and oust Noriega from power, and the determination to impose long-term hegemony, have not been accompanied by a similar commitment at the level of the economy. One result of this failure to grapple with the destructive consequences of two years of U.S. financial sanctions, the invasion, and its aftermath, has been the disintegration and almost total collapse of the client Endara regime's political base of support. At a broader level, this incapacity or unwillingness to promote economic reconstruction in Panama illustrates a fundamental principle of imperial-state policy in the Third World during the Reagan-Bush era: the enormous gap between America's power to dominate countries militarily and ideologically and its inability to rebuild economically viable client states.

Notes

1. See "The Panamanian Invasion, A Year Later," *Washington Report on the Hemisphere*, December 26, 1990, p. 5. The source for the casualty figures is the United Nations Human Rights Commission.

2. Frederick Kempe, *Divorcing The Dictator: America's Bungled Affair With Noriega* (New York: G.P. Putnam's Sons, 1990), p. 301.

3. Joe Pichirallo and Patrick E. Tyler, "Countdown to an Invasion," *Washington Post National Weekly Edition*, January 22–28, 1990, p. 32

4. Quoted ibid., p. 31.

5. Quoted in the *Philadelphia Inquirer*, December 21, 1989, p. 15A.

6. John Dinges, *Our Man in Panama* (New York: Random House, 1990), p. 305.

7. Quoted in Bob Woodward, *The Commanders* (New York: Simon & Schuster, 1991), p. 128. Secretary of State James Baker made essentially the same point during congressional testimony. See Andrew Rosenthal, "U.S. Considered Aid to Panama Rebels," *New York Times*, October 5, 1989, pp. 1, 14.

8. Dinges, *Our Man in Panama*, p. 305.

9. Kenneth Freed, "Some Blame Rogue Band of Marines for Picking Fight," *Los Angeles Times*, December 22, 1990.

10. Dinges, *Our Man in Panama*, p. 312.

11. See Seymour M. Hersh, "Why Democrats Can't Make an Issue Of Noriega," *New York Times*, May 4, 1988, p. 27.

12. Kempe, *Divorcing The Dictator*, p. 170.

13. Joseph B. Treaster, "U.S. Says Noriega Seems to Direct Attacks in Panama," *New York Times*, December 23, 1989, p. 1. Also see Andrew Rosenthal, "Bush Raises Force in Panama by 2,000," *New York Times*, December 23, 1989, p. 13.

14. *Philadelphia Inquirer*, December 24, 1989, p. 1.

15. Quoted in the *Philadelphia Inquirer*, December 23, 1989, p. 7A

16. *Philadelphia Inquirer*, December 24, 1989, p. 9A.

17. Quoted in the *Philadelphia Inquirer*, December 21, 1989, p. 15A.

18. Quoted in the *Philadelphia Inquirer*, December 24, 1989, p. 9A.

19. Quoted ibid.

20. See, for example, James Brooke, "U.S. Denounced By Nations Touchy About Intervention," *New York Times*, December 21, 1989, p. 24; Robert Pear, "Quayle Trip: Resentment Dramatized," *New York Times*, January 31, 1990, p. 16.

21. See Dinges, *Our Man in Panama*, passim; Kempe, *Divorcing The Dictator*, passim; Seymour M. Hersh, "Panama Strongman Said to Trade in Drugs, Arms and Illicit Money," *New York Times*, June 12, 1986, pp. 1, 14.

22. Assistant Secretary of State for Inter-American Affairs Elliott Abrams, April 1986 congressional testimony, quoted in Dinges, *Our Man in Havana*, p. 207.

23. Quoted ibid., p. 243.

24. For a discussion of the State/Defense debate during 1987 and 1988, see Kempe, *Divorcing The Dictator*, pp. 293–304; Pichirallo and Tyler, "Countdown to an Invasion," p. 31.

25. See "Counting on the U.S. for Stability," *Latin American Monitor: Central America*, January–February 1991, p. 865; "PRD Returns to Haunt Endara," *Latin American Monitor: Central America*, March 1991, p. 877; "Efforts to Regain Financial Credibility," *Central American Report*, October 12, 1990, p. 311.

26. Quoted in Michael Massing, "New Trouble in Panama," *New York Review of Books*, May 17, 1990, p. 47.

27. See "Privatizing to Mop Up Debt Arrears," *Latin American Weekly Report*, May 30, 1991, p. 9.

28. See Laura Brooks, "US, Panama Spar Over Aid Pact," *Christian Science Monitor*, September 20, 1990, p. 3; Mark A. Uhlig, "Panama Resisting Move to Clean Up Banking System," *New York Times*, October 22, 1990, pp. 1, 8.

29. Clifford Krauss, "Panama-U.S. Accord Set on Bank Records," *New York Times*, April 3, 1991, p. D1.

30. See Kenneth Freed, "Panama Is Seen as a Hub of Drug Traffic," *Los Angeles Times*, April 28, 1991, p. A11.

31. See Mark A. Uhlig, "Panama Drug Smugglers Prosper As Dictator's Exit Opens the Door," *New York Times*, August 21, 1991, pp. 1, 2; Laura Brooks, "A Tide of

Cocaine Rises in Panama," *Christian Science Monitor*, October 11, 1990, p. 6; Freed, "Panama Is Seen as a Hub of Drug Traffic," pp. A1, A11.

32. See ibid., p. A1.

33. Quoted ibid.

34. See ibid., p. A11.

35. Molly Moore, "U.S. Seeks to Rebuild Structure," *Washington Post*, December 30, 1989.

36. See America Watch, *The Laws of War and the Conduct of the Panama Invasion*, (New York: May 1990), pp. 44–45.

37. Quoted in Brook Larmer, "Panama Forges Police Force From Members of Noriega's Military," *Christian Science Monitor*, December 29–January 4, 1991, p. 2. Also see Howard W. French, "Noriega's Troops Now Form Police With U.S. Aid, Panamanians Say," *New York Times*, July 24, 1990, pp. 1, 6.

38. See Clifford Krauss, "Dependence and Sovereignty Pull at Panama's Equilibrium," *New York Times*, February 11, 1991, p. 15.

39. Quoted in Laura Brooks, "Crime Wave, Corruption Tie Up Panama's Police," *Christian Science Monitor*, August 28, 1990.

40. See Mark A. Uhlig, "U.S. Yielding its Police Role in Panama to Rebuilt Force," *New York Times*, October 30, 1990, p. 8; Clifford Krauss, "Rebels Are Posing Threat in Panama," *New York Times*, January 21, 1991, p. 3.

41. See Eric Schmitt, "U.S. Helps Quell Revolt in Panama," *New York Times*, December 16, 1990, pp. 1, 13; Lee Hockstader, "U.S. Army Guarantees Endara Stays in Power," *Washington Post*, December 16, 1990, pp. A51, A52.

42. Quoted in Kenneth Freed, "U.S. Quietly Helps Panama Organize Intelligence Office," *Los Angeles Times*, December 21, 1990, p. A5. Also see Lee Hockstader, "Panamanian Intelligence Service's Biggest Secret—Who Pays the Bills?" *Washington Post*, December 25, 1990, p. A29.

43. See "Economic Improvements Not Attacking Poverty,"*Central American Report*, January 18, 1991, p. 20; "Coalition Shaken By Corruption Row," *Latin American Weekly Report*, March 21, 1991, p. 5.

44. See "Endara Fights for Survival," *Latin American Monitor: Central America*, April 1991, p. 879; "PDC Prepared for Opposition Role," *Latin American Monitor: Central America*, May 1991, p. 901.

Revolution and Counterrevolution

5

Cuban Socialism: Rectification and the New Model of Accumulation

Introduction

The setting for an understanding of Cuban development in the 1990s is the basic shift from dynamic growth to economic stagnation and austerity. The decade and a half between 1970 and 1985 was a period of economic growth, expanding incomes and consumer spending, liberalized markets, and generous Soviet aid. At the same time, expanded health and educational services forced down infant mortality rates, increased life expectancy, and created a more skilled labor force. But the structure of the Cuban economy remained basically unchanged: In the absence of new export industries, excessive dependence on volatile primary commodity exports to finance imports necessary for producing goods for domestic consumption continued unabated; market diversification was neither pursued nor possible; sugar sales and oil reexports to the Soviet Union continued to predominate in the external sector.

Beginning in the mid-1980s, however, these persistent structural vulnerabilities converged with shifts in the international environment to produce a marked downturn in the Cuban economy, generating a number of political, economic, and social changes by the revolutionary leadership: Centralized political control at the top was matched by widespread criticism from the bottom of the middle-level bureaucrats; more centralized direction of the macroeconomy and increasingly decentralized management at the microeconomy level; moralization campaigns attacking inequality and corruption; and the initiation of a new period of austerity.

Preceding and paralleling these changes was a major internal policy debate over how best to confront Cuba's economic stagnation and its hard-currency balance-of-payments problem. On the one side were those who argued for greater integration into the Council on Mutual Economic Assistance (COMECON) and the need to more closely approximate the new Soviet model (economic liberalism and political openness) unfolding under Gorbachev. On the other were those, including Fidel Castro, who countered that to combine political openness with economic austerity could provoke serious political polarization and the consequent weakening of the revolutionary leadership. This latter argument carried the day. Castro's decision to tighten up the pre-1985 "openings" while Gorbachev moved in the opposite direction reflected the Cuban leadership's different evaluation of the international political/economic setting (e.g., continued U.S. hostility) and the impact of the post-1985 economic crisis. For the Cubans, the declining external sector did not indicate that the time was propitious for internal liberalization since the latter could well have upset the existing social equilibrium. Nonetheless, while restrictions on domestic market activity may have political payoffs and provide social symbolic gratification, they still don't address the unfilled economic needs resulting from the incapacity of the state distribution system to provide goods and services that the private sector supplied—even if at a certain political cost.

Against the background of this economic crunch—the need to export and become more globally competitive—Castro launched a major critique of the functioning of the party and the state institutions in early December 1986. In the course of the speech, he attacked the key problem of labor indiscipline, low productivity, and high costs (overinflated payrolls and resource squandering).[1] But he neglected to explore perhaps the most critical source of the absence of motivation: the political structures that centralize power and decision-making at the top and alienate workers from the power to make their own decisions and set their own levels of work and rewards.

In late December, the revolutionary regime established the context for political rectification and recentralization/decentralization with the announcement of an austerity program that involved cuts in consumer goods, price increases, and the elimination of automatic wage bonuses and bureaucratic perks.[2] The new economic sacrifices were not to be accompanied by greater political openness in order to avoid the likelihood of public protest and a weakening of regime authority. To counteract internal pressures for greater centralized planning and economic market mechanisms, Castro responded with an egalitarian moralistic approach; to compensate for external weaknesses and possible declining Soviet subsidies, he emphasized the necessity of labor discipline. By balancing consumer cutbacks with the elimination of some bureaucratic/managerial perks, the government hoped to forge a new internal consensus.[3]

Early in June 1987 Castro replaced the editor of the government newspaper, *Granma*, and the press began to attack state managers; popular forums to express mass discontent with corruption were encouraged; reports on inadequate services were publicly aired. Anticorruption campaigns against high officials were launched. Castro returned to a kind of selective glasnost—an alliance of the top and bottom against the middle. Even the top elite was not immune, though the elite structure remained intact. Mass populace mobilized to attack middle levels of power became the basis for relegitimizing the leadership. This policy weakened the intermediary sectors, strengthened the political elite, and defused popular discontent. Openness was directed toward strengthening state policy by producing focused objects of criticism. But while black marketeers, currency speculators, and self-aggrandizing bureaucrats were all worthy targets of opprobrium,[4] the government again refused to confront the deeper structural issues to explain why longstanding, senior officials such as General Arnaldo Ochoa resorted to counterrevolutionary or corrupt activities. The leadership failed to present systematic explanations for such extravagances and "lack of revolutionary education." Yet, if they were appointed or approved by Castro, doesn't that say something about his responsibility, or at least that of the system by which they are selected, promoted, and protected?

Meanwhile, according to Fidel, the shortage of hard currency (decreasing imports from market economies), foreign debt payments, and the absence major new sources of funding will dictate the continuation of the austerity program into the 1990s. At the same time, "liberalization" has not been totally eliminated. Rectification did not mark the end of the private sector in Cuba. As many as 50,000 workers are employed in the private sector despite the prohibition on unlicensed individuals, which has led to an erosion of services to the public, causing widespread shortages and discontent.[5] While the regime has eliminated the 250 private markets opened in 1980, it has also promoted private farms, through incentives (improved water supplies, access to machinery, etc.), in order to increase food production for the domestic market.[6] Finally, accompanying the regime's centralization of the economy to limit imports and impose austerity so as to save hard currency has been its willingness to "liberalize" the export tourist sector in the search for such currency.

In his speech to the Cuban people on July 26, 1988, the thirty-fifth anniversary of the Moncada uprising, Castro articulated two major themes, blending pragmatic short-term economic interests with long-term ideological concerns: the need to accumulate hard-currency earnings constitutes the instrumental and practical basis for the shift from material to "moral" incentives; and work is part of an individual's collective responsibility to society and the means for increasing collective rather than individual welfare.

Prelude to Rectification

From the mid-1970s to the mid-1980s, while Latin America's market economies sank in a deepening crisis of negative growth and triple-digit inflation and incomes plummeted, Cuba's noninflationary growth was an island of sanity and stability. Industrial, agricultural, and material product continued to experience an impressive annual growth rate. Between 1980 and 1985, real gross social product (GSP) increased by an average annual rate of approximately seven percent in striking contract to a 1.7-percent yearly fall in the rest of the hemisphere's real per-capita gross domestic product (GDP).[7] Since the end of the era of rapid expansion, however, real economic growth rates have been either minimal or negative—a decline which cannot be understood without reference to the liberalization policies of the pre-1985 period.

The dynamic growth decade of 1976 to 1985 was based on a deepening of Cuba's external dependence on the global economy. Consequently, shifts in the behavior of international economic forces after 1985 adversely affected Cuba as well as (albeit to a much greater extent) the rest of Latin America. Andrew Zimbalist details these factors and their impact on the Cuban economy:

> Low sugar prices, plummeting petroleum prices, devastation from Hurricane Kate, several consecutive years of intensifying drought, drastic dollar devaluation, the tightening U.S. blockade, growing protectionism in Western markets—all combined in 1986 to reduce Cuba's hard currency earnings by nearly 50 percent or $600 million. Cuba's failure at the summer 1986 Paris Club negotiations to obtain a new $300 million loan led to severe shortages of needed imported inputs. The ensuing shortages of outputs greatly diminished the possibilities for material incentives to function properly. This fact provides the objective backdrop to the subjective re-examination of the use or material and moral incentives.[8]

While external factors provoked the "subjective re-examination," the internal sociopolitical configuration of power was also deeply implicated, not only in the policy changes, but in developing the overall orientation of the regime in the preceding period. And thus it too figures in the reformulation of policy. Moreover, the issues raised went far beyond problems of incentives—as important as they are—but touched on the style of life, institutions, and behavior of the social structure from top to bottom. This suggests that the economic policies pursued in Cuba during the period of dynamic growth profoundly contributed to changes in societal structures and the value system, and that these transformations, both at the internal and external level, created a series of contradictions which the 1986 Communist Party Congress began to confront.

In the 1970s, Cuba initiated an economic liberalization program based on market mechanisms, material incentives, financial accountability, private consumer markets, and greater managerial/ministerial autonomy within the overall pattern of central planning. These internal changes were accompanied by increasing ties to external financial and trade markets which secured greater material rewards but within a framework of weak or nonexistent democratic worker accountability, thus giving license to the emergence of a new class of privileged managers, party functionaries, and globe-trotting technocrats (on expense accounts and with access to hard currency). The members of these social strata were willing and able to participate and secure the high-price consumer goods in the "free market" and hard-currency stores. While the economy was expanding, the political and social consequences of these inequalities were mitigated by general increases in incomes across the class spectrum. Worker salaries and consumption levels increased, although at a more modest rate, along with those of the new class of entrepreneurs, technocrats, and managers.

However, the economic crunch of the mid-1980s rendered this situation intolerable—the conditions and lifestyles of the organizers and principal beneficiaries of economic liberalization stood in stark contrast to the austerity demands now imposed on the majority of the labor force. Moreover, the negative impact extended to the most productive sectors of the economy. Within the top echelons of the Cuban social structure, one could identify two groups: those tied to domestic production, who derived their income from increasing productivity, eliciting worker/management cooperation, securing inputs and markets—who functioned within the discipline of the productive process; and those tied to the reexport of imported commodities (mainly sugar and petroleum), who were engaged in the "buying and selling" process, acting as intermediaries between different producers. This latter group thrived on market speculation and, in time of windfall profits, financed and stimulated greater imports and consumption. During the 1970s and early 1980s the two groups functioned in tandem, the incomes from one financing the other. Nevertheless, the easy sources of income generated by buying and selling weakened market discipline and postponed needed structural reforms while simultaneously intensifying Cuba's dependence on overseas suppliers and financiers. The post-1985 economic crisis initially affected the compradore sector but soon reverberated throughout the economy, also impacting on the productive sectors.

It was within this context of a shift in the balance of socioeconomic forces—between compradores and producers—that Castro launched his rectification program: Essentially, it reflected an effort to strengthen the productive classes in the face of the faltering performance of the compradores. Unregulated compradorism is incompatible with the social relations of industrial production, most of all in the context of austerity and a class-conscious working class. At the social psychological level, the uneven gains undermine social solidarity and the notion of common sacrifice; at the structural level, they undermine and distort resource flows from public to private sectors, undermining the calculations of investment decision-makers and disrupting the productive process.

The regime targeted the free-wheeling style associated with the compradores for concentrated attack: not only the farmers' markets and private-home builders but also the high-spending consumers, many of whom were able to accumulate small fortunes through their unrestricted external ties. The July 1989 trial of the narco-General Arnaldo Ochoa publicly exposed the self-aggrandizing behavior emblematic of a whole stratum of ministerial compradores who linked "legitimate" compradore activity to illicit profiteering.

The rectification process was based on Castro's effort to mobilize the productive classes against the compradores: to subordinate the former to the latter, while mobilizing both for a relaunching into the world market place. Rectification involved "reforms" because while the farmers' "free market" was abolished, the state-controlled parallel market was left untouched.[9] The "reforms" led to personnel changes in some cases, but retained the vertical control structure; they increased the technocratic presence, but tightened central allocation of hard currency. The process of change is not a generalized shift toward some abstract notion of "centralization" but a complex process of centralization and decentralization that focuses on strengthening the productive sector at the expense of the compradores. Zimbalist well describes these complex shifts:

> There is centralization in the sense that more activities are being brought back into the public sphere. There is also centralization with regard to control over resources linked to foreign exchange expenditures. There is, however, an ongoing effort at decentralization within the planning system. Direct contracting between enterprises for many inputs is being promoted, enterprise reports to their ministries are being cut back, the number of administrative personnel in the planning system is being reduced, enterprise self-financing of investment is being extended, worker participation in management and plan formulation is more extensive than ever before, the decentralization of enterprise management into smaller units (brigades) with greater worker control is being universalized in agriculture and extended in industry and the role of parallel markets where prices are set according to conditions of supply and demand is growing at an accelerated pace.[10]

There is also a second tendency in the rectification process which goes in a different direction, explicitly taking its cues from the capitalist marketplace and conforming much more closely with the export-market strategy which increasingly defines Cuban political economy. The export sector generated a series of "corporacions" (corporations), each with its specific economic functions. These, in turn, were divided into "real" and "fictitious" entities. The former included a number of "mixed enterprises"—joint ventures in which foreign capital predominates. The latter were dummy corporations managed by individuals closely linked with the principal nucleus of power in the government—the Politburo and the ministries of Defense and Interior. These corporations were set up to evade the U.S. economic blockade and import scarce and strategic products. (It was these fictitious corporations—out of public scrutiny—that fostered the corruption and illicit speculative activity of the Ochoa group.) Alongside of the emergence of "corporate structures" in the export sector was the widespread presence of highly specialized military officials in key sectors of the economy, giving the impression of a militarization of civil society. The Ochoa trial was less an effort to revert back to civil power than to rein in the "absolutist" power tendencies that military officials tend to transfer from one sphere to the other and an effort to affirm the principle of political party supremacy.[11]

The third observable tendency in Cuba's rectification is the basic shift in policy-makers' views of the labor process, with increasing emphasis on learning from Japanese and U.S. managerial and organizational experiences. The Cuban approach is to retain public property ownership and introduce profit maximizing and capitalist organizational principles. Carlos Aldana, head of the Cuban Communist party's Revolutionary Orientation Bureau, highlights the new directions in Cuban economic policy:

> We are applying Soviet economic calculation [enterprise profitability]; but within much more precise limits than in the U.S.S.R. In the basic system that will follow this sometime in the future, the Japanese and North American experience should be contemplated. Experts from the Rockefeller Group are already advising us on enterprise management. We think we should incorporate capitalist experience in the organization of production, in work payment and in quality control. We are not going to change the system of collective property, but we will apply scientific methods in the global organization of work. We have a great deal to learn from capitalism in this sense.[12]

Thus, the shift in the Cuban model in the late 1980s represented a deepening of the liberalization process and, in the context of scarcity and austerity, an increase in technocratic and managerial power ("scientific methods") over the working class. There was an explicit rejection of the "populism" (general income and consumer increases) and job protection ("paternalism") that accompanied the earlier variant of liberalization during the previous expansive decade in favor of cost efficiency and a flexible labor force (unemployment). According to Aldana:

> We have had to rectify previous lines. More than 70 decrees and decree-laws have been eliminated. The old permanent employment of workers in an enterprise is incompatible with our own modern model of economic calculation. We do not think that in production the collective will should have primacy; the work post belongs to the most qualified worker. Of course, the Cuban road to labor force efficiency does not pass through automatic unemployment as under capitalism. . . . Here we will adopt . . . gradual approaches. . . . We think there are democratic formulas in the relation between firm and worker, as in Japan [*sic*], but we have already learned the error of a forced march toward socialism.

Cuban income policies, however, were to be oriented toward favoring the lower class at the expense of the new "middle class":

> Our priority is to raise the welfare of these [low-income sectors]. Not as before, by raising the average level. Here there is a "middle class" that already has satisfied its necessities, including an excess, while others are confined to urban slums. It is a "middle class" that says that the revolution is going badly when it cannot conserve its level of life. They are bothered now because the priority is the popular strata, the workers who are quite below their status.[13]

It appears that the Cubans are trying to combine a progressive income policy, a strengthening of management prerogatives, and an increased emphasis on enterprise cost accounting, while holding down incomes of the "middle class." Given the qualifications in the application of the 'reforms' (on employment, for instance) and the split between increasing management authority and restricting 'middle-class' income levels, it remains to be seen how effective their implementation will be.

The Rectification Campaign and Cuban Development

In analyzing Cuban policy since the mid-1980s and, in particular, the rectification campaign launched by Fidel Castro, it is important to sort out what is ideological from what is expedient or pragmatic: which measures reflect underlying principles and methods of socialist development and which reflect adaptations to externally or internally imposed exigencies? It is necessary to examine the rectification policy in terms of whether it reflects a major historical turn involving a decisive shift in the internal structure of society or is simply a product of conjunctural circumstance, subject to modification with changes in the external environment (read: marketplace).

Several questions emerge regarding these alternative hypotheses. Did the rectification campaign result from internal struggles from below, from confrontations between contending social forces over the direction of Cuban development? Or was it a product of an internal-faction fight between contending elites over how to respond to external economic problems in which issues of personal power and authority were mixed and/or cloaked with ideological issues? Was the rectification campaign part of an effort by Castro to go back to the original roots of the revolution in the 1960s, to renew the spirit of egalitarianism, voluntarism, and idealism, or was it a product of an economic crisis in which the government, left with few material resources, fell back on the moral and symbolic strengths of the revolution to implement unpopular economic measures?

To what extent has the population responded favorably to the rectification campaign? Which changes have evoked support and which have provoked opposition? Has the Castro leadership been successful in recreating the revolutionary mobilization of the earlier period? Or conversely, without much "mobilization" has the regime been able to carry out unpopular austerity programs without evoking countermobilizations?

There is no doubt that by launching a campaign from above against some of the popularly disliked features of Cuban socialism—corruption, managerial abuses, private appropriations of public transport, etc.—the government at least preempted any campaign from below against the restrictive economic measures imposed by the regime (increases in prices, reductions in salaries, increased costs for utilities and transport, etc.). By simultaneously attacking the profiteering of the market and the work rules and salary/bonus structure of labor, the regime neutralized the potential for large-scale discontent.

The radicalism of the rectification was localized in time and place, adding substance to the notion that it reflected the convergence of a specific set of forces. The rectification campaign was launched as the economic constraints (particularly balance of payments in convertible currency) began to fully emerge in 1985 and intensified as the crisis continued toward the end of the decade. The radical measures, ostensibly based on a renewal of socialist egalitarianism, were accompanied by an aggressive effort to expand and deepen ties with capitalist regimes, especially in Latin America and Western Europe. The appeal to socialism internally was matched by the deliberate policy of relegating socialism in foreign relations to the back burner and adopting a "broad front" strategy in Latin America which at least raised the possibility of alliances with any civilian "democratic" regime in the region, no matter how reactionary, which had diplomatic and commercial relations with Cuba.

This apparent paradox of Cuban policy—a radical "Guevarist" rectification campaign at home and a broad front hemispheric policy that surpassed the blandest formulations of local Communist parties—reflects the dual effort of the Castro leadership to lessen domestic consumption while creating a competitive export sector based on a disciplined labor force and opening markets externally. Unlike the 1960s when radical egalitarianism was linked to an alliance with international revolutionary movements, the current campaign of sacrifice and moralization is directed toward very dissimilar goals—the reducation of labor costs, the creation of nontraditional export sectors, the search for new markets to compensate for declining hard-currency income, the effort to compensate for reductions in Soviet subsidies, as well as a means of responding to increasing pressure from Western and Japanese banks to keep up debt payments. In the late 1980s and early 1990s the (world) market, not (revolutionary) politics is in command, even as the peasant market has been abolished and socialist exhortations abound.

Unlike the Soviet and Eastern European counterparts who were also pursuing economic restructuring to compete in the world market, Castro chose the strategy of recentralization rather than decentralization, of selective criticism of middle functionaries rather than wholesale attacks on the top leadership, of cloaking the whole endeavor in the symbols of the national revolutionary past rather than in the contemporary modernist liberal rhetoric of the West.

Perhaps more than the rest of the Communist world—probably because of his proximity to the United States—Castro was keenly aware of the destructive and uncontrollable centrifugal forces which could be unleashed by discarding existing political structures and authority without having an alternative political base. The foreign-exchange crunch of the 1980s provided few possibilities for sustaining private consumption, particularly of imported items. The problem was cutting back on individual consumption and imports and increasing exports and productions while retaining basic collective welfare services. "Free market" rhetoric and glasnost were perceived by Castro as ideologies and practices compatible with a period of expanding consumption and social consensus. That is why they were tolerated and promoted to some extent during the decade preceding 1985. The present period of austerity and increasing demands on labor calls for an ideology and practice of centralized socialism—strong state control to mobilize resources for the external market. For that policy, public authority must be sustained.

Hence, in order to secure popular respect a powerful moralization campaign was launched to ensure state legitimacy while pursuing unpopular economic policies. In other words, the rectification campaign focuses on the personal moral attributes of the policy-makers, rather than on the overall socioeconomic policies being pursued. Personal enrichment and individual profiteering is condemned, while the economic system extracts and transfers income to the international bankers and finances investment in market-competitive enterprises.

Speaking of the difference between Gorbachev's perestroika and Castro's rectification, a senior Cuban Communist party official stressed the rhythm and range of modifications undertaken:

> In the Soviet Union there has been an abrupt change from a closed society, archaic and police-state, to the present situation. The paradox is that the change has been provoked from power, but it is power which remains in question. Glasnost has unleashed all the demons at once, but it can only deal with one at a time, and the rest continue to [run] loose. In this fashion, Soviet society has become disarticulated. The great error of the U.S.S.R. in the period of Breshnev is having remained in isolation after having achieved strategic parity with the United States. The isolation was cultural, ideological and political. Then, from one day to the next, the Soviets discovered North American style democracy, Disneyland, Donald Duck, pizza. [Within the Soviet leaderhip today] there is an evident fascination for the North American model, that leads to decentralization of the economy, to the re-establishment of capitalist values. We also want to modernize the economy, take on the flexible aspects of capitalism and its capacity for immediate response to problems [*sic*], but we cannot abandon the centralization of the economy; we cannot permit ourselves the luxury of each self-managed enterprise dissipating national resources in hard currency.[14]

This attempt to find a middle road between bureaucratic isolationism and indiscriminant liberalization combines the introduction of market techniques and central planning; a Cuban way of promoting political openings and the continuity of political authority; and the selective retention of the revolutionary past rather than its wholesale debunking in order to avoid the disarticulation of the structure of power and the collapse of the social structure. This account fits in with our analysis of the Cuban perspective—prudent transition toward as export-oriented, welfare-based model, rather than following a radical liberalization lacking any solid basis of political support, a formula more likely to lead to the Latin Americanization of the Eastern countries than to their Western Europeanization.

Nonetheless, Cuban economic "restructuring" still confronts two key obstacles: (1) the entrenched bureaucratic party political machinery which resists efforts to reorient from the existing patterns and the mutual support system which extends this behavior across enterprises; and (2) workers who are likely to object to harder work for less wages, scarcer consumer goods, and fewer opportunities to earn extra income through sideline employment.

The austerity and readjustment measures have provoked some discontent. Castro has responded by taking certain populist measures to alleviate disaffection: punishing corrupt officials, attacking profiteers, and canvassing neighborhoods to discuss the measures. He has evoked revolutionary symbols and reaffirmed basic social gains to mitigate against the application of the new economic rationalization of work and rewards. The opening of the press to critical debate, within political-party guidelines, and the liberalization of migration are two areas which could also serve to ease the pressure on the domestic front. The regime hopes that by increasing production for domestic consumption through private farms it can compensate for increased exports. Whether high-enough levels of production can be attained in a reasonably short time to serve both increased export targets and domestic consumption is debatable. In any case, the centralized political and economic structures are effective levers in neutralizing autonomous bases of opposition. At the same time, the success of the export model depends to a considerable degree on Cuba's capacity to produce quality products on demand at competitive prices, and that depends, sooner or later, on unleashing technical and skilled labor from the bureaucratic fetters of the authoritarian personalist regime.

What seems clear is that Cuba's labor-oriented productive system and its new export-oriented development system are in conflict. The attempt to mesh the two seems to lead to the worst of both worlds: declining incomes and productivity at home in the absence of any major expansion in overseas markets. The export strategy seems to require a wholesale restructuring of at least the leading economic sectors and the resocialization of labor along the lines of long-term delayed gratification, a restratified salary and wage system, and heightened managerial prerogatives. It combines efforts to implement a program of consumer austerity and the rationalization of wage/productivity norms in the context of a political campaign against managerial incompetence and leadership corruption.

The key to any successful conversion to an export strategy is the emergence of a managerial elite capable of organizing the factors of production and penetrating overseas markets. It is not clear how the economic changes at the bottom will translate into efficient use of resources at the top if the current managers and officials are denounced, replaced, or demoted. Will a new group of entrepreneurial technocrats emerge from the current campaign primed to pursue the new strategy, mindful of the trade unions' criticisms of managerial abuses? Will the weakening of the consumer power of the workers be amply compensated by the symbolic gratifications emanating from the anticorruption moralization campaign? And, finally, will Cuban managers have the resources to compete internationally if the government continues to pay out much of its hard-currency earnings to service its foreign debt?

The Cuban effort to contain and limit the negative consequences of the economic restructuring accompanying the turn toward the export market is evident in Castro's constant denunciation of corruption and in his recognition that the unregulated market dissolves the elementary social bonds that tie state and society in a workable relation. Pursuing an export-market strategy and regulating internal-market differentiation may seem a contradictory halfway-house approach, and it may even be creating bottlenecks to the effective pursuit of the overseas markets, but it also reflects the prudence of a political leader who is deeply aware of the corrosive effects which the market has on the social solidarity that sustains state power. The tensions, and ebb and flow, of Cuban policy in the coming period will reflect the pressures emanating from the contradictory demands flowing from the collectivist-worker traditions and the exigencies of market competition.

Economic Restructuring Within the Socialist Bloc: Comparing the Cuban, Soviet, and Chinese Approaches

Both Castro and Gorbachev had the same economic restructuring goal based on increased labor discipline, rising productivity, and greater export competitiveness and management accountability, as well as a deeper insertion into the capitalist marketplace. The means employed, however, varied significantly, based on different assessments of the obstacles and problems. For Castro, the problems of securing social cohesion and political order in pursuing restructuring were primary. Given Cuba's proximity to the United States and the latter's continued belligerence, Castro couldn't risk any broad opening of market forces which might result in deep cleavages and the rapid escalation of opposition (in part funded by external sources). The road to cohesion in Cuba was based on evoking the egalitarian goals of the past, the revolutionary symbols of "uncorrupted idealism" and the populist denunciation of managerial abuses. Thus restructuring began with a vertical alliance from the top to the bottom to confront "the middle"—a melange of corrupt officials, technically incompetent "old revolutionaries" and pro-Moscow Communists who perhaps want to liberalize prematurely in imitation of Gorbachev. The populist measures, however, were linked to a strengthening of ties with the technocratic managers, and the armed forces, the Ministry of Interior, and the trade union apparatus.

Gorbachev, on the other hand, simultaneously promoted the restructuring of the Soviet economy (perestroika) and broad electoral openings (glasnost) that undermined existing party authority without creating an alternative structure. Change precedes order and authority and was presumed to derive from the favorable public response to it. But the consequences of Gorbachev's experiment suggest that widespread glasnost in a period of economic retrenchment accompanying restructuring does not generate political cohesion. On the contrary, political freedom and freeing of markets can undermine restructuring by increasing short-term internal demands, thus preempting long-term changes oriented toward strengthening the external sector. In this, Gorbachev may indeed have been more innovative, but he was less realistic, than Fidel Castro.

The Cuban road to restructuring also exhibits similarities to and differences from the Chinese approach. In contrast to China's mass of petty commodity producers demanding private ownership, Cuban agriculture, particularly its export crops, is organized in large cooperatives or state farms. Hence, restructuring in Cuba, unlike China, does not involve privatization of the agricultural export sector. Nevertheless, while suppressing the private farmers' market, Castro is promoting increased small-farmer production of food for local consumption. Likewise, because of the small size of its domestic market, Cuba is unlikely to attract large-scale foreign investment, such as has happened in China. Rather, economic sectors with large overseas foreign market appeal are being targeted for joint ventures with foreign capital. In the case of tourism, West European investors holding fifty percent equity have been given total control over management and work rules in the particular enterprise.[15] In February 1991, as part of its continuing effort to encourage foreign investors to participate in joint venture projects, the government granted tax exemptions on imported materials and eliminated all restrictions on profit remittances abroad.

The Cubans differ from the Chinese substantially on the scope and timing of restructuring and its articulation with the internal private market. Beijing simultaneously began to deepen the scope of the internal market through indiscriminate lifting of state controls, privatization, and loosening of price controls—leading to massive pillage of the public sector, strong inflationary pressures, and the weakening of state authority. The result was widespread discontent—highlighted by the student/worker mass protests in April–June 1989—eventual repression by the armed forces, and the centralization of political power. In Cuba the process of restructuring has followed a different path: the internal market has been suppressed, moralization of the economy has been launched, and selectively directed dissent has been permitted, thus precluding the deep economic cleavages, the wholesale public corruption and open-ended mass rejection of public authority. Populist centralization preceded restructuring, thus limiting the intensity of opposition and preventing movements toward decentralized decision-making such as occurred in China. The revolutionary regime drove a wedge between a potential opposition alliance of discontented workers adversely affected by the restructuring and Western market-oriented intellectuals by abolishing the internal market and taking preemptive action against two vital targets of Chinese protests, corruption and elitism, while retaining the authoritarian political structure. By taking a piecemeal and prudent political course in restructuring, the Cubans were able to avoid the extremes of China: rapid and disruptive shifts from total collectivism to the market, from mass popular protest to brutal terrorist state repression.

The Cuban strategy of separating internal market changes from external restructuring and providing limited populist dissent, while avoiding general glasnost, seems to have ensured greater stability and cohesion than either Gorbachev's or Deng's strategy.

The export strategy adopted by the so-called "market socialists" in the former Communist countries tends to underestimate the effects of inequality in bargaining with Western bankers and investors, to look for short-term benefits at the expense of long-term liabilities, and to fail to recognize that the consumerism of the West is the product of a long-term process of accumulation, not an immediately realizable product, least of all for relatively weak export economies opening their markets to powerful financial-investor countries. Equally important, the sociopolitical consequences of the type of polarized and uneven development that almost universally appears with the export model are rarely examined by the market socialists, leading to new waves of political confrontation. The inequalities of power under collectivism are translated into the inequalities in access to the newly privatized enterprises, to land, and to credit when the market is introduced. Corruption and private abuse of public power become the normal accompaniments of the return to the market. Private concentrations of power based on kinship networks reemerge, with the rupturing of political and social constraints.

The New Model of Accumulation and Cuba's Foreign Policy

The rectification campaign is not simply a series of discrete policy measures but part and parcel of a larger effort to create a new accumulation model—and thus part of the restructuring and adjustments inherent in the transition. The model ascendant in the 1970s and the first half of the 1980s—specialization in primary goods exports and imported finished and capital goods, in order to build and diversify, and meet the consumer needs of, the domestic market—was largely financed by deficits and by subsidies from the Soviet Union. In a period of expansiveness in the Socialist bloc, as well as in the West, this model functioned quite successfully: Cuban GSP grew at a rate far above the average for Latin America; consumer incomes improved substantially and industrial growth rates were acceptable.

By the mid-1980s, however, this model of accumulation based on external financing for internal growth began to exhaust its historical possibilities. The prices of sugar and oil declined precipitously; the Socialist bloc countries began to reallocate their external financial resources toward internal modernization and to look toward greater integration with Western markets; Cuba's hard-currency balance-of-payments account deficits widened; and debt payments to Japanese and West European bankers increased pressure on hard-currency reserves and export earnings.[16] Cuban economic policy began to shift from an "internal market import substitution strategy" to an "export strategy"—combined with an intensified effort to create the internal structural conditions to compete successfully in the world market. In entering the world market and adopting the export strategy, labor was increasingly seen as a factor of production, a cost, and salary and labor relations were geared accordingly.

The transition from an "inward-oriented consumer economy" to an "outward-looking export economy" implied a number of internal socioeconomic dislocations as well as shifts in Cuba's foreign policies. The first basic structural shift was increased investment in means of production and increased charges for public services: economic resources were reallocated away from consumption toward production, and hopefully export production. Second, efforts were directed toward lowering labor costs through readjusting the wage/salary/bonus payments, linking them to actual increases in production. Third, efforts were made to separate party control from day-to-day management of economic enterprises: Professional managers and technocrats increasingly replaced older political-party stalwarts. Fourth, efforts were intensified to promote new lines of foreign exchange earnings—principally through tourism and attempts to forge new links with market economies in Europe, Latin America, and elsewhere.

This effort to promote a new model of accumulation took place within the shell of a centrally planned economy and was accompanied by constant reaffirmations of Marxist-Leninist principles.[17] The regime placed a premium on sustaining ideological-organizational continuities in order to cushion the inevitable shocks and discontent accompanying the transitional period. Castro purposely sought to avoid the problems of simultaneously weakening ideological and political control while implementing deep structural changes that were likely to have adverse results for the population.

The change in the accumulation model led to a series of socioeconomic dislocations: salary/bonus payments declined while public-service costs increased, engendering some discontent and real declines in income; the abolition of the private markets and the promotion of state-regulated parallel markets provoked protests from former beneficiaries; the elimination of unlicensed service workers produced widespread protests over the loss of services and income. Consumer goods shortages, tighter work norms, and (probably) increasing disguised or real unemployment are part of the dislocations accompanying the transition period.[18] The changes instituted, however, are not temporary; they must be routinized if Cuba is to make an effective transition to an export-oriented economy: It cannot return to the relaxed atmosphere, excessive-absenteeism, and high consumption of the early 1980s.

The new export model has also had a profound impact on the broad thrust of Cuba's international relations. Above all, it has meant that foreign relations are now increasingly determined by market possibilities, not revolutionary politics. Cuba is pursuing economic and political ties with existing regimes, irrespective of their domestic or foreign policies—provided, of course, the minimum condition of diplomatic recognition is accepted. Cuba seeks to play an important role in Latin American economic organizations, promoting common commercial and investment policies, while intensifying its efforts to increase financial and economic ties with the European Economic Community (EEC), Japan, and Canada. To the extent that Cuba's debt position has weakened its import capacity, its actual trade relations with the advanced capitalist countries have declined, and Cuba has turned to South-South trade talks, mostly with the more dynamic regional countries such as Brazil, Mexico, and Argentina. Castro has advocated a doctrine of ideological pluralism in Latin America and a collective front against the foreign debt; he has tried to avoid any socioeconomic criticism of the internal policies of what he describes as democratic regimes in the hemisphere: These are efforts to break Cuba's isolation and to promote Cuba's new export-accumulation model.

Externally, this attempt to shift to a new model of accumulation faces several formidable challenges: increasing competition from all Third World countries adopting export strategies; growing protectionism in the Western capitalist countries which limits market access; problems presented by the EEC, particularly the privileged access granted to former colonies; the probable downturn in the world economy in the early 1990s; the increasing linkage between Eastern Europe and the advanced capitalist countries; and, last but by no means least, foreign debt payments and restrictions on fresh financing.

Nevertheless, there are also a number of positive signs. Cuba has built bridges to the EEC and expanded its economic relations with Spain and Italy. Canada is seeking to strengthen trade ties while Japanese government officials have expressed interest in tourist-sector investment opportunities.[19] Two-way trade with China reached $500 million in 1990 (an eleven-percent increase over 1989) and can be expected to blossom further amid rising sugar purchases by Beijing and its agreement to build a bicycle factory in Cuba.[20] In the Mideast and the Horn of Africa, the Castro government signed economic pacts with Iran, Iraq, and Ethiopia during 1990–1991.[21] Perhaps most significant has been the development of closer links with Latin American producers and markets. Trade with the hemisphere increased from $359 million in 1985 to $1.33 billion in 1988 and since then has continued its upward spiral. In 1990, Brazil purchased $130 million of Cuba's meningitis B vaccine—equivalent to the total value of two-way trade during 1989. The value of Cuban-Mexican commercial ties is expected to double between 1990 ($130 million) and 1991, bolstered by joint-venture investments in the island's tourist, agricultural and construction sectors.[22]

The tourist industry has grown at a faster rate than any other economic sector, earning $125 million in hard currency in 1988, $149 million in 1989 and $250 million in 1990—profits likely to increase severalfold in future years. Attracted by new majority foreign-ownership laws, hundreds of millions of dollars in new (primarily European) foreign investment have poured into this sector since 1990.[23] Major high-technology biotechnical laboratories are also coming on stream as part of the government's export offensive. Recent successes have included the marketing of the meningitis B vaccine as well as other kinds of medicines and medical equipment. Not the least among Cuba's resources is its abundance of skilled professionals who can compete, particularly in servicing lesser-developed countries. Finally, global and regional political developments could add to Cuba's economic prospects: the decline of U.S. hegemony and the pressures of a diversified competitive world economy will inevitably weaken the U.S. blockade; the demise of liberal electoral regimes in Latin America may produce successor governments interested in furthering Cuban trade and investment.

The Foreign-Debt Dilemma

Cuba has fallen into the same Latin American debt trap Castro has so eloquently denounced in recent years: borrowing at exorbitant interest rates, pursuing the risky commodity-export-based development game, rescheduling and capitalizing an increasingly insurmountable debt, imposing austerity programs to continue the flow of foreign funding, and trying to increase exports in a period of declining prices and restricted markets. Efforts to promulgate the notion of Cuban "exceptionalism" cannot be sustained: The terms of payment, interest rates, rescheduling costs, and time frames established by Japanese and European creditor banks were no different from those demanded of other regional governments by American private multinational banks.[24]

Although Cuba invested its loans in productive activity this does not change the *global relations*, shaped by creditor classes and nations, that affect the terms and consequences of payment. Moreover, Cuba did not invest sufficiently in productive activity with a *hard-currency export component* to enable it to pay back the loans in kind. Like other Third World debtors, it gambled on high commodity prices to sustain its interest payments—underestimating the instability of the market and its historical tendency to work against primary producers. This despite Castro's long and detailed discourses on the subject of unequal exchange. . . . Since 1985, the prices of Cuban sugar and oil exports have declined significantly at a time of exports being pegged to the falling U.S. dollar, and imports and debt payments being pegged to the appreciating Japanese yen and West German mark, thus increasing trade deficits—while moving interest rates have simultaneously pushed up interest obligations to foreign creditors.[25] Meantime, in the absence of sufficient sources of long-term, low-cost financing, the revolutionary regime faces the onerous prospect of more austerity and declining economic growth as it pursues domestic policies and an export development-accumulation model resembling that of the rest of Latin America.

This domestic austerity-export strategy logic that the Castro leadership has embraced raises a difficult question that needs to be addressed: As debt payments to the West mount and trade opportunities decline,[26] is the solution to be found in deepening market ties, increasing dependence on external funding, and making more market adjustments to increase exports at the cost of declining local consumption and greater subordination to foreign capital? Devaluations will not necessarily increase exports (given the constraints on access to overseas markets) while increasing the price of the imports and the cost of financing the debt. Decentralization and marketization could imply a worsening of the debt while decreasing the central government's capacity to control the variables affecting world trade.

In searching for answers to the above, a further set of questions emerge: First, should Cuba consider reducing its convertible currency needs instead of mapping strategies to increase them—under conditions that are unfavorable? Second, is it time for Cuba to start moving to lessen its dependence on its middle-person role reselling sugar and oil for foreign currency and for it to begin producing its own competitive commodities? Third, should Cuba repudiate its foreign debt and reorient its economy away from the market?

Growing indebtedness is only the first step toward greater integration into the market *on its own terms:* eroding domestic consumption, increasing labor discontent, deepening inequalities, and promoting foreign control of the economy via debt swaps, joint ventures, and the like. The greater the debt, the greater the need to find new sources of hard currency, the more concessional agreements, leading to a spiralling debt and a greater need to sell off resources, cheapen labor power, and sacrifice consumer living standards—until nothing is left of socialism. In other words, socialist relations of production and worker-oriented welfarism increasingly come into conflict with the exigencies of an export-oriented development strategy that primarily benefits overseas lenders. Instead of a decentralized market economy, the end result of this scenario is a foreign-controlled, polarized society vulnerable to the decisions and cycles of the capitalist marketplace.

Paradoxically, as Cuba attempts to broaden its market ties, commercial trading opportunities are diminishing: trade with capitalist countries declined from twenty-two percent to twenty-five percent of total trade in 1980–1981 to less than fourteen percent in 1986. Between 1986 and 1987, the total value of this trade fell from $1.6 billion to $1.25 billion.[27] While Cuba struggles to find new sources of external financing what it generally receives is old-debt refinancing. With declining market and financial opportunities in the capitalist world and few medium-term prospects for any dramatic shift in either area, it seems unrealistic for Cuba to squander its economic resources in plying uncooperative market players. A new direction might involve deepening its import substitution policies, diversifying its processing of sugar into local sources of energy and other uses, and bringing its investment rates down to levels that can balance with consumer needs.

Cuban-Soviet Relations

It was one of the peculiarities of Cuban-Soviet relations during the latter half of the 1980s that the "center" wanted to end the "periphery"'s dependence—to diminish the historic process of large-scale, long-term net transfers from East to South. The shift in Cuban policy toward an "export strategy" and, in particular, its effort to penetrate market economies was supported by the resource-short Soviets, who desired to redeploy as much of their Cuban transfers as possible to bolster their own economy and finance their own restructuring. The inward turn of the Soviets under Gorbachev was accompanied by Moscow's encouragement of Cuba's outward turn. The convergence of Soviet and Cuban policy on the new directions in Cuban economic strategy was indisputable.

The shift to the new export-accumulation model as well as internal economic restructuring did not, however, mean any distancing from the Soviet Union. These changes were building on the foundations of the existing bilateral relationship, at least for the foreseeable future. But as the political and economic crisis in the Soviet Union deepened, it placed additional, more serious strains, on Moscow's ties with its closest Third World ally over the past three decades—triggering new criticisms and controversies on both sides.

During 1989–1990, the debate over aid to Cuba featured prominently in Soviet policy-making circles and the media. Amid the anti- and pro-Cuban statements, it was possible to identify three broad schools of thought: the "continuators," who favored critical support of Cuba; the "compromisers," who want to retain ties with Cuba but insisted on substantial changes in the relationship and disapproved highly of the island's economic structure; and the neoliberal "Westernizers," who supported the counterrevolutionary exile forces and advocated a rupture in relations between Moscow and Havana.

Fortunately for Castro, most of the Gorbachev's senior foreign policymakers were numbered among the continuators. When the two countries signed the 1990 bilateral trade agreement worth $15 billion (an approximate nine-percent increase over the record 1989 accord), the vice-chairman of the USSR Council of Ministers, Leon Abalkin, called it a reaffirmation of "our historically good relations" with Cuba. While acknowledging the need to institute some changes in the relationship "to match the conditions of the world market," he admonished those attempting to link the Cuban aid program to shortages in the Soviet economy. Abalkin stressed the complementary nature of the trade: an end to Cuban sugar, nickel, and citrus-fruit imports would force Moscow to spend scarce hard currency and pay higher prices for these products in the world market. Cuba was still a valuable economic asset and represented an important indirect source of savings—estimated at around $2 billion annually.[28]

On October 11, 1990, a senior Soviet military officer, General Mikhail Moiseyev, told Cuban officials that the cooperative relationship was not under threat: "We are faithful today to the roots of our friendship and especially to the obligations of contractual agreements established after the visit of President Gorbachev [April 1989] which includes economic, political and military relations."[29] Two months later, the head of the Soviet foreign ministry's Latin American department, Valery Nikolayenko, dismissed speculation of an end to economic ties with Cuba. The Soviets would continue to service Cuba's vital needs "regardless of what the Soviet Union has or doesn't have." Discussing Moscow's decision to shift all trade from subsidized barter to hard currency in January 1991, he said that in the case of Cuba "we are going to try to implement this more slowly, to avoid damaging the Cuban economy."[30]

At the same time, despite support for maintaining trade ties among senior

Soviet officials, the signs were not all promising for the future. During 1990, for instance, the twenty-percent reduction in Soviet fuel shipments to Cuba totally eliminated one of the island's two major sources of foreign exchange earnings— the reexport of Soviet crude (which topped $620 million in hard currency in 1985).[31] The requirement that Cuba now purchase Soviet petroleum with hard currency at world market prices was likely to further reduce the flow of crude into the former's economy. Nor was it clear whether Cuba will benefit from now having to bargain with individual Soviet republics and state companies instead of negotiating business deals with the central government alone, as was the case under all previous trade pacts. Moreover, disruptions caused by the erosion of Soviet central planning resulted in more and more delays in shipping vital spare parts to Cuba and in the transport of perishable fruits from the island to the Soviet Union. Delivery problems forced the Castro leadership to tighten the distribution of food, clothing, and household appliances and to expand the number of rationed items. Adding to these problems, the neoliberal "Westerners" seemed to be gaining strength within the Soviet political arena in their pursuit of a full-scale "reconsideration of all habitual relations with Havana," leading to an end to Cuban "subsidies."[32]

While challenging the "Westernizers'" one-sided interpretation of trade relations—emphasizing the large amounts of hard currency Moscow saved by trading with Havana, and the latter's tolerance of shipment delays and the often poor quality of Soviet manufactured exports—the Cubans were clearly anticipating more significant changes in the bilateral relationship. In December 1990, expressing concern over future prices for Soviet oil and Cuban sugar in the context of a hard-currency squeeze, Vice President Carlos Rafael Rodríguez predicted "five or six very difficult years ahead."[33] To offset the potentially devastating impact of any abrupt deterioration in economic ties, the Cubans began implementing a number of precautionary measures including food rationing and an emergency plan to drastically reduce energy dependence in the event the Soviets decided to halt all petroleum exports. The latter is based on an increased use of animal power instead of tractors in the agricultural sector and the purchase of hundreds of thousands of bicycles (mostly from China) to wean motorists away from their cars.

The decision to place economic links with Cuba on a more commercial basis— replacing rouble-based trade by trade in convertible currency—reflected the transition to a new bilateral relationship which would take greater account of Soviet domestic needs. However, the 1991 trade and economic agreements pact did indicate a willingness on Moscow's part to cushion the impact of the changes on Cuba's economy: Sovier sugar imports remained at the 1990 level; Soviet grain and flour exports to, and purchases of biotechnic and medical products from, the Caribbean island increased substantially; and the Gorbachev leadership agreed to continue funding eighty economic development projects begun during the previous (1986–90) five year plan. But these positive expressions of support were accompanied by more negative developments. First, Cuban trade with the Soviets fell by twenty five percent during the first half of 1991. Second, Soviet oil exports declined by approximately thirty percent. Third, lowered Soviet prices for Cuban sugar, nickel and other commodities resulted in a net loss of purchasing power of over $1 billion compared with 1990. Finally, 1991 witnessed major delays in the arrival of Soviet goods in Cuban ports. Under the terms of the one year pact, Moscow contracted to export goods valued at close to $4 billion; by September 30, only $1.3 billion worth of exports had reached the island.[34]

Thus, even prior to the Soviet political upheaval in late August 1991, economic relations between the two countries were on a downward trajectory. The failed coup against Gorbachev, and the emergence of Boris Yeltsin as the dominant figure on the Soviet political landscape, signalled almost certain moves to further retrench what was left of the country's overseas economic commitments. Cuba seemed a prime target, especially given the Bush administration's insistence that a complete rupture in economic relations with Havana was a necessary precondition for large scale U.S. funding of Soviet economic reconstruction. In the months following the August events, Soviet leaders emphasized that future trade with China would be on a strictly nonsubsidized basis while indicating a greater disposition to accomodate Washington's demands for concessions in the international arena in return for badly needed financial support.

Cuban-Soviet frictions over global and regional political developments have paralleled, and been interrelated with, disagreements over the right mix of domestic political change and economic restructuring, and shifts in the nature of the commercial relationship since 1986. Cuba, for instance, has been very concerned about the Soviet's disarmament policies, contemplating the possible shift from a bipolar world to one dominated by a country that remains unremittingly hostile to the revolutionary regime. Castro has repeatedly questioned the benefits of superpower detente to Cuba, given the continuing imperialist pressures and threats, "The news that there may be peace, that there may be detente between the United States and the Soviet Union, does not necessarily mean that there is going to be peace for us."[35] A related source of considerable irritation to Castro was Gorbachev's willingness to negotiate with Washington about Latin American and other Third World issues of concern to Havana without prior consultation, and his new penchant for making public pronouncements about major changes in the bilateral relationship without informing the Cubans first. The most recent example of the latter was the Soviet President's September 1991 statement that Moscow would soon begin discussions with Cuban authorities about withdrawing Soviet military personnel from the island.

Clearly, taking into account the growing ascendancy of those forces within the Soviet Union interested in pursuing deep structural links with the West at the expense of the Cuba relationship, Soviet policy, even prior to August 1991, seemed unlikely to remain one of continuing to provide substantial economic aid to Cuba as an incentive to deepen the process of export growth based on increasing productivity, diversified products, and expanded markets. Pressure on the revolutionary government to find new markets and sources of financial support are increasing, and likely to become greater than even in the 1990s.

Cuba and Latin America

The foundation stone of Cuban foreign policy has been the need to sustain the continuity of ties with the Soviet Union to safeguard essential national security and economic interests. Ideological reductionists, however, grossly simplify Cuban foreign policy by failing to examine the way in which these *primary* relations were articulated with a *wider set of ties* and the *direction* and *thrust* of Havana's international relations *over time*. Cuba's policy is a very complex, multilayered phenomenon, operating on the principle of consolidating essential ties that secure the continuity of the state, and then reaching beyond that to deepen regime-to-regime ties, expand markets, and consolidate a role in regional political and economic organizations. Moreover, Cuba's foreign relations are moving in the direction of emphasizing the market over politics, but never to the extent of cutting political relations with revolutionary movements *if and when* conventional ties are ruptured and international threats of isolation resurface.

Cuba's Latin American policy has moved in a consequential manner toward promoting greater market/financial ties and political/diplomatic integration within the region. By mid-1989, Cuba had diplomatic and economic relations with all countries except Chile, Colombia, and Paraguay. Its message of ideological pluralism was accepted throughout the hemisphere as a recognition of mutual acceptance of existing state structures—publicly affirmed later that year by the unanimous support for Cuba's election to a seat on the United Nations Security Council. In some of his public pronouncements, Castro even offered advice to capitalist regimes on how to avoid "social explosions" (revolution). But the key to Cuba's regional strategy is the consolidation of state-to-state ties. These are of two kinds: diplomatic/economic, particularly with major countries like Mexico, Brazil and Argentina; and political/ideological, with countries such as Nicaragua under the Sandinistas. The former is the most important and represents a policy of accommodation to the status quo—weakening ties with revolutionary movements in pursuit of deeper integration at the level of the market. The result is a uniform emphasis on positive interstate relations and a downplaying or total absence of class struggle and revolutionary politics. Put another way, Cuban policy is based primarily on maximizing short-term economic gains at the expense of possible favorable strategic ideological/political gains.[36]

Paralleling the promotion of bilateral relations, Cuba's regional strategy also involves active participation in, and promotion of, regional organizations, particularly those which have economic functions. Once more, revolutionary links are subordinated to market concerns. This reaching out for external market linkages accompanies the internal rectification program; revolutionary élan is harnessed to earning foreign exchange.

At the nongovernmental level, Cuba's regional strategy is linked to developing ties to a broad array of political parties, personalities, and social movements around specific overarching issues (like the foreign debt) that cut across class boundaries.[37] The Cubans describe the policy as the broad front. In practice, the broad front policy has not made much headway: for example, neither the populists turned free marketeers (Carlos Menem in Argentina) nor the social democrats turned fiscal conservatives (Carlos Perez in Venezuela, Michael Manley in Jamaica) have expressed the least interest in a collective approach to dealing with the continent's foreign debt. They prefer to accord the demands of overseas creditors national priority. Speaking of which, Castro's behavior on this issue is hardly exemplary. The bilateral pursuit of the same marginal favors, debt restructuring, making interest payments (despite the rhetoric)—all weaken those who argue for debt repudiation, moratoriums, or even debt ceilings.

While the broad front policy has had little direct impact on regional governments and has not produced any ongoing intraregional organization, it serves two important purposes: First, it defines a critical pole from which other state and regional policies can be evaluated without endangering Cuba's state-to-state relations. It serves much as a pressure group, offering alternatives and analyses that contrast with those practiced in official circles. Second, some of those nongovernmental participants may in the near future become members of governments, in which case Havana will, at least in theory, have co-thinkers at the regime and state-to-state level—at least on discrete issues.

In addition to the broad front policy, the Cubans have developed new sets of ties with church groups. Catholic and Protestant church officials have visited Cuba, exchanged views, discussed public issues, and found agreement in several specified areas—ranging from human rights and church/state relations to migration and the foreign debt.

And, finally, in the area of nongovernmental relations, the Cuban government has retained ties to revolutionary and progressive movements challenging certain dictatorial or authoritarian-electoral regimes such as those in Chile (pre-December 1989) and El Salvador. But it is possible that this support is conditional on the nature of the regime and its relationship to Cuban state interests. The transition to electoral politics in Chile, where conservative Christian Democratic president Patricio Aylwin in effect shares power with the Pinochet military state, and the July 1991 decision to normalize diplomatic relations with Cuba, is likely to result in Castro adopting the same friendly position taken toward the Cerezo regime in Guatemala (1985–1990) that cohabited with the terrorist military state of the preelectoral period. In brief, movement ties are subordinated to state-to-state relations; market pragmatism permeates Cuba's international relations in the late 1980s and into the 1990s. Or, as Trade Minister Ricardo Cabrisas phrased it in

May 1991: "We're in a position to work toward integration in Latin America without the difference in social systems becoming an obstacle."[38]

Cuban-American Relations

Given its belief that normalized bilateral relations are important to the success of its new model of accumulation, the Castro government has made all manner of overtures and concessions to the United States since the latter half of the 1980s in pursuit of a diplomatic accommodation. These included the signing of a new immigration accord, an agreement to withdraw 50,000 troups from Angola, a crackdown on drug trafficking, proposed joint drug programs, support for the various Central American peace proposals, acceptance of pro-American regimes throughout the hemisphere (the primacy of state-to-state relations), steps to improve relations with the Catholic Church, according greater latitude to internal opposition groups including regular meetings with foreign journalists and diplomats, the release of hundreds of political prisoners, and invitations to human rights monitoring organizations (Red Cross, United Nations, Amnesty International, etc.) to visit the island.[39] The absence of virtually any kind of reciprocity on Washington's part is testament to the "set in concrete" character of imperial-state policy. Hence, the paradox: While Cuba moves toward the market and signals declining support for revolutionary and antiimperialist forces in the Third World, the Unites States remains wedded to its historic posture of unremitting antagonism, essentially refusing to contemplate any modus vivendi prior to the demise of the Castro leadership.

The Reagan-Bush approach is exemplified in the sustained efforts to maintain Cuba's regional political isolation and global economic isolation, as well as by the extraordinary determination with which both administrations have pursued the revolutionary regime over the issue of human rights—despite the lack of documented widespread violations and during a decade when U.S. clients in El Salvador, Guatemala, and elsewhere in the region were revealing themselves to be among the worst human rights' abusers in the entire Third World.[40]

The 1980s witnessed no letup in Washington's increasingly tattered and discredited policy of seeking to maintain Cuba's isolation within Latin America. "The principal U.S. response to Cuba," a senior State Department Cuba specialist remarked in mid-1987, "remains to try to keep Havana's [regional] options limited and to support friendly governments economically, politically and militarily."[41] But hemispheric governments spurned repeated U.S. pressures and warnings that Cuba still constituted a political and military threat to their security. To some degree the growth in diplomatic and economic ties between Havana and other Latin capitals was a consequence of Cuban policy shifts, notably Cuba's active support for negotiated settlements of Central America's various political conflicts—including a willingness to withdraw its military personnel from Nicaragua and pressure revolutionary movements in El Salvador and Guatemala to speak with pro-U.S. military-controlled civilian regimes.[42] In part, Cuba has also benefited from the failures of U.S. policy—the obsession with military buildups in Central America rather than solving economic problems in South America.

In November 1987 Washington received a major rebuff when the presidents of eight of the most important Latin American countries agreed that Cuba should be invited to rejoin the Organization of American States and other regional organizations. According to Brazilian President Jose Sarney, "there was a consensus among the presidents that we ought to struggle for the total integration of Cuba into the inter-American system. . . ." The Reagan administration was unmoved, announcing its opposition to any such move on the grounds that Cuba's foreign policy still constituted "a danger to the stability of the hemisphere."[43] Weeks later, it enlisted the support of Honduras to veto a Guatemalan government proposal to invite Fidel Castro and a senior U.S. official to the January 1988 Esquipulas III meeting of the Central American presidents to review the progress of the peace plan.[44] The following August, Reagan officials vented their anti-Cuba spleen with Costa Rican President Oscar Arias over the latter's personal request for help from Castro in extracting concessions from the Sandinistas and his public declaration that the Cuban leader "has a very important role to play if we are to achieve peace" in Central America.[45]

The transition from Reagan to Bush was not accompanied by any appreciable change in Washington's regional isolation policy. Within days of Bush's inauguration, the U.S. ambassador to Venezuela, Otto Reich, made an unsuccessful attempt to persuade the newly elected Venezuelan president, Carlos Andres Peres, not to invite Castro to his inauguration.[46] In April 1990, State Department officials indicated that the administration would strongly oppose reported new moves by a number of Latin American countries to bring Cuba back into the Organization of American States.[47] Instead of isolating the revolutionary regime, imperial policy continued to produce the opposite: the further isolation of the United States within the hemisphere. This was even evident in such international forums as the United Nations, where Latin American governments gave their complete backing to Cuba's candidacy for a Security Council seat in 1989 and have been manifestly reluctant to support U.S. efforts to have Cuba targeted as a major human rights' violator.[48]

American policy has given no support or sustenance to Cuba's export-oriented accumulation model. On the contrary, it has sought, where possible, to maintain the bilateral, regional, and global economic blockade, pressuring allies such as Japan not to buy Cuba sugar, blocking nickel and other nonsugar exports to the market economies, thus limiting the island's access to convertible currency and exacerbating its foreign-debt crisis. The Reagan White House also rigorously enforced the bilateral trade embargo despite the fact that U.S. enterprises were losing an estimated $750 million annually as a result.[49] In November 1988, prompted by a National Security Council directive calling for a "tightening up" of the economic blockade, the Treasury Department announced new rules applying to U.S. firms sending funds from Miami residents to relatives in Cuba—part of the ongoing effort to halt the flow of hard currency to the island.[50]

The Bush administration has been just as, if not more, zealous in prosecuting the ongoing economic war against Cuba. "There is a policy to isolate Cuba," announced White House Press Secretary Marlin Fitzwater in early 1990—"a total embargo against everybody and everything going to Cuba. . . ."[51] This included stricter enforcement of regulations governing travel by U.S. citizens to the island, "encouraging" the new Endara regime in Panama to crack down on front companies reexporting U.S. goods to Cuba, and withholding licenses to prevent U.S. corporations from televising (ABC) or providing drug-testing equipment (Hewlett-Packard) for the 1991 Pan American Games to be contested in Havana.[52] The objective was the same as it had always been: to limit the flow of American dollars (ABC had agreed to pay $8.7 million for exclusive television rights, of which approximately $6.5 million would go to the Cuban government) and goods that can be traded for U.S. currency into the island economy. (Reexports from Panama in 1989 totalled an estimated $82 million.)[53] Other targets were the import of goods containing Cuban-origin materials into the U.S. market and Cuban purchases of goods from third countries containing "significant" U.S.-origin materials. In May 1991, for instance, Washington blocked the sale of five Brazilian passenger-transport planes to Cuba because they included several American-made components.[54]

Thus, we see the paradox of Castro reaching out to the market, as well as to the United States, only to confront implacable imperial-state hostility—unlikely to evaporate short of a fundamental restructuring of the island's political and economic system. Washington's posture has also served to trigger a renewed militancy on Castro's part (appeals to self-sufficiency, declarations of support for regional revolutionary movements, antiimperialist rhetoric, etc.), which gives the appearance of being an integral part of the new accumulation model.[55] In reality, however, such statements can only be understood, and located, in terms of the Reagan-Bush rejection of Cuban overtures and concessions and Castro's desire for expanded economic relations with the capitalist world, including the United States.

Another major focus of White House policy since the latter part of the Reagan presidency has been to mobilize international condemnation of Cuba's human rights record and to demand concessions in this area as a precondition for any movement on the bilateral relationship. In early 1987, the United States launched a full-court diplomatic press to force a resolution through the United Nations Human Rights Commission (UNHRC) denouncing Cuba for human rights' abuses. President Reagan telephoned heads of state, United Nations Ambassador Vernon Walters personally lobbied five Latin American presidents, U.S. ambassadors in forty-two capitals made representations to host-country foreign-ministry officials, and Washington sent out more than 400 cables to member governments urging support for the resolution. Remarked one Western government delegate to the commission: "The Americans pushed people into corners and twisted arms wherever they could." The outcome, however, was a diplomatic embarrassment for the administration. The commission voted nineteen (including all five Latin American members) to eighteen, with six abstentions, not to debate the resolution.[56]

In March 1988, ignoring the Cuban government's decision to allow almost 400 former and current political prisoners to migrate to the United States as part of a major campaign to improve the country's human rights image, the Reagan White House once again "pulled out all the diplomatic stops" in an attempt to force the United Nations to cite the revolutionary regime for human rights' violations. This time it was forced to withdraw a draft resolution putting the Human Rights Commission on record as expressing concern over reported abuses and directing the U.N. secretary general to request information from Havana on the charges. Instead the United States had to accept a substitute resolution proposed by Argentina, Colombia, Mexico, and Peru to dispatch a special mission to Cuba—at the invitation of Castro himself—to investigate the allegation of human rights' abuses.[57]

While Reagan officials were busy denouncing Cuba in the UNHRC, an unofficial American delegation arrived on the island in the last week of February 1988, under an agreement reached with the National Union of Cuban Jurists, to survey the country's prisons. They were given unrestricted access to prisons and prison inmates. In a report on the visit, delegation member Aryeh Neier, a senior official of the human rights organization Americas Watch, highlighted a number of shifts and changes in official Cuba policy:

> The most important aspect of my visit to the Cuban prisons, I believe, is that it took place at all. . . . A few weeks later Cuba opened its prisons to Amnesty International. Now it has invited the United Nations Commission on Human Rights to visit . . . external pressure has already produced another change of considerable significance in protecting human rights: that is, two human rights groups with which we met are now able to work in Cuba."[58]

When Amnesty released its report in September, although critical of aspects of government policy and the country's legal system, it acknowledged significant improvements in the prison system, noting shorter sentences, better living conditions, less executions, and the release of many long-serving inmates. In February 1989, the United Nations mission issued its report on the human rights situation in Cuba, which basically confirmed the Amnesty assessment. Despite continuing constraints on political liberties, human rights' abuses had declined, and there had been a major improvement in the treatment of political prisoners.[59]

Notwithstanding these Cuban concessions, the incoming Bush administration declared that one of the funamental obstacles to any U.S.-Cuban rapprochement was the fact that Havana "persist[s] in its internal repression and violation of the basic human rights of its citizens."[60] Subsequently, the U.S. renewed its efforts in the UNHRC to increase the pressure on Cuba for reforms—only to suffer a humiliating diplomatic setback similar to that suffered by the Reaganites when the commission rejected Washington's attempt to get the organization to agree to monitor Cuba's human rights performance during 1990.[61]

Undeterred, the Bush White House continued to pressure the United Nations throughout 1989 over this issue. Although Secretary General Javier Perez de Cuellar refused to bow to Washington demands that he submit a report on alleged human rights' abuses based on his talks with Cuban officials to the UNHRC in January 1990, in March the United States did succeed in cajoling the commission to authorize the secretary general to appoint a special representative to monitor Cuba's human rights behavior.[62] In January 1989, on the eve of the first Cuban troop withdrawals from Angola and only days after Castro announced the release of 225 political prisoners, U.S. President-elect George Bush assured his right-wing supporters in Miami that there would be no change in existing Cuba policy.[63] In March, Secretary of State James Baker wrote in a confidential policy memorandum that "Cuban behavior has not changed *sufficiently* to warrant a change in U.S. attitudes." Despite overwhelming evidence to the contrary, he accused Cuba of "military adventurism abroad" and continuing to support "subversive movements in the Western Hemisphere." Ignoring Havana's myriad concessions to American demands in recent years in pursuit of improved bilateral ties, Baker concluded that the Castro government "has not changed its basic policies."[64] That June, President Bush added that Cuba would have to do "much more" before his administration would even consider a policy shift. The much more included Soviet-style economic ("free market") restructuring and political reforms (elections), additional human rights concessions, and substantial cuts in military spending and the armed forces—the most excessive demands by a U.S. president since the early 1960s. "I am not," he told the *Miami Herald*, "about to shift our policy toward Fidel Castro."[65] Since then, senior Bush foreign-policy officials have placed the onus entirely on Cuba for any movement toward normalized ties: "U.S. policy . . . will remain constant until Cuba takes steps to remove the impediments to improved relations."[66]

The Reagan-Bush rejectionist approach toward Cuba can be explained partly in terms of a need to placate the Republican party's right-wing constituency (especially the anti-Castro forces headquartered in Miami). At the same time, this may be less of a factor than in the past in light of an extensive survey of Cuban-American conducted by the Johns Hopkins University Cuban Studies Program in late 1988, which found that seventy-three percent of its respondents favored normalization of relations between the United States and Cuba.[67] A more likely explanation is that in the new era of superpower detente and the Soviet's wholehearted turn to the market under Gorbachev, Washington saw this process as offering real possibilities for achieving historic strategic objectives in Cuba. President Bush appears to have concluded that the shift in Soviet policy held the key to "softening up" the Cuban economy, thus making Castro more amenable to economic and political changes Washington desires.

To hasten this process, the Bush White House deliberately exploited the Soviet Union's desperate need for Western, especially U.S., economic assistance. In testimony before a committee of the Soviet Parliament in February 1990, Secretary of State Baker urged Moscow to cease its support for Cuba. This refrain was repeated at every opportunity by U.S. officials—the prospects of large-scale aid would be considerably enhanced if the Soviets substantially cut, or preferably totally halted, all economic and military aid programs to their Caribbean ally.[68] Thus, in the hope that continuing changes in Eastern Europe would eventually rupture economic relations between Moscow and Havana, the United States ignored Cuba's opening to the market and foreign-policy concessions and pursued the politics of hostility—until the combined external pressures force Cuba to make wholesale internal changes closer to the Soviet version of perestroika which, in turn, would force changes in the political system. Current imperial-state policy is designed not simply to accommodate the demands of a right-wing ideological constituency; it also seeks to undermine the island's economic and political structures, leading to a reassertion of America's hegemonic status.

Conclusion

Cuba's foreign policy has become increasingly oriented toward establishing greater links with the capitalist marketplace. But what needs to be recognized is that this policy orientation is not a linear process; nor is there a single specific marketplace to which the Cubans are tied. Moreover, the openings to overseas markets have in many cases been preceded by diplomatic/political linkages which, in turn, clearly indicate the basic shift in Cuban economic strategy. Essentially, *Cuba's push to deepen the role of the world market in its accumulation process has been accompanied by the increasing role given to establishing or cultivating state-to-state relations.* International cooperation and pragmatic ties with existing regimes concerning global economic issues such as the debt and economic integration, not class struggle and revolution, are Castro's current priorities.

While Cuba has been relatively active and successful in building out from its foundation ties with the Soviet Union toward a complex array of regional relations in Latin America, the axis of its foreign relations increasingly seem to be evolving toward deepening its ties (where possible) to the advanced capitalist countries— namely, Western Europe, Japan, and Canada—at the level of debt, credits, hard-currency loans, and hopes for future earnings via exports, tourism, and the like. Notwithstanding the fall in overall trade with the advanced capitalist countries during the 1980s, Cuba's policy has been, and more and more will be, directed toward finding a niche in these markets, negotiating financial loans and rescheduling its debt, securing technology, and all the while scrambling to find economic resources to compensate for shortfalls resulting from shifts in economic policy among the liberalized economies of Eastern Europe. The key point about this ordering of Cuban foreign relations is that it is not a matter of Cuban choice so much as on response dictated by international necessities and/or constraints—not least Washington's continuing efforts to maintain a regional and global economic "iron curtain" around the island nation. The reality is that Cuban policy-makers do not have open-ended trade opportunities.

If Castro and Gorbachev had any conflicts in relations they were *not* the result of *differences* but derived from *common* policies. Both focused on opening new export markets, deepening ties with incumbent regimes (no matter how politically and socially reactionary), and distancing themselves from revolutionary movements in favor of state-to-state relations. The differences were over the methods of carrying out their policies.[69] Castro's concern was always that in Gorbachev's wholesale pursuit of Western markets, Cuba might get frozen out. Furthermore, Castro wished to retain ideological continuities (the new accumulation model is accompanied by constant reaffirmation of Marxist-Leninist principles) while Gorbachev wanted to combine economic restructuring with an ideological rupture. Still, Cuba's liberalization strategy—the pursuit of Western markets, the debt ties with capitalist creditors, the promotion of foreign investment and tourism, and the broad front policy—belies those who see in Castro's attack on peasant markets and material incentives a return to a socialist vision.

The internal difficulties provoked by the debt-payment policy and the ineffectiveness of the broad front strategy due to the interlock between local regimes and classes and international finance capital suggest that Castro's liberalization politics will need heavy doses of populist rhetoric to contain discontent. The fact that Castro relies on the ministry of the interior to mobilize against "liberal bourgeois tendencies" suggests that he wants to control the site and source of any attack on "liberalism." The placement of a new generation of technocrats in power may increase *efficiency* and lessen corruption, but it will not necessarily strengthen socialist tendencies from below. On the contrary, the new managers and technocrats can become prime supporters of the new liberal shift toward market integration. While Castro may continue to direct public wrath against the emergence of the "new millionaires" and the mentality of the "small entrepreneur,"[70] his international economic policy is forcefully directed at promoting new ties with foreign investors and maintaining existing relations with overseas bankers.

Castro is a shrewd-enough analyst to know that his moves toward international liberalization must be legitimated by a resort to populist measures and moral exhortations at home. He walks a middle course between raising the question of debt repudiation and practical accommodation with Cuba's foreign bankers, between reaching out to the market externally but cracking down internally, between cutbacks domestically but spreading the burden equally. It is a hard act to carry out but it would be a mistake to underestimate Castro's political skills.

Notes

1. "PCC Told to Deal with Criticisms," *Latin American Weekly Report*, December 11, 1986, p. 3.

2. A.R.M. Ritter, "Cuba's Convertible Currency Debt Problem," *Cepal Review*, No. 36, December 1988, p. 133.

3. "'Liberal' Reforms are Outdated," *Latin American Regional Reports: Caribbean*, July 24, 1986, p. 2.

4. See "Police Crack Down on Speculators," *Latin American Monitor: Caribbean*, December 1988, p. 613; "Black Market Crackdown," *Latin American Monitor: Caribbean*, April 1989, p. 709; "Crackdown on Black Market," *Latin American Regional Reports: Caribbean*, November 2, 1989, p. 2.

5. "Ideologue Hits at 'Private Sector,'" *Latin American Weekly Report*, November 12, 1987, p. 9.

6. "Private Farmers to Play Bigger Role," *Latin American Regional Reports: Caribbean*, March 31, 1988, p. 6.

7. See Andrew Zimbalist, "Cuban Political Economy and Cubanology: An Overview," in Andrew Zimbalist, ed., *Cuban Political Economy* (Boulder: Westview Press, 1988), pp. 2–3; Andrew Zimbalist and Susan Eckstein, "Patterns of Cuban Development: The First Twenty Five Years," *World Development*, Vol. 15, No. 1, January 1987, pp. 10–17; Claes Brundenius, *Revolutionary Cuba: The Challenge of Economic Growth with Equity* (Boulder; Westview Press, 1984).

8. Andrew Zimbalist, "Cuban Political Economy and Cubanology: An Overview," p. 11. Also see "Smile Off the Faces of Policy-Makers," *Latin American Regional Reports: Caribbean*, January 22, 1987, p. 3; "A Negative Balance for 1986," *Latin American Regional Reports: Caribbean*, October 1, 1987, p. 2.

9. "Castro Shuts Down Peasants' Markets," *Latin American Weekly Report*, May 30, 1986, p. 2.

10. Andrew Zimbalist, "Cuban Political Economy and Cubanology: An Overview," pp. 12–13.

11. See "Purge Continues After Executions," *Latin American Regional Reports: Caribbean*, August 24, 1989, p. 2.

12. Quoted in *Brecha* (Montevideo), June 23, 1989, p. 4.

13. Ibid.

14. Ibid.

15. See Howard W. French, "Cuba Flirts With Capitalism to Stave off Collapse," *New York Times*, December 5, 1990, p. 18.

16. Ritter, "Cuba's Convertible Currency Debut Problem," especially pp. 127–132; "Cuba Warns Creditors on Loans and Trade Squeeze," *Latin Americal Regional Reports: Caribbean*, May 9, 1986, p. 1.

17. See, for example, "Revolution's 'Marxist-Leninist' Principles Will Not Be Aban-

doned, Says Castro," *Latin American Regional Reports: Caribbean,* January 19, 1989, p. 1.

18. The unemployment rate, for instance, was six percent in 1988 compared with 3.4 percent in 1981. Economist Intelligence Unit, *Quarterly Economic Review of Cuba,* No. 2, May 1989, p. 12.

19. Cuba is the first non-European member of COMECON to have diplomatic ties with the European Community. On Cuba's links with the EEC, see *Latin American Regional Reports: Caribbean,* July 21, 1988, p. 8, and November 3, 1988, p. 8. On Canada and Japan, see *Cubainfo Newsletter,* Vol. 2, No. 16, October 5, 1990, p. 3, and Vol. 2, No. 20, December 14, 1990, p. 4.

20. See Economist Intelligence Unit, *Quarterly Economic Review of Cuba,* No. 1, March 1990, p. 21; *Cubainfo Newsletter,* Vol. 3, No. 2, February 14, 1991, p. 3; Majorie Miller and Richard Boudreaux, "Cuba Faces a New Life on Its Own," *Los Angeles Times,* April 7, 1991, p. A10.

21. See Economist Intelligence Unit, *Quarterly Economic Review of Cuba,* No. 2, May 1990, p. 18; *Cubainfo Newsletter,* Vol. 3, No. 2, February 14, 1991, p. 3.

22. See Gillian Gunn, "Will Castro Fall?," *Foreign Policy,* No. 79, Summer 1979, p. 138; *Cubainfo Newsletter,* Vol. 3, No. 3, February 28, 1991, p. 3; "Cuba Kicks Off Plan to Export Medical Supplies," *Times of the Americas,* May 29, 1991, p. 14.

23. See Economist Intelligence Unit, *Quarterly Economic Review of Cuba,* No. 2, May 1989, p. 17; French, "Cuba Flirts With Capitalism to Stave Off Collapse," p. 18; Michael White, "Castro Courts International Visitors," *Christian Science Monitor,* July 13–19, 1990, p. 10B; "Cuba Tries Self-Help," *Washington Report on the Hemisphere,* Vol. 11, No. 13, April 3, 1991, p. 6; "Betting on Tourism as Exchange Earner," *Latin American Weekly Report,* June 13, 1991, p. 8.

24. Ritter, "Cuba's Convertible Currency Debt Problem," p. 119.

25. Ibid., p. 134; "Cuba's Debt Rises as US Dollar Weakens," *Latin American Regional Reports: Caribbean,* November 2, 1987, pp. 4–5.

26. Between September 1987 and the first quarter of 1989, Cuba's hard-currency debt increased by over $1 billion. See Robert Graham, "Austerity . . . and Experiment," *Financial Times* section III, February 17, 1989, p. 3; "Rise in Cuba's Hard Currency Debt," *Latin American Regional Reports: Caribbean,* November 2, 1989, p. 5. On declining trade with the market economies, see note 27.

27. Ritter, "Cuba's Convertible Currency Debt Problem," p. 121; The John Hopkins School of Advanced International Studies, Cuban Studies Program, *Opportunities For U.S.-Cuban Trade,* June 1988, p. 11. Also see "Castro Warns of Further Belt-Tightening," *Latin American Regional Reports: Caribbean,* February 25, 1988, pp. 4–5; Economist Intelligence Unit, *Quarterly Economic Review of Cuba,* No. 4, November 1988, p. 13.

28. Quoted in *Sovetskaya Rossia,* May 5, 1990.

29. Quoted in *Cubainfo Newsletter,* Vol. 2, No. 17, October 19, 1990, p. 2.

30. Quoted in Anne-Marie O'Connor, "Soviets Tell Cubans They'll Give Aid Until U.S. Drops Embargo," *Cox News Service,* December 5, 1990.

31. See Lee Hockstader, "Castro's Cuba, at 32, Faces Stiffest Economic Test," *Washington Post*, January 1, 1991, p. A18; *Cubainfo Newsletter*, Vol. 3, No. 7, April 25, 1991, p. 3.

32. Quoted in *Moscow News*, March 11, 1990.

33. Quoted in *Cubainfo Newsletter*, Vol. 2, No. 20, December 14, 1990, p. 1.

34. See "Soviet Move to the Right May Help Cuba," *Latin American Monitor: Caribbean*, Vol. 8, No. 2, March 1991, p. 874; "Castro Under Mounting Pressure," *Latin American Monitor: Caribbean*, Vol. 8, No. 7, September 1991, p. 931; "Cuba: Foreign Trade," *Latin American Monitor: Caribbean*, Vol. 8, No. 9, November 1991, p. 955; "Spain-Cuba Venture to Make Energy Savings in Cuban Industry," *Reuters News Dispatch*, November 11, 1991.

35. Quoted in Joseph B. Treaster, "Castro Scorning Gorbachev Model," *New York Times*, January 11, 1989, p. 10. Also see "'Stormy' Talks with Gorbachev Delayed," *Latin American Regional Reports: Caribbean*, January 19, 1988, p. 2.

36. Castro quoted in " 'No Strings' to Co-Operation," *Latin American Regional Reports: Caribbean*, September 29, 1988, p. 2; "Castro Returns to Latin Roots," *Latin American Monitor: Caribbean*, December 1988, p. 206, Robert Graham, "Back in the Fold," *Financial Times*, section III, February 17, 1989, p. 3; Economist Intelligence Unit, *Quarterly Economic Review of Cuba*, No. 3, August 1988, p. 17, and No. 1, February 1989, pp. 17–18.

37. See, for example, "Castro Wins Some, Loses Some at Havana Debt Meeting," *Latin American Regional Reports: Caribbean*, August 23, 1985, p. 1.

38. Quoted in *Cubainfo Newsletter*, Vol. 3, No. 9, May 31, 1991, p. 4.

39. On relations with the church, see "Improving Church-State Relations in Cuba," *Latin American Regional Reports: Caribbean*, June 16, 1988, pp. 4–5. On the immigration agreement, see Neil A. Lewis, "U.S. and Havana Agree to Restore Immigration Pact," *New York Times*, November 21, 1987, p. 1. On drug trafficking, see Michael Oreskes, "Castro Urges U.S.-Cuba Cooperation in Drug War," *New York Times*, December 16, 1988, p. 18; "Cuba Says it Wants Help on Drugs," *New York Times*, July 26, 1989, p. 3.

40. See, for example, Americas Watch, *A Year of Reckoning: El Salvador A Decade After the Assasination of Archbishop Romero* (New York: March 1990); Americas Watch, *Messengers of Death: Human Rights in Guatemala* (New York: March 1990).

41. Kenneth N. Skoug, Jr., director of Office of Cuban Affairs, "Cuba's Growing Crisis," address, Minneapolis, May 27, 1987, reprinted in *Department of State Bulletin*, Vol. 87, No. 2126, September 1987, p. 89. Also see Richard Beeston, "U.S. Warns Latins on New Ties to Cuba," *Washington Times*, May 11, 1987, p. 1A.

42. See "Fidel Puffs Peace Signals to U.S.," *Latin American Regional Reports: Caribbean*, February 22, 1985, p. 4; "Ready to Join Contadora Plan," *Latin American Weekly Report*, April 18, 1986, p. 11.

43. Quoted in Larry Rohter, "8 Latin Chiefs Urge Cuba Role in Their Region," *New York Times*, November 29, 1987, p. 1.

44. See "Return to the OAS Now Possible," *Latin American Regional Reports: Caribbean*, February 25, 1987, p. 7.

45. Quoted in Eugene Robinson, "Arias Asks Castro for Help with Nicaragua," *Washington Post*, August 12, 1988, p. A20.

46. See "Moscow Chill vs. Nod From Bush," *Latin American Weekly Report*, February 19, 1989, p. 10.

47. See Martin McReynolds, "Allies in OAS Begin Bid for Cuba," *Miami Herald*, April 15, 1990.

48. See "Support Grows for Cuban Comeback," *Latin American Weekly Report*, November 2, 1989, pp. 6–7; *Cubainfo Newsletter* Vol. 3, No. 4, March 15, 1991, p. 1.

49. See, for example, "Cuba Warns Creditors on Loans and Trade Squeezes," p. 1; *Latin American Monitor: Caribbean*, July–August 1987, p. 445; *Caribbean Update*, August 1987, p. 3; The Johns Hopkins School of Advanced International Studies, *Opportunities for U.S.-Cuban trade*, p. 1.

50. Quoted in Jacquelyn Swearingen, "Rules Tighten for Cash Relays to Cuba," *Miami Herald*, November 24, 1988.

51. Quoted in Ann Devroy, "U.S. Employs 'Verbal Policy' in Attempt to Isolate Castro," *Washington Post*, April 3, 1990.

52. See ibid; Mimi Whitefield, "U.S. Begins Cuba Travel Crackdown," *Miami Herald*, December 22, 1989; Mimi Whitefield, "Trade Ban Snarls ABC's Plan to Air Games from Cuba," *Miami Herald*, December 15, 1989; Christine Brennan, "Havana Site Poses Potential Problems for Pan Am Games," *Washington Post*, February 6, 1990.

53. See Whitefield, "Trade Ban Snarls ABC's Plan to Air Games from Cuba;" Laura Brooks, "Cuban Economic Woes Reduce Trade with Panamanians," *Christian Science Monitor*, November 9, 1990.

54. *Cubainfo Newsletter* Vol. 3, No. 9, May 31, 1991, p. 2.

55. See, for example, Castro's July 26, 1988, speech on the thirty-fifth anniversary of the Moncada uprising.

56. Elaine Sciolino, "Reagan's Mighty Effort to Condemn Cuba," *New York Times*, March 24, 1987, p. 28.

57. Paul Lewis, "U.N. Is Pressed to Cite Cuba for Rights Abuses," *New York Times*, March 6, 1989, p. 6; Edward Cody, "U.N. Team to Probe Rights Abuses in Cuba," *Washington Post*, March 11, 1988, p. A22.

58. Aryeh Neier, "In Cuban Prisons," *New York Review of Books*, June 30, 1988, pp. 21, 22.

59. Peter Sleven, "Amnesty Finds Abuse on Decline in Cuba," *Miami Herald*, September 6, 1988; "U.N. Finds Some Gain in Cubans' Rights," *New York Times*, February 29, 1989, p. 3.

60. Secretary of State James Baker, quoted in "Baker: Cuba Blocks Chance for Better Ties," *Chicago Tribune*, March 29, 1989, p. 2.

61. Paul Lewis, "U.N. Rights Panel Avoids Cuba Issue," *New York Times*, March 11, 1989, p. 5.

62. See Paul Lewis, "U.S. to Press U.N. Chief on Human Rights in Cuba," *New York Times*, January 27, 1990, p. 8; Paul Lewis, "Move by U.N. Chief on Cuba Irks U.S.," *New York Times*, January 30, 1990, p. 11; Paul Lewis, "Rights Panel Scolds Cuba, Not China," *New York Times*, March 7, 1990, p. 3; *Cubainfo Newsletter*, Vol. 3, No. 4, March 15, 1991, p. 1.

63. Joseph B. Treaster, "U.S.-Cuba Enmity May be Relaxing," *New York Times*, January 6, 1989, p. 3; Julia Preston, "Cuba Says It Will Free Last Political Prisoners," *Washington Post*, January 4, 1989, pp. A1, A14.

64. Quoted in "Baker: Cuba Blocks Chance for Better Ties," ~~~~~~~ ..phasis).

65. Quoted in Andres Oppenheimer, "Pr~~~~~~ ~~o Improvement in Havana Ties," *Miami Herald*, June 27, 1989.

66. Deputy Assistant Secretary of State Michael Kozak, quoted in Mimi Whitefield, "U.S. Relations with Cuba Likely to Remain on Ice," *Miami Herald*, November 17, 1990. Also see President Bush, quoted in *Cubainfo Newsletter*, Vol. 3, No. 9, May 31, 1991, p. 1.

67. See "Washington's Cuba Policy Remains Rigid," *Washington Report on the Hemisphere*, April 26, 1989, p. 4.

68. See Thomas L. Friedman, "Baker Braves the Gauntlet in the Moscow Parliament," *New York Times*, February 11, 1990, p. 20; David Hoffman, "Proposals to Assist Soviets Pose Dilemma for West, Bush," *Washington Post*, June 29, 1990; David Hoffman, "Bush Holds off on Economic Aid to Soviets," *Washington Post*, June 30, 1990, p. A23.

69. "Our methods cannot be similar," declared Castro in his July 26, 1988, address to the nation. "It would be erroneous to copy other countries." Quoted in "Cuba Shuns Gorbachev's Reform Policies," *Latin American Regional Reports: Caribbean*, August 25, 1988, p. 4.

70. Quoted in "CDRs Urged: Stamp Out Corruption," *Latin American Weekly Report*, October 9, 1986, p. 5.

6

The Electoral Defeat of the Sandinistas: Critical Reflections

Introduction

The electoral defeat of the Sandinistas in February 1990 demands a critical reexamination of their political strategy, their economic policies and, not least, the way in which they viewed their relationship with the major centers of world capitalism. While the United States indubitably played a central role in influencing the electoral outcome, the Sandinistas' long-term political and economic strategies—toward Washington, the Nicaraguan economic elites, and the country's urban working class in particular—were decisive factors in the voting debacle and loss of political power. The central thesis of this essay is that the Sandinista National Liberation Front (FSLN) strategies and polices essentially undermined and dispersed the socioeconomic forces that most actively supported the revolution without eliciting equivalent support from those other forces—the domestic elites and the overseas capitalist states—that its policies were designed to attract. The regime's initial mixed-economy formulation contained the seeds of its own downfall, which was increasingly evident as the particular mix between private and collective power unfolded over the decade of revolutionary rule.

During the postelection period, the Sandinista bourgeois elite further distanced itself from the working poor—the core constituency of the FSLN in power—by collaborating with the center-right Chamorro government, which was intent on dismantling the still-intact socioeconomic gains of the revolutionary period. Responding to exhortations from Washington and the overseas ("international" and private) banks, the new regime proceeded to build on the "free market" foundations of the late Sandinista years, enacting even harsher austerity measures to attract new inflows of foreign capital. In these endeavors, it received essential support from the FSLN political leadership—even though the Chamorro "stabilization" policies worsened the living standards of an already-impoverished Nicaraguan populace.

Sandinista Political Strategy: Elections Within a
Counterrevolutionary Framework

Critical to an understanding of the FSLN's profoundly flawed political strategy is the nature of Reagan-Bush policy. In seeking to overthrow the Sandinista revolution, Washington adopted a dual approach: a prolonged war of economic and military attrition combined with a political/electoral strategy. Bilateral and global economic sanctions were intended to block development projects and social reforms; counterrevolutionary warfare aimed to destroy infrastructure facilities and productive units, force the government to increase its military spending at the expense of development and social projects, and systematically intimidate the civilian population. This long-term, large-scale "outsider" offensive was keyed toward the "insider" political/electoral strategy which involved organizing and funding the opposition political parties, media outlets, and propertied elites— to enable them to exploit the socioeconomic conditions created by the external military/economic pressures in the electoral arena.

In September 1984, the Reagan administration waged an active campaign to discredit the process of redemocratization in Nicaragua, pressuring and bribing opposition political leaders to withdraw their candidacies from the national election process, because imperial-state strategy was still unfolding; insufficient time had elapsed to wreak maximum havoc on the economy and the FSLN's social base of support.[1] By 1989, after five more years of intensified U.S. warfare and accumulating Sandinista concessions, the Bush administration deemed the time was now right to implement the political/electoral strategy. The Sandinistas fell into the trap, committing the fundamental strategic mistake of agreeing to organize and hold another national election in the midst of this externally orchestrated devastation. By so doing, they reversed the logic of revolutionary politics: Instead of insisting that elections follow the termination of hostilities, the demobilization of the contras, and the "takeoff" of economic reconstruction and development, the FSLN organized the process on terrain created by the counterrevolution. To Managua, elections became the panacea: They would end the war and reverse the economic slide.

The Sandinista decision to endanger the revolutionary process by holding national elections in the midst of war and economic disintegration was not made on the basis of an examination of the conditions of the working class, the peasantry, and the urban and rural poor. Above all, it was taken in response to U.S., European, and domestic elite demands. Moreover, the political process leading up to the February 1990 elections was marked by a series of open-ended unilateral concessions that progressively strengthened the internal and external opposition—at the expense of consolidating the regime's historic support base.

The Bush administration came into office in January 1989 promising "to keep the pressure on the Sandinistas" both economically and militarily.[2] Maintaining the Reagan opposition to any Central American peace process in the absence of a change of regime in Nicaragua, the new White House opposed the recent agreement by the five area governments in favor of disbanding and demobilizing the contra forces as soon as possible. As one senior Bush official put it: "Our policy is and has been that we would not like to see demobilization before the elections."[3] Secretary of State James Baker and other high-ranking American diplomats lobbied Washington's Central American clients, especially Honduras, in an effort to sabotage the accord on the contras.[4] Through February 28, 1990 [the date of the election], the Bush White House consistently opposed contra demobilization and refused to terminate aid to these mercenary exiles.

Despite Washington's pro-contra stance, Sandinista President Daniel Ortega announced in February 1989 that the government had agreed to reschedule promised 1990 elections from November to February and would discuss changes to the 1988 electoral law with the domestic opposition (which ultimately led to additional reforms). Beginning in January 1988, the Sandinistas had begun to open up the political system—lifting censorship, easing constraints on political party activity, etc.—under pressure from the United States and its regional clients and in the absence of equivalent concessions from these governments. This lack of reciprocity was the dominant feature of the "peace process" that came from the August 1987 Esquipulus accords signed by the five Central American presidents prior to the February 1990 Nicaraguan elections: "None of the nations which the U.S. considers its democratic allies in Central America . . . complied as thoroughly with the spirit and letter of the Esquipulus Accords [in regard to electoral reform, political democracy, media reforms, halting outside support to insurgent forces, etc.] as has Nicaragua. Yet at every turn, the United States was able to minimize the concessions made by Nicaragua and to keep the focus of world attention on Nicaragua instead of on Central America as a whole."[5]

On April 23, 1989, the Nicaraguan government took steps to comply with the February Tesoro Beach Agreement by passing new electoral and media laws in preparation for the elections. Despite having now put in place an electoral code that was one of the most liberal in Central America, the U.S. response was to minimize the changes and demand more concessions. State Department officials and President Bush characterized these reforms as a "tragic setback" which would create "a stacked deck against freedom." They further complained about the "procedures for ensuring the presence and unlimited access of international election observers," ignoring the fact that the United Nations and Organization of American States monitoring teams were already established in Nicaragua to oversee the entire operation through February 1990.[6] This contrasted sharply with Washington's approach toward elections held by client regimes. During the March 1989 elections in the terrorist "democracy" of El Salvador, the only monitoring of the process took place on election day and was confined to a team of United Nations officials.

The Bush administration continued to charge the Sandinistas with fixing the election, to demand new concessions, to question whether it was possible to hold free and fair elections in Nicaragua as long as the FSLN remained in power, and persistently attacked the new democratic voting procedures in language reminiscent of the Reaganites at the time of the 1984 election, terming them unacceptable and a "sham."[7] For its part, the FSLN leadership continued to do all in its power to facilitate the opposition's electoral campaign. When funds destined for the UNO coalition or UNO-supported organizations were slowed down both in Washington and Managua, for example, the government responded by expediting the release of monies from the Central Bank for the National Organized Union (UNO) and a pro-UNO institute that was heavily funded by the National Endowment for Democracy (a counterrevolution political arm of the U.S. established during the Reagan presidency), whose mission was to train anti-Sandinista poll watchers for election day. Efforts to conciliate Washington and accommodate its demands for more concessions also continued apace. "In the period immediately before the election," the U.S. Latin American Studies Association Commission monitoring the process reported, "the U.S. acted through the various opposition parties and four other states in Central America to change already quite liberal electoral laws to include unprecedented concessions such as the legalization of foreign funding of campaigns."[8]

Nonetheless, right up until the eve of the election, the State Department preferred to ignore the findings of United Nations, Organization of American States, and other electoral observer delegations and declare that "there is serious doubt about Sandinista intentions to conduct a free and fair election and to relinquish power if they lose."[9]

External concessions defined the trajectory of the so-called peace process: Nicaragua accepted continuous and minute scrutiny of its electoral procedures in the absence of equivalent monitoring of the terrorist "democracies" in Guatemala and El Salvador and in the absence of contra demobilization as demanded by the peace accords; contradicting years of the FSLN exhorting its constituents to support the FMLN guerrillas in El Salvador, President Ortega, under pressure from Washington's regional clients, even signed a document characterizing the military–death-squad rightist Cristiani regime in El Salvador as "legitimate" and "democratic."

Internally, the pattern of rejecting and then conceding opposition positions or demands was a feature of the process, culminating in the decisions to allow the Bush administration to bankroll the UNO presidential campaign and the freeing of 1,150 contra terrorists less than two weeks before the election. In the case of the former, the massive U.S. organizational and financial intervention on the side of the anti-Sandinista forces was initially denounced by the FSLN leadership and then meekly accepted. The domestic supporters of foreign armed intervention against the government were given the "green light" to receive millions of dollars in outside funding and to operate publicly in pursuit of political power! In the case of the Sandinista turnabout on freeing the imprisoned mercenaries, apart from the injustice done to the victims of their terror, the release of these individuals had the effect of blurring the lines between revolutionary politics and the opposition for the majority of the population, who were not deeply involved. Conceivably, it led some to conclude that the jailed were not guilty or were even fighting for a just cause. Undoubtedly, it demoralized many Sandinistas who had participated in the anticontra war (to defend the revolution) to encounter their torturers and assassins on city streets handing out leaflets in the electoral campaign.

The cumulative effect of these one-sided Sandinista concessions to the UNO, Washington, and hostile U.S. client regimes was to reinforce the ideology, image, and authority of the internal opposition as a major power center in society. The government's constituencies saw each and every position that they had believed in, fought for, and defended conceded to their adversaries. Only Sandinista "cheerleaders" in Washington, New York, Paris, and Bonn viewed the policy of unilateral and unreciprocated concessions as clever politics. On the basis of this conciliatory behavior, they hoped to convince liberal and social democratic legislators that the regime in Managua was "reasonable and flexible" and not controlled by "orthodox Marxists"—and therefore worthy of economic and political support. But the strategy produced few instances of concrete support; rather it resulted in demands for more Sandinista concessions and new funds flowing into the opposition electoral coffers.

The Sandinista strategy of reaching upward, outward, and to the right eroded previous coherent class and popular positions. The politics of pandering to the elites—the "new realism"—weakened the allegiance of the regime's less committed supporters: They could not be expected to follow the contradictory policy shifts and the rightward drift in the hope of finding the golden chalice in an uncertain future, particularly since all the Sandinista byways were leading toward orthodox market-oriented austerity programs.

The last and somewhat bizarre effort of the Sandinistas to follow in the footsteps of their Western adversaries involved the election campaign itself. The FSLN leadership resorted to media-cum-celebrity politics and "lavish handouts of imported presents"[10] in the context of a highly polarized and destitute electorate—workers and peasants looking for relief from hunger and oppressive economic conditions, only to be confronted by an affluent, well-financed, and externally connected elite. The image and personality politics of the Ortega campaign, and its willingness to spend large amounts of money on campaign "events" in the midst of such poverty, were well captured in a description of one electoral rally: "[Ortega] bounded onto the stage with awkward hops, reminding me of a late 1950s rock 'n roller. He was wearing a passion-flower orange shirt and cowboy boots. . . . The rally culminated with a gaudy blaze of fireworks."[11]

Undoubtedly, part of the responsibility for the making of this electoral disaster resides with the Sandinistas' Washington consultants and liberal advisors. But it was FSLN policy to allow structural and class divisions to persist in Nicaraguan society, to permit the ruling-class leaders to deepen the existing cleavages, and to decide to formulate a campaign that overlooked past relationships of power and provided no class strategy for the future. On the contrary, the course marked out for Nicaragua in the 1990 campaign by the Ortega leadership was based on freeing the market and opening up the economy to foreign investment.[12] Ortega's pathetic adaptation to the rock star electoral campaign style, however, didn't cut much ice with a population suffering the effects of declining wages and consumption, rising prices, concessions to the domestic bourgeoisie—and promises of more of the same. Sandinista "political will" was incapable of overcoming the class realities of politics.

Sandinista Economic Strategy: Falling Between Two Chairs

In underdeveloped societies with a substantial petty commodity sector, the notion of a mixed-economy development model, in the sense of retaining elements of private property ownership, is a sensible one. However, the Sandinista resort to a mixed-economy approach was fundamentally flawed insofar as it allowed the strategic export sectors—the main instruments of accumulation—to remain in the hands of the pre-1979 agricultural and commercial elites. Instead of confronting the agro-export economy, the Sandinistas accepted it in toto—and even attempted to expand and deepen its role in the accumulation process—while reforms were largely confined to the sphere of distribution. In other words, they attempted to harness the Somocista agrobusiness structures to a welfare state. The result was that the agro-export elites absorbed resources (subsidies, etc.) but remained hostile to the revolution; instead of making new investments, they exported hard-currency earnings abroad and helped finance the counterrevolution. Additionally, the continuation of this sector prevented alternative structures from emerging. The economic mix promoted by the Sandinistas created an incongruous and unstable situation between a popular revolutionary state and a counterrevolutionary ruling class that monopolized the means of production. The class could not control the state but the state could not develop the economy. One or the other would have to concede.

During 1988 and 1989, the Sandinista government implemented a series of shock-treatment economic measures, harsher than the typical IMF "stabilization" program, in an attempt to reign in hyperinflation, stabilize the financial system, and encourage a hostile domestic bourgeoisie to make new, large-scale investments in agriculture and industry, thereby arresting sustained declines in production levels. The measures taken included three major currency devaluations, massive cuts in public-sector spending and direct state investments, job losses involving tens of thousands of public employees, the lifting of price controls on basic foodstuffs, the removal of almost all government subsidies, the abolition of index-linked wage rises, and numerous concessions and incentives to the private sector—especially the large agro-export producers—and to foreign investors.[13] Although draconion in content, these "adjustments" failed to achieve their stated objectives while simultaneously eroding the social-welfare gains of the revolution's first half-decade.

These belt-tightening measures were indicative of the extraordinary lengths to which the regime was prepared to go to conciliate the Nicaraguan bourgeoisie. Yet, offered all manner of additional incentives such as "favorable access to dollars and subsidies on inputs,"[14] repeated assurances of security for their investments and the continuation of the mixed-economy model, and new, extremely generous tax breaks, the private sector showed little or no interest in any kind of reciprocity.[15] On the contrary, they redoubled their economic-sabotage activities: operating on the black market, moving capital overseas, and deliberately orchestrating production slowdowns in their factories.

The Sandinista decision to bend over backward to try and accommodate a politically and economically antagonistic domestic bourgeoisie had devastating consequences for its own social base. The burden of the austerity measures fell most heavily on the wage-working and peasant populations in the form of food scarcities, skyrocketing prices for basic commodities, falling real wages and consumption, rising unemployment, and deteriorating public services:

> As the economic crisis worsened, subsidies to the middle-class and wealthy entrepreneurs were increasingly financed by cutting back on consumption, income and living conditions of the revolution's natural base of supporters. . . . Physical rationing of basic commodities, which guaranteed access for everybody, was eliminated in favor of market rationing by making prices affordable only to the richest and plunging peasants into debt.[16]

Even Defense Minister Tomas Borge acknowledged the direct link between government handouts to the agricultural and industrial elites and declining living standards for the great majority of the country's urban and rural workers:

> It is no accident that the bourgeoisie have been given so many economic incentives . . . we ourselves have been more attentive in giving the bourgeoisie economic opportunities than in responding to the demands of the working class. We sacrificed the working class in favor of the economy as part of a strategic plan.[17]

The impact of Sandinista economic policies on wage, employment, and consumption levels was truly staggering. Over the decade, real wages plummeted by more than ninety percent while per capita income declined from $1,000 to $300. But even these figures understate the scope of the contraction during the high point of the austerity programs. Between January and December 1988, the value of the average wage dropped by seventy-five percent; over the same period, the value of state workers' salaries declined by 93.7 percent. The inclusion of wage increases in the January 1989 stabilization program failed to arrest the impoverishment process because they were more than offset by accompanying price rises in public transport fares (up 20,000 percent), fuel and petrol costs (up to 140 percent), and a large number of basic consumer goods (up as much as 100 percent). Given such trends, compounded by an unemployment level that had soared to around forty percent, it is not surprising that individual consumption during the 1980s fell by an astronomical seventy percent.[18]

The deepening economic crisis triggered growing political discontent among the Sandinista rank and file which had a threefold focus. The first related to the impact of the crisis on overall living standards. "We used to eat three times a day, like normal people," said a wage laborer in Managua in late 1989. "But [now] I can only afford to eat twice, and it is the same with everybody I know."[19] The second questioned the government's priorities in a situation of widespread and worsening poverty such as the decision to allocate a large amount of scarce financial resources to build a lavishly endowed discotheque, Lobo Jack, to cater to the domestic bourgeoisie and foreign tourists. As a schoolteacher told President Ortega at a public meeting soon after the opening of the state-owned facility in May 1989: "We don't want more money to go to concerts or discotheques—we just want enough to eat."[20] The third main source of growing worker disillusionment with the government was an increasing perception that the costs of the austerity seemed not to have touched the lifestyles of the top-echelon figures in the government and the state institutions. An urban worker summed up this feeling that the full brunt of the "recovery" measures were being borne by those least able to absorb the "punishment": "The only ones who can afford to eat are in the Government."[21] Extensive interviewing of urban workers in both the public and private sectors during the latter half of 1989 revealed considerable unhappiness over the government's handling of the economy. "Many indicated that their lack of confidence in the government['s ability] to solve the economic crisis would lead them to vote for Mrs. Chamorro in the [February 1990] elections."[22]

While the economic "adjustments" disproportionately impacted on the country's urban and rural poor, the FSLN leadership responded harshly to strikes and demonstrations against their policies. When taxi drivers, teachers, and coffee growers publicly protested in June 1989 over another round of price increases stemming from a further currency devaluation, the regime cracked down with considerable vigor. Accommodations with each group were finally reached, but not before riot police had tear-gassed taxi drivers demonstrating over a 100-percent rise in petrol prices and what they considered an unsatisfactory deal stitched together between their union and the government—and not before land belonging to three leaders of the coffee-growers' association had been confiscated.

Throughout the 1980s, Sandinista policy oscillated between threats, pressures, and concessions to the agrocommercial elites: The latter became increasingly ascendant toward the end of the decade. The economic damage wrought by this version of a mixed economy was only exceeded by the political consequences: the elites, with bases intact and receiving funds from both the Nicaraguan and

U.S. (CIA) governments, remained strategically placed to mount a struggle to regain hegemonic status—particularly in rural areas among small and medium-size farmers hardest hit by the U.S. economic warfare.

The Sandinista economic strategy was also constructed on two other flawed assumptions: that it was possible to revive prerevolutionary relationships with the major international capitalist lending institutions by accepting foreign-debt obligations inherited from the Somoza regime, and with the United States through the politics of conciliation and concession. Hence, they renegotiated the debt owed to the private commercial banks in 1980 and continued to make interest payments to creditor banks and governments until funds were exhausted—in no small measure due to the refusal of the private banks and the "international banks" (World Bank, Inter-American Development Bank) to provide new loans—the latter in response to enormous pressure exerted by the Reagan (and Bush) administrations. Likewise, Sandinista expectations of a continuation, or renewal, of trade and aid ties with the United States proved illusory—no matter the extent of their willingness to capitulate to imperial-state demands. Managua's persistent and forlorn hope of a change in U.S. policy only served to increase the effectiveness of the economic sanctions. To the degree that FSLN policy of making political and economic concessions to the internal opposition and its imperial adversaries was geared to terminating the U.S. economic blockade, it fell between two chairs: It failed to gain the support of the latter while strengthening the position of the former. While the Sandinistas gained tactical victories (small loans and limited trade) by maneuvering among its Western capitalist adversaries, these hostile governments gained strategic allies within the Nicaraguan political economy.

Under the stress and pressures of the contra war, the FSLN beat a disorderly economic retreat after 1985, shifting from a regulated economy and agricultural cooperatives to the anarchic forces of the "free market" which, in turn, unleashed hyperinflation and triggered price rises, black-marketeering, speculation, disincentives to work for a wage, and incentives to buy and sell. The IMF-type economic policies devastated the living standards of the major social base of the revolution—the working class and the working poor—and vastly expanded the petty-commodity-speculative strata linked to "liberal economics" and counterrevolutionary politics. (At the time, Sandinista theoreticians rationalized this process of class restructuring by attacking orthodox class analyses and inventing new amorphous categories such as the "popular classes" or "intermediary classes" and imputing to them a transformative role—overlooking their relationship to the market and exaggerating the autonomous role of culture and political will.)

Within this matrix of large-scale structural continuities, state economic elite contradictions, and working-class restructuring, Sandinista policy evolved from a mixed regulated economy toward a deregulated market, culminating in the imposition of harsh IMF-style economic stabilization measures. The new austerity programs of 1988–1989 savaged wage and salaried workers, and the rural and urban poor, while increasing profits for the economic elites in a fashion not dissimilar from the economic policies implemented by reactionary regimes across Latin America during the 1980s. This "silent coup" almost certainly induced many former FSLN supporters to take their revenge at the ballot box. Sandinista economic policy, played out on the terrain of the capitalist class and confirming the power of the agrobusiness elites, had the effect of substantially eroding the government's support among its working lower-class base without gaining the confidence or votes of the petty bourgeois and property-owning classes.

The turn to economic orthodoxy hollowed out the Sandinistas' revolutionary political appeals and disillusioned their historic base of support. Campaign electoral commitments to further open up the economy to the vagaries of international capitalist forces played directly into the hands of the UNO opposition and were probably the last straw for many voters: If both sides are articulating the same economic vision for the future based on external ties, then perhaps it makes most sense to choose that candidate (Violeta Chamorro) linked to, and financed by, international capital.

The Chamorro Government and Sandinista Power: The Politics of Conflict and Collaboration

Bouyed by the electoral victory of the Chamorro forces, Washington aligned itself with the rightist elements in the new governing coalition, centered around the ambitious Vice President Virgilio Godoy, who wanted to oust the Sandinistas from all positions of power in the state and civil society. To facilitate this objective, Bush officials warned Mrs. Chamorro that a decision to retain Sandinista commandante General Humberto Ortega as head of the Nicaraguan Army could imperil not only projected U.S. aid programs but also new loans from the international banks. Furthermore, the White House gave its tacit backing to the contras' refusal to demobilize unless the senior ranks of the army were purged of Sandinista officers. For her part, the new president was committed to dismantling the Sandinista welfare state, privatizing the state sector, and deepening the already-in-place "free-market" strategies—differing with the U.S.-Godoy coalition only over the pace, scope, and timing of the envisaged changes. In part, this reflected Chamorro's belief that a wholesale attack on the still-powerful Sandinista presence in the state and civil society was a possible recipe for a new outbreak of civil war.

Meanwhile, the evolving response of the Sandinista movement to its loss of political power was two fold: (1) The Ortega political leadership were prepared to collaborate with Chamorro in implementing new "free-market"–austerity measures in return for limited concessions. (2) The organized working class and the Sandinista mass organizations desired to aggressively confront any center-right offensive to roll back revolutionary gains.

Having assumed control of an economy mired in recession, the Chamorro government accorded the highest priority to regaining favor with Nicaragua's major pre-1979 overseas funding agencies—namely, the U.S. government and the international banks. From the outset, the Bush administration, the World Bank, the IMF, and the Inter-American Development Bank had implicitly or explicitly conditioned new aid flows on the implementation of "sound economic policies," which meant, in the words of an involved Agency for International Development official, a "market economy. What we are looking for is the standard orthodox stuff."[23] The attack on the Sandinista agrarian reforms began in May 1990 with the announcement of two presidential decrees permitting the lease of state lands to private producers and the privatization of state and collectively owned land and businesses—including the return of nationalized properties to their former owners. The land takeovers provoked a number of work stoppages on some of the largest agro-industrial enterprises. That same month, 60,000 members of the National Confederation of Public Employees went on strike demanding wage increases and greater government consultation with the Sandinistas on key policy issues.

Between May and July, the Sandinista unions put the government on notice that they were determined to challenge the drift toward an IMF-type "free-market" economy. This groundswell of popular opposition to job layoffs, wage cuts, and the privatization of state enterprises reached its peak in July when an estimated 90,000 public-sector workers left their jobs, bringing most of the economy to a standstill. The immediate Chamorro response was to declare the strike illegal and threaten harsh measures against the protesters. She mobilized the pro-Sandinista army and police, who dismantled workers' barricades set up during confrontations with extreme rightist elements but refused to take direct action against the strikers. The intercession of the FSLN bourgeois political elite ultimately resolved the impasse. On July 12, the government reached an agreement with the Sandinista unions under which the public sector workers would receive an immediate forty-three-percent wage increase, those fired from their jobs would receive compensation pay, and the plan to return nationalized properties to their Somocista-era owners would be suspended. But these "concessions" were only temporary and the reality was that thousands of state workers still lost their jobs—victims of the same kind of austerity programs the Ortega leadership implemented in the late 1980s.

During September, a series of meetings took place between Daniel Ortega; Mrs. Chamorro's most trusted advisor, the minister of the presidency, Antonio Lacayo; and the U.S. ambassador to Nicaragua, Harry Shlaudeman, aimed at forging a consensus that would support the government's economic program. Subsequently, under pressure from the FSLN leadership, the Sandinista National Worker's Front (FNT) agreed to participate in a national "concertacion economica y social." To mollify organized labor, the regime said it would place a temporary freeze on job firings in the state sector, honor all existing labor agreements with the FNT, and not privatize the state-run properties formerly owned by the Somoza family. However, the state would relinquish control of the banking system and foreign trade to the domestic elites. On October 10, the "concertacion," unanimously supported by the FSLN and the fourteen UNO coalition parties, was endorsed by the Nicaraguan legislature (National Assembly). Once again the Sandinista politicos indicated their preference for collaborating and making deals with the government rather than defending urban and rural working-class interests. This strategy "at best," as Spence and Vickers observe, "has [only] been able to cushion the blows."[24] In supporting the establishment, and the maintenance of this social pact—tantamount to political support for the regime—the FSLN effectively abrogated its role as the major opposition force to the extreme rightist UNO Vice President Godoy and his supporters.

By early 1991, the Chamorro government had still not passed the "creditworthy" test to the satisfaction of the Bush administration. Only $207 million of the $541 million pledged by the White House and authorized by Congress had actually been disbursed on the grounds that the pace of deregulation and privatization was falling behind Managua's original commitments. Appeals by the Chamorro government for a more flexible approach on Washington's part were summarily rebuffed. "This is as flexible as it gets," said one U.S. official. "Our only conditions are the targets in their economic plan."[25] The aid lever was also being wielded in an attempt to pressure Nicaragua to withdraw its case against the United States in the International Court of Justice (and the $17 billion judgement against the imperial power) over the mining of the country's harbors in early 1984.

In its bid to extract new credits from Western governments and banks and renegotiate its private foreign debt, the Chamorro regime unveiled an IMF-approved plan to privatize 200 state enterprises, ranging from telecommunications networks to agricultural estates. The president of the National Assembly, UNO's Alfredo Cesar, put it bluntly: "Everything is up for sale."[26] Then, in March, the president announced a new round of shock-therapy measures including a fivefold devaluation of the currency and increases of more than 400 percent in the prices of basic food staples. The latter totally wiped out the one "concession" in the package: a 200-percent wage increase for 105,000 state employees (all other workers' salaries remained frozen).[27] The senior cabinet minister Antonio Lacayo called it "the toughest stabilization plan in Central America."[28] But they confronted a Sandinista political leadership, most notably Daniel Ortega, who, despite repeated threats of "government from below" to safeguard the gains of the revolutionary period, endorsed the rightest regime's "stabilization" blueprint. Sandinista deputies in the National Assembly offered their unqualified support for the Chamorro plan and Ortega subsequently played a central role in defusing this latest manifestation of working-class struggle to prevent a further erosion of living standards.[29] Former FSLN Vice President Sergio Ramirez even travelled to Washington with Lacayo to jointly present the March plan to representatives of the World Bank, the Inter-American Development Bank, and the prospective donor governments.[30]

The Chamorro-Sandinista economic cohabitation has deepened the recession and worsened the conditions of life of the country's workers, peasants, and urban poor. In 1990, the gross national product shrank by 5.7 percent—in relative terms a greater contraction than occurred in the last year of FSLN rule; agricultural and industrial production continued in a downward spiral, hyperinflation topped 13,500 percent, and unemployment remained above forty percent. In the social-welfare area, the deterioration was equally dramatic: the average daily caloric intake fell to 300 calories below the level considered adequate by nutrition experts; a measles epidemic claimed over 600 lives; public hospitals ran out of 303 of the 327 types of medicines deemed critical by international health agencies; and dozens of free clinics were closed due to the austerity budget cuts. By year's end, seventy percent of the population was eking out an existence below the poverty line.[31]

At the same time, many of the top Sandinista leaders who were lecturing workers on the need for austerity and sacrifice made it clear they were not about to forgo the bourgeois lifestyle they had become accustomed to while in office. These self-styled revolutionaries insisted on retaining those assets accumulated during the 1980s and also began to investigate ways of accumulating additional wealth, often through external ties. Daniel Ortega, when not junketeering in the United States in search of a six- or seven-figure advance from publishers for his memoirs, was busy fending off efforts to force him to return a complex of houses, roads, and a small baseball field belonging to a wealthy Nicaraguan exile which he acquired when the FSLN held power. The passage of special property laws during those years allowed a large number of party influentials to purchase houses at absurdly low prices when they did not get them for nothing.[32] Members of this bourgeois elite were also active in "capital-raising ventures" with the help of overseas linkages they developed during the revolution.[33]

Conclusion

The Nicaraguan revolution took place in a poor and underdeveloped country only to be confronted by an intransigent imperialist power willing to destroy the economy in order to terminate the process. Forced by the pressures of war and economic necessity to make difficult choices, the Sandinista leadership resorted to strategies to consolidate the revolution that had the reverse effect: Unilateral political concessions to external and internal elites opened space and provided historically unprecedented opportunities for the revival and expansion of the counterrevolutionary movement. The FSLN failed to anticipate the political and social costs of economic policies based on conciliating and accommodating these adversary forces. Finally, reversing the logic of revolutionary politics, they made the fundamental strategic mistake of convoking national elections *prior to,* rather than following, military/political stabilization and economic reconstruction.

The outcome of the February 1990 election was a setback to the forces of social and economic change not only in Central and South America but in the Third World in general. Nevertheless, a number of painful lessons can be extracted from the Nicaraguan experience. *First,* nationalist or revolutionary governments cannot take their initial popular support for granted and presume that a reordering of economic priorities in favor of domestic capitalists and international bankers can be done with impunity. The retention of popular support depends on a *continuing* congruence between strategic socioeconomic policy and the interests of the revolution's social base. *Second,* the interests of internal class supporters must take precedence over the demands and pressures of external "supporters"— liberal and social democratic policy-makers and other "influentials"—to make concessions to imperial states and foreign financial institutions. *Third,* revolutionary pluralist-socialist democracy either establishes the boundaries for political activity or it self destructs. The democratic process cannot allow itself to be subverted by political parties subsidized by external powers; nor can supporters and advocates (in the political system, economy, mass media, etc.) of foreign-financed and -armed enemies be allowed to claim a legitimate place within that process. *Fourth,* class-based democracy rooted in the workplace is essential if production and distribution are to assume precedence over speculation and commercial exploitation in the government's socioeconomic program, and if the regime is to remain accountable to those who made the revolution. *Fifth,* the export economy should be subordinated to the domestic market. Small and medium-size decentralized enterprises oriented toward local needs should be given precedence in economic planning over large-scale bureaucratic and private sector, export-oriented projects. *Sixth,* the consolidation of state and regime power (the elimination of armed external enemies and their internal allies) and the processes of economic reconstruction and development are the *essential prerequisites* of open and democratic elections in Third World revolutionary societies.

In a world-historical perspective, the electoral defeat of the Ortega leadership in Nicaragua signals a major reversal in the nationalist/populist revolution. But even in Nicaragua itself, the struggle for state power in the post-Sandinista era is far from resolved: The bourgeoisie has gained control of government but working-class power is still influential in civil society (through the trade unions and mass organizations) and in the state (through the Sandinista-dominated army, police, and judiciary). Attempts by the rightist pro-contra forces in the UNO government to purge the state of Sandinista influence and repress the popular organizations have been resisted by Mrs. Chamorro in an effort to minimize conflict and on the grounds that such actions could possibly ignite a new civil war.

Given Daniel Ortega's embrace of electoral politics and "free-market" economics and the Chamorro leadership's policy of limited confrontation with the centers of working-class power in the state and civil society, it is not surprising that negotiations, and even a de facto form of power sharing, should have become the order of the day. On the other hand, while Ortega has demonstrated a consistent willingness to accommodate the interests of domestic property owners, overseas bankers, and Washington policy-makers, he has been careful not to lend his support to proposed policies that would reverse the Sandinista land reforms and restore titles to the prerevolutionary owners.

North American interventions in Central and South America and the Caribbean during the postwar period have only produced longer or shorter detours to popular revolutions. The latter—delayed transformations in which nationalist, democratic, and social demands converge—have inevitably turned out to be much more radical. United States installed electoral regimes in the hemisphere over the past decade have, without exception, been unable to consolidate their political power or resolve the underlying socioeconomic problems—despite the rhetoric of the campaign period. Within this context, the 1990 electoral outcome in Nicaragua is but a temporary and partial setback in a larger historical process.

Notes

1. For a detailed analysis of U.S. policy toward the 1984 elections, see Roy Gutman, *Banana Diplomacy: The Making of American Policy in Nicaragua 1981–1987* (New York: Simon and Schuster, 1988), pp. 232–257.

2. Bush quoted in Carla Anne Robbins, "New Look in Latin America," *U.S. News and World Report,* December 26, 1988/January 2, 1989, p. 58.

3. White House spokesman Marlin Fitzwater, quoted in John M. Goshko and Ann Devroy, "U.S. Endorses Contra Plan as Prod to Democracy in Nicaragua," *Washington Post,* August 9, 1989, p. A15.

4. See ibid.; Robert Pear, "U.S. Envoy Urges Honduras to Let the Contras Stay," *New York Times,* March 14, 1989, pp. 1, 5.

5. *Electoral Democracy Under International Pressure*. The Report of The Latin American Studies Association Commission to Observe the 1990 Nicaraguan Election (March 15, 1990), p. 9.

6. Quoted in "Nicaragua Implements Electoral and Media Reforms," *Washington Report on the Hemisphere,* May 24, 1989, p. 5.

7. See, for example, "Quayle Calls Managua Vote Plan a Sham," *New York Times,* March 14, 1989, pp. 1, 5.

8. *Electoral Democracy Under International Pressure,* pp. 4–5.

9. Quoted in Council on Hemispheric Affairs, *News and Analysis,* February 23, 1990.

10. Carlos M. Vilas, "What Went Wrong," *NACLA Report on the Americas,* Vol. XXIV, No. 1, June 1990, p. 14.

11. Julia Preston, "The Defeat of the Sandinistas," *New York Review of Books,* April 12, 1990, p. 27.

12. See, for example, "Campaign to Attract Foreign Investment," *Central America Report,* August 25, 1989, p. 262.

13. See "Between Intervention and the Market," *Latin American Monitor: Central*

America, August 1988, p. 577; Mark A. Uhlig, "Sandinistas' Medicine," *New York Times,* February 1, 1989, pp. 1, 7; "Overtures to the Private Sector," *Latin American Monitor: Central America,* March 1989, p. 630.

14. "UNO Election Victory" U.S. Ousts Sandinistas, but Revolutionary Achievements Survive," *Central American Bulletin,* Spring 1990, p. 9.

15. On tax breaks for the bourgeoisie, see "Adjusting the Financial Screws," *Central America Report,* September 15, 1989, p. 184.

16. Vilas, "What Went Wrong," p. 12.

17. "Tomas Borge on the Nicaraguan Revolution," *New Left Review,* No. 164, July/August 1987, p. 58.

18. See "Yankee Blamed for Economic Disaster," *Latin American Regional Reports: Mexico and Central America,* February 16, 1989, p. 2; Mark A. Uhlig, "Nicaraguan Study Reports Economy in Drastic Decline," *New York Times,* June 26, 1989, p. 1; Mark A. Uhlig, "A Sandinista Promise Gone Sour Alienates Nicaragua's Working Class," *New York Times,* November 7, 1989, p. 10.

19. Quoted ibid.

20. Quoted in Tim Coone, "Managua's Disco Mix Fails to Keep Wolf from Door," *Financial Times,* June 7, 1989, p. 3.

21. Quoted in Uhlig, "A Sandinista Promise Gone Sour Alienates Nicaragua's Working Class," p. 10.

22. Quoted ibid.

23. Quoted in William I. Robinson, "AID to Nicaragua: Some Things Just Aren't What They Seem," *In These Times,* October 24–30, 1990, p. 12.

24. Jack Spence and George Vickers, "The Chamorro Government After 200 Days," *LASA Forum,* Vol. XXI, No. 4, Winter 1991, p. 10.

25. Quoted in Richard Boudreaux, "Nicaragua Kinder and Gentler, but Poorer, Under Chamorro," *Los Angeles Times,* April 14, 1991.

26. Quoted in "Testing Time for Violeta Chamorro," *Latin American Weekly Report,* March 21, 1991, p. 4. Also see "Privatizations Pave Way for IMF Deal," *Latin American Monitor: Central America,* March 1991, p. 876.

27. See "U.S. Visit Fails to Bring More Aid," *Latin American Monitor: Central America,* May 1991, p. 896; David Adams, "Nicaraguans Unite in the Battle to Heal the Economy," *The Independent,* March 11, 1991.

28. Quoted in Boudreaux, "Nicaragua Kinder and Gentler, but Poorer, Under Chamorro."

29. See "Chamorro Wins Breathing Space," *Latin American Monitor: Central America,* April 1991, p. 888.

30. See Edward Cody, "No Truce for Nicaraguan Poor," *Washington Post,* April 7, 1991, p. A24.

31. See Mark A. Uhlig, "Nicaragua Sinks Further as Chamorro's Magic Fails," *New York Times,* January 15, 1991, p. 3; "Economic and Social Stability Threatened,"

Washington Report on the Hemisphere, February 6, 1991, p. 4; Boudreaux, "Nicaragua Kinder and Gentler But Poorer, Under Chamorro."

32. See Nancy Nusser, "Sandinista President Ortega Now Battles for his Real Estate," *Cox News Service,* May 12, 1991; Janine Di Giovanni, "Where are the Sandinistas Now?" *The Spectator,* May 4, 1991, p. 5.

33. Spence and Vickers, "The Chamorro Government After 200 Days," p. 11.

7

The Retreat of the Intellectuals

Introduction

It is painfully evident that intellectuals no longer play a major role as protagonists of working-class politics. Indeed, for some the "working class" no longer exists; for others, the very notion of class is "problematical."[1] Marxism has become a term of opprobrium, imperialism has been replaced by "discourses," socialism is usually put in quotation marks, and the loud cries of crisis have been replaced by claims of failure, disintegration, and demise.

The paradox in the posture struck by these intellectuals is that they claim to have uncovered new social, political, and economic realities that make the Marxist categories outmoded, while proceeding to dredge up a melange of mainstream concepts from the most commonplace orthodoxies: "rational individuals," economic equilibrium, distributive equity, procedural democracies, individual preferences.[2] The retreat from Marxism is accompanied by a reversion to liberal democracy and neoclassical economics. We are back to the debates of the 1950s (or is it the 1850s) with one proviso: The intellectual optimism that accompanied the earlier orthodoxy was anchored in an expansionary capitalist world economy in which industrial growth, a strong labor movement, and welfare-state politics still held sway. The orthodoxy of the 1950s, based on an upswing in the capitalist cycle, could be excused for proclaiming an "end to ideology." The conformist intellectuals of the earlier period could point to a semblance of "equilibrium" and democracy, particularly if they excluded women, blacks, and Third World nations. They could point to Stalin's Russia and argue about the monolithic, unchanging, and repressive collectivist regime as an unattractive alternative.

Today's intellectuals' flight has little basis for proclaiming the failure of Marxism, despite the pseudoscientific pretensions of some. With millions unemployed in the European Economic Community, and three-quarters of the new jobs in the capitalist world of a temporary, low-paid, low-skill service variety, with the Latin American market economies in a decade-long crisis that has brought living standards below those of the early 1960s and left financial leaders waiting for the next economic crisis to happen, there is scant basis for any optimism rooted in the fragile structures of Western capitalism. The successes of capitalism are elsewhere: in the spheres of the paper economy, in speculation and in pillage of the state. Those intellectuals who have forsaken Marxism strengthen the power of speculators and neoliberals in their out-of-hand attacks on "statism"—in the name of an elusive conception of civil society.

The retreat of the intellectuals from Marxism in particular and the scientistic posturing occurs precisely when the ruling classes are most robustly ideological and mince no words in defending class power with straightforward expositions of doctrinaire unregulated capitalism and income reconcentration at the top. Corporate policies increasingly bind owners and managers through bonus and stock plans that bring them closer together, undermining notions of managerial dominance. Never in this century have the bonds between capitalism and the state been so transparent as during the 1980s; and never has control over the state and production had such a direct impact on "distribution" of income. Yet it is precisely in this period that the former Marxists choose to emphasize the autonomy of the state from class power and the autonomous role of ideological discourses in shaping historical development, while dissociating "distribution" from capitalist ownership of production.[3] One of the principal issues facing these analysts is the striking divergence between their new ideological positions and the unfolding political and socioeconomic relations and processes of the present period.

The "demise of Marxism" thesis is largely based on a series of invented strawpersons, on sloppy theoretical and methodological reasoning, and an unwillingness to apply the test of facts to propositions. First, a careful reading of the financial pages of the most influential Western print media confirms the Marxist prognosis for and analysis of the inner logic of capital: its concentration and centralization, the mergers into even larger conglomerates, the increasing sway of financial over productive capital, and the growing subordination of national competitive capital to these movements.[4] Second, the increasing diversion of society into wage and salaried workers and capital has advanced even further than Marxists projected due to the enormous growth of low-paid workers who have come to dominate the labor force in the so-called service sectors.[5] Third, the Marxist analysis of the tendency for capital to intensify the rates of exploitation under competitive pressures has been writ large by the dismantling of the welfare states, by the declining share of income accruing to labor as against capital, and by the continuing transformation of work forces into temporary labor—burdened with the increasing costs of social reproduction and health care, as well as pension losses and the like.[6] Fourth, the confrontationist postures adopted by the leading capitalist states toward their trade-union movements throughout the 1980s is visible testimony to the class nature of the state and to its role as the manager of the ruling class. From U.S. President Reagan's smashing of the air controllers' strike to British Prime Minister Thatcher's savaging of the miners' union to Spanish President Gonzalez's efforts to break the December 1989 general strike of the labor confederations, and in a host of other circumstances, there is overwhelming evidence that the class state is a far more rigorous analytical tool in understanding the decline of labor and the dissolution of workers' power than notions of state autonomy and "mediation."

By avoiding an analysis of the major processes of large-scale, long-term *structural change* that confirm the Marxist analysis, the former Marxist intellectuals focus on the *behavior* of the working class (their lack of "class identification," the influence of nonclass factors).[7]

There are several problems with these analyses. First, they all tend to conflate class formation with class consciousness: by denying the latter, they deny the former. If you don't hear the workers shout revolution, they don't exist. The social division of labor and the interdependent position of producers separated from the means of production are obscured and in their place we are presented with "rational individuals" subject to a multiplicity of determinations.[8] The social relations which exist *independent of the will of the producers or employers*—in their individual capacities—are a product of the operations of the profit motive in the marketplace. Against this, the ex-Marxists counterpose abstract notions of individual free choice to the realities of the market compulsions to sell labor power or starve.

Marxism's multilevel dialectical analysis of political and social action is caricatured into a singular mechanical/structural simplification: Class position equals class consciousness equals revolutionary action. The technique of oversimplifying adversarial positions involves attributing the distorted position to "anonymous," "orthodox," "classical" Marxists who probably only exist in the polemical excesses of the former Marxists. A brief survey of Marx's life—the long, tedious hours spent trying to build the organization of the First International, the pedagogical efforts and travels to worker educational conferences, the ideological struggles devoted to clarifying theoretical and practical issues for the workers' movement[9]—should suggest to the adherents of post-Marxism that for Marx, Lenin, Trotsky, Gramsci, and contemporary Marxists, the transformation of a class in itself to a class for itself required political organization, education, and ideological debates. These interrelated processes, however, are situationally located in the context of the class division of society and within the process of class struggle—located in a variety of social sites (workplace, housing, political movements for democratic rights).[10]

The works of Lenin have suffered from a dual distortion. He is falsely accused of being either an economic reductionist or a "voluntarist organization man." On one level, however, Lenin's discussion of revolution revolves around a detailed concrete analysis of the impact of capitalism on the specificities of the Russian class structure; on another, it centers on the problems of highly differentiated and uneven development of class consciousness; on a third level, it provides an analysis of the political conditions (nature of state, levels of repression) that influence the type of political organization; and, finally it emphasizes the centrality of ideological and programmatic debate and clarification within the workers' movement. Lenin's complex multilevel interactive model of analysis cannot be forced into any of the simplistic categories elaborated by the anti-Leninists.[11]

The same could be said for the former radicals' treatment of contemporary Marxists. Their efforts to repudiate Marxism revolve around their discovery of the obvious: that the workers' movement is reformist with limited or weak class consciousness and that "nonclass factors" are determinants of working-class behavior. Contrary to the "reductionist" charges, Marxists have combined an analysis of the *objective processes* of class formation (capitalist accumulation and reproduction based on class differentiation and exploitation) with an analysis of the subjective responses in the most varied social and political situations. While Marxists have taken account of reformist consciousness, they insist that the only means to transform capitalism is through the development of a class-conscious, organized working class. Marxism is analytical and prescriptive. Its purpose is not only to describe but to change the world, and the two are interrelated. The objective processes form the basis for the prescriptive action. Inherent systemic processes establish the basis for political intervention. In that sense, the Marxist theory of revolution is both historically determined and politically problematical.[12]

There are in the United States several strands of "post-Marxist" thought and not all have made their peace with the status quo. Samuel Bowles, Herbert Gintis, Derek Shearer, and Martin Carnoy have attempted to formulate a radical-democratic critique of capitalism while taking exception to basic analytical concepts and perspectives of Marxism.[13]

The writings of the radical-democratic intellectuals, while differing on substantive issues of politics, method, and analysis with many of the post-Marxist writers, unfortunately share with them an inadequate understanding of the distinctions between state and regime and thus underestimate the enduring and deeply entrenched nature of the class constraints on reformist socioeconomic change. The radical-democratic intellectuals emphasize policy-making structures rather than the larger economic institutional setting; they focus on the permeable character of the political regime over and against the rigidities of the permanent state apparatus. And, on the basis of regime permeability and policy-making structures, they elaborate a critique of Marxism and a reform strategy designed to ameliorate the gross inequalities of U.S. society.

In contrast to the radical-democrats, so-called "state-centered theorists" have overlooked the most elementary distinctions between regime and state in their analyses.[14] The state functionaries, the permanent body of nonelected officials linked to the enduring class institutions who control the means of coercion and fashion economic policy, are subsumed with the transitory electoral officials operating inside the boundaries of the state and defining the political regime. By "permanent body of nonelected officials" we refer to the officials of the Federal Reserve, Treasury, Defense, and State departments, the CIA, and the other executive-branch agencies that are the key determinants of the great bulk of the federal budget, of the level of state repression and tolerance, and of the direction and conduct of U.S. foreign policy and overseas economic activity. By enduring class institutions, we mean the major multinational corporations, banks, and financial and real-estate houses that define the levels of investment, income shares, and divisions in society. Hence, we have the chronic intellectual muddle in which most "state theorizing" finds itself: describing *regime* behavior and character and calling it the democratic *state*.[15] By focusing exclusively on competitive, interest-group-based regimes, it fails to grasp the authoritarian, hierarchical, class-dominated state and how the latter constrains the former, and it always creates the possibility of reversing whatever working-class gains a welfare regime might evoke in a period of upsurge.

If the ex-Marxists have omitted basic analytical political distinctions in their haste to assert the "autonomy" and "specificity of the political," in the economic realm their redefinition of exploitation outside of the realm of production to "distribution," and the accompanying rejection of the labor theory of value, strips political economy of its most fundamental analytical point of departure: the social relations of production.[16] The capital/labor relations and the issues of power, alienation, insecurity, and domination are set aside and the problems of income distribution and consumption are artificially inserted. Artificially because income is correlated with power derived from ownership of capital—productive and speculative. Moreover, the social relations of production have been and are today the major point of contention between capital and labor, and this has been the site for most of the significant organization that has challenged in one form or another the organized power of capital.[17]

The repositioning of exploitation into the realm of distribution conflates the positions of labor and capital in production, and this becomes the formula for the policies of class collaboration and "social contracting": both are interdependent "productive factors" involved in producing income. Conflicts are over the appropriate income policies. The deterioration of workers' power in relations of production has been instrumental in changing the conditions for the reproduction of labor and the structure of social organization and social action. It has also affected family relations, personal worth and identity, and quality of neighborhood life. In the lexicon of the post-Marxists, these *consequences* of capitalist relations of production are "theorized" as "new sites" of action stripped of their systemic attributes. "Movements" and "actors" intervening against these derivations from the capital/labor relationship are counterposed to labor/capitalist "workplace" conflict as if they could be separated by a Chinese wall.[18]

The fragmentation of knowledge is the hallmark of the former Marxists—the emphasis is on self-contained and generated phenomena, "indeterminacy," and elaborate mathematical exercises based on oversimplified assumptions.[19] The procedure of "methodological individualism" involves the dissolution of social reality into abstracted individuals and subsequently the imputation of a liberal economic calculus stripped of all prior social bonds, traditions, and struggles. This becomes the point of departure for reconstructing social reality. In contrast, Marxism focuses on the dynamics of collective interaction with crisis, on state action (repression, war, etc.), on social mobilization, and on social power. The real world in which "individuals" live and work cannot be understood through discussions of social identity based on interviews of isolated individuals in private settings: The results reproduce the method.

Analytical Marxism is a halfway house between the radical past and a reconciliation with orthodox neoclassical economics, mainstream pluralist politics, and microsociology. Having emptied the structural foundations of radical change, reform proposals emerge as pious "normative" wishes operating and conflicting with the dominant market and state imperatives. It would not be surprising to see the ultimate extension of this logic and resolution of this tension in the direction of market rationality and the celebration of capitalist democracy.

The Global Nature of the Retreat

Retreating intellectuals are not a new phenomena. During the 1930s and 1950s a similar process took place. Under the pressure of events, whole contingents of Marxists abandoned working-class politics and began the sojourn to the center and beyond. In a brilliant essay, Leon Trotsky dissects and analyzes the retreat of James Burnham and a host of New York intellectuals who discovered the "autonomy" of the state in the bureaucratization of world politics, the convergence of social systems, and the irrelevancy of class.[20] Many ex-Marxists ended up supporters of the Cold War, some joined in the McCarthyite purges, while others retained residual welfare commitments with their visceral anticommunism.[21]

In the 1950s, Isaac Deutscher described a new wave of former radicals, which included those who began as left-wing critics of Stalinism and eventually dissolved their left positions and became collaborators with the imperial ventures of the West.[22] The ex-leftists' conversion to liberalism was not the end of the process. In the 1960s, during the student, civil rights, and peace movements in Berkeley, Chicago, and New York, a number of leading academic ex-radicals became ardent defenders and intellectual spokespersons for police repression and critics of mass democratic movements. Seymour Lipset, Nathan Glazer, Lewis Feuer, Bruno Bettelheim, to name a few, equated democratic mass politics with the Nazis and put forth the idea of democracy as a process of elite negotiations and contracts.[23] They argued that imperial intervention in Vietnam and "Stalinist" liberation movements were equally condemnable, but that "Western values" were still preferable. This melange of ex-Trotskyist and ex-Communist intellectuals was the immediate forerunner of the current group. They, too, claimed to have gone "beyond Marxism" and class reductionism, discovering the intrinsic values of capitalist democracy and the success of free enterprise, while criticizing "pockets of poverty" as part of a faulty distribution system. For all of their scientific pretensions, the ex-radicals of the 1960s did not anticipate the burning of the fifty major urban centers during the black uprisings, the killing of three million Asians during the U.S. invasion of Indo-China, or the dismantling of the welfare state during the 1980s. They falsely assumed that the welfare state was intricately bound up with "mature capitalism" and the enduring social consensus. The flawed analysis of one generation of former Marxists has been handed over to another: the methods, discourse, and theories of one generation of post-Marxists is repeated by another.

The intellectuals' retreat from Marxism is not merely a Western European and North American phenomena. It is evident in Eastern Europe and the Third World—particularly in Latin America. While the intellectual shifts in each region reflect the influence of specific conditions, many of the ideas and theories seem to originate in Western Europe and North America and to be diffused toward other regions, with the aid of foundation funding and state-subsidized intellectual joint ventures.

The "internationalization of capitalism" and the rapid diffusion of capital through the electronic networks is accompanied by the "internationalization" of post-Marxist ideologies, rhetoric, and scientistic "discourses." With a striking and almost banal regularity, the same unfounded criticisms of Marxism are leveled from Paris to Buenos Aires, from Warsaw to Chicago. The retreat has become a rout—celebrated in the mass media as further confirmation of the superiority of the free-enterprise system.

The style and substance of the retreat have several characteristics which are generally observable. First, there is the turn from public to private discontents: the disconnection of private anxieties and decisions from their systemic sources. It is not the structure of capital but the structure of language that is the key to understanding the condition of classes in society: Symbols preempt substance as the retreating intellectuals seek to dominate center stage, relegating the uninitiated masses to be passive spectators.[24]

The critical role of the intellectuals in "naming the system" and the processes— capitalist democracy, imperialism, exploitative relations of production—is replaced by evasion and the vacuous language of discourse babble. The style of language reveals the substance of the perspective. The retreating intellectuals no longer address a class-specific constituency (the working class) but "democratic" forces, Europe, the managers of the status quo—the cultural watchdogs, the political rule-makers, the elite negotiators of social and political pacts.

Accompanying their declaration of the "failure of Marxism" is a tendency to accommodate to the programmatic positions of liberal democratic parties and their rules of the game. The celebration of capitalist democracy occurs through the elaboration of theories devoid of autonomous class action, class struggle, and a vision that transcends the existing configuration of power. In the East many dissident intellectuals have moved from anti-Stalinist rituals to blind eulogies of the West. Some have substituted their earlier docile submission to the productive forces of bureaucratic collectivist society for the imitative submission to the consumer forces of "free-market" capitalism. The thought processes of the pro-Western Eastern intellectuals are a mirror image of those of their former Stalinist tormenters: undifferentiated, noncontradictory utopias laden with good tidings. The escape from the class contradictions of the East into the mirage of a classless consumerist West is the opium of these intellectuals.

For others, the "realists," the retreat from revolutionary Marxist opposition to Stalinism has carried them onto the terrain of neoliberal orthodoxy. The former Marxist theorist Jacek Kuron, the Solidarity labor minister, speaks to the interests of the working class in terms of unemployment and soup kitchens to "cushion" the post-Marxist "reforms."[25] The Eastern intellectuals' embrace of soup-kitchen capitalism for the workers and state-subsidized public-enterprise sell-offs to private investors spells not the end of Marxism but the end of Western radical illusions about Solidarity's leadership and direction.

Many of the Gorbachevian intellectuals have few claims to intellectual originality in post-Marxist "rethinking." They move within the narrow bounds of simple-minded evolutionism: *from* vulger theories of automatic breakdown of capitalist society and the predetermined transitions to the assumedly superior Soviet socialism *to* the newer incarnation of the automatic growth and assumed superiority of "free-market" capitalism. From defining human progress as a conflict between state blocs, they now define it in terms of global classless cooperation.

In many cases, the "retreat" from Marxism has never occurred because most of the Eastern intellectuals were never critical Marxists. They rarely reflected on class struggle and class movements. Today and yesterday they were "state-centric"—the only change is in the state and states that dominated their thinking.

The Eastern intellectuals demonstrate little evidence of having studied the behavior of real existing "free-market" capitalism (and not the ideological constructs of neoclassical theory). Otherwise, they would have examined how in the United States it has undermined working-class security, trade unions, and communities and driven tens of thousands of farm families into bankruptcy. They ignore the massification of mental illness, destitution, lumpen classes, and homelessness which dominates whole areas of major American city thoroughfares. They pass over the tens of millions of workers in Third World countries who, following "free-market" prescriptions, have seen their incomes decline fifty and sixty percent over the past decade. Otherwise critical Marxists tended to tolerate these pernicious notions among Eastern intellectuals under the mistaken idea that Stalinism was the only problem. In the aftermath of the political changes and the rise of the intellectuals to power, we can now observe how the tyranny of the market has replaced the state.

If in Poland the ex-Marxist-intellectuals-turned-government-functionaries are discussing the virtue of markets and the necessity of unemployment and soup kitchens, in Western Europe, Spanish ex-Communists like Fernando Claudin and Ludolfo Paramio became the main defenders of NATO-democracy, liberal economies, and the Gonzalez regime's effort to break the ten-million-strong general strike in this time of postmodern working-class decline.[26] In France, the intellectual retreat from working-class politics has been wholesale, ranging from ex-Maoists turned ultrarightists and linguistic hair-splitters (Derrida) to enthusiasts of U.S. positivism (decision-making studies) to defenders of the independent and freedom-loving French nuclear arsenal (Debray).

The Latin American retreat has taken its own unique form: splicing quotes from Gramsci between defenses of electoral regimes cohabitating with military torturers and packaging the ensemble as "democratic realism" while debunking popular opposition as "Jacobin."[27] The Anglo-Latin foundation intellectuals add to this mystification by emptying democracy of its institutional and class context and reducing it to a set of procedures.[28]

In the United States, the shift from Marxism takes at least three directions: (1) a reform–democratic based critique of contemporary capitalism within the framework of progressive politics (Bowles and Gintis);[29] (2) an abstract theorizing divorced from popular struggles and tied to methodological individualism and rational choice;[30] and (3) a state-centered conception of political conflict anchored in elite-directed change (Skocpol).[31] This worldwide retreat of the intellectuals is best understood as a response to a common political/economic context in which there has been a decisive shift in the balance of class forces.

The Decline of Working-Class Power and the Retreat

As noted above, the tendency in recent years has been for capitalist development to extend wage-labor relations (salaried professionals, incorporation of women, expropriation of farmers, etc.) and to deepen the polarization between classes (speculator real-estate millionaires vs. low-paid temporary service workers), thus confirming the orthodox Marxist analytical framework for analyzing capitalism. The retreating ex-Marxists do not address these structural developments. Their analysis grows out of a different matrix of "facts": the obvious decline of working class power (at the firm, national, and international level, as well as in the economic/social and political spheres); the rise of right-wing business influence accompanied by the all-pervasive extension and deepening of neoclassical economic doctrines and liberal democratic ideology.

Accompanying the ascendancy of capitalist power in the West has been the crisis in the bureaucratic collectivist societies (existing socialist states) and the growing influence of pro-Western capitalist political forces (Solidarity, Hungarian "reformers"). The new Eastern liberal ideologists exploit the issues of corruption and authoritarian practices and structures, amalgamating bureaucratic politics with Marxist concepts, laying the groundwork for the profoundly anti–working-class policies favored by Western bankers and investors (austerity in wages, permissiveness in profit-taking, supply-side state incentives, and state-enforced demand-side contraction).

In the Third World, the Western-financed state-terrorist regimes (Argentina,

Uruguay, Chile, Indonesia, Zaire [ex-Congo], Guatemala, etc.) exterminated a whole generation of Marxist intellectuals and activists. They have been replaced by Western-funded "institutional intellectuals" who are more "open" to the notions of market based development and "nonclass" democracy. In the case of radical states like Cuba, Vietnam, Nicaragua, Mozambique, and Angola, either terrorist wars waged by Western-backed surrogates have destroyed their productive base or global economic embargoes have served the same end, forcing them to seek economic and ideological compromises on terms favorable to the capitalist countries. These shifts in the South and East have, in turn, limited the options available to ongoing Third World liberation movements (e.g., the FMLN in El Salvador), creating pressures for accommodations with the reactionary pro-Western regimes.

It is clear that the *contemporary political/ideological matrix created by Western capitalist and bureaucratic collectivist regimes is as unfavorable to Marxist analysis as the socioeconomic developments are favorable*. The retreating intellectuals are responding to the former—being more sensitive to the political/ideological pressures and substantially less influenced by the impact of the economic system on the class structure. Under conditions of maximum capitalist power (as exists presently—with little in the way of organized working-class power), the cost to the intellectuals of retaining their Marxist commitments goes up and the benefits go down, increasing the incentives to rationally choose to operate within the framework of neoliberal political economics.

Dissociated from working-class struggles, striving for upward mobility, the retreating intellectuals incorporate the values and norms of neoliberal hegemony and transmit them into left-wing intellectual arenas. The retreating intellectuals do not respond to the failures of capitalism—to the rigidity of the state in enforcing wholesale downward "restructuring" of the working class; rather, *they respond to the political/ideological power of capital*. The fragmentation of the working class is rather inelegantly repackaged as "individual" preferences; the ideological impositions of ascending capitalist power over a weakened working-class movement are described as the noncorrespondence of working-class "positions" and "interests."[32] The partial transformation of the working class from industrial to service employment is described as the decline of the working class and the growth of a postindustrial service economy.[33] The decline in the labor movement—a result of its bureaucratization and class-compromise policies—becomes the basis for questioning the very existence of "classes" and for making their existence contingent on their action.

While some deny the restraints imposed upon "democracy" by capitalist power, others incorporate those restraints ("rules of the game") and argue that they could or should work to the advantage of workers.[34] The elasticity of formulation belies the dubiousness of the assumptions.

The importance of social power in creating cognitive dissonance among the retreating intellectuals is manifest in their inability to theorize the major transformation of capitalist structures—from industrial to speculator, from U.S. dominant to interimperial rivalries—in their analysis of post-Marxist nonclass politics. Instead, what we have is an undifferentiated capitalism, operating in an undifferentiated capitalist world system. Rising or falling empires, imperial and nonimperial states, fall into the memory hole. Massive capitalist pillage of the state does not inhibit the use of market-centered neoclassical assumptions; the degradation of labor as the basis for their declining purchasing power does not prevent the focus on "distribution."[35]

If there are no classes because there is no class struggle, what emerges is a plurality of "social groupings" and free-floating individuals, the stuff of pluralist interest-group theory.[36] The universe—the forces that shape the rules and fragment the class and define the boundaries of issues—is left unexplained. If the analytical categories of the post-Marxists are warmed-over recitals of David Truman, orthodox U.S. political science resurfaces in their discussion of "political consciousness": From a notion of "action," they deduce or impute consciousness. If we substitute "behavior" for "action," we can see the methodological affinity between our post-Marxist and the behavioralist ideologies of an earlier period.[37] We are told that when workers act as if they can improve their material conditions within the confines of capitalism, they consent to it.[38] Action in conformity with the capitalist system can be the result of coercion, intimidation, manipulation, or limited choices. It is retreating intellectuals who arbitrarily impute their notion of "consent" to the action. And, of course, it is a weakened and fragmented working class that is the object of their theorizing. The retreating intellectuals contribute to the strengthening of capitalist hegemony through their ideological construction of capitalist Utopia based on reified individuals bargaining over constantly rising incomes in a world of expanding opportunities. The virtual absence of trade unions in most American states, the subordinate position of union officials in management-controlled teams, the undemocratic nature of almost all national trade-union conferences (the predominance of appointed officials), and the socioeconomic differences between bureaucratic officialdom and the members suggest that the basic issue facing the working class is not the question of whether they have class consciousness but rather the absence of representative democratic organizations to articulate their interests. And if there is a lack of representative institutions of the working class, the ex-Marxist's key concept, "civil society," is bereft of substance. The issue of the relationship between state and civil society is overshadowed by the overpowering reality of a state exclusively responsive to capital confronting an almost-atomized working class. Problems of "class compromise," of working-class consent, take on different meaning within the concrete parameters of real, existing capitalist society.

Retreating Intellectuals: Routes, Destinations, and Regional Variations

There is no single line of retreat that describes the defecting intellectuals' trajectory. Diverse routes have been taken, reflecting the particular academic disciplinary pressures that they adapt to and the professional orthodoxies they accommodate. In some cases, they have traded in their critical intelligence for elaborative quantification (or algebraic formulas) based on orthodox neoclassical assumptions. The critique of Marxism embraces a variety of theories and methods and extends across the map. Moreover, the political-intellectual destination of the intellectuals in flight is still unclear as they are still in flux. Some have, at least temporarily, settled in liberal or social-democratic positions. Others have moved on to neoliberal and right-wing nationalist perspectives. Not infrequently, they quote each other's work to reinforce their common position, while others engage in polemics among themselves, purporting to detect residual influences of the "reductionist" doctrine.

Among the many routes away from Marxism, several stand out: Gramscian revisionism, the doctrine of indeterminacy, neoclassical economo-Marxism (to be referred to as hyphenated Marxism), and the policy-advisory perspective. Undergirding the retreat is the assumption of the underlying stability and flexibility of capitalism. From this perspective it is a short step toward anchoring politics in cultural contradictions and cross-class social movements that reflect fragmented, partial conflicts within capitalist society. From this cock-roost they seek to provide the governing class with prescriptions on how to manage the system better, gratuitous advice to save capitalism before it self-destructs.

One of the principal victims of the ideological apostates is Antonio Gramsci. Using somewhat questionable methods of citation, the revolutionary socialist writings of Gramsci are put at the service of neoliberal political regimes. In Argentina, the Gramscian revisionists provided the intellectual defense for the Alfonsin regime (1983–1989), which reduced workers' incomes by fifty percent, pursued IMF austerity and "free-market" policies, and exonerated hundreds of police and military officials implicated in gross human rights' violations.[39] In Spain, they have been busy defending the doctrinaire neoliberal/speculator Gonzalez government.

The process of distorting the Gramscian intellectual legacy follows two procedures. First, his political practice and writings during his years as a Communist leader in the working-class struggle are ignored. Second, the epigones focus on reinterpreting his metaphorical and elliptical writing during his imprisonment. Metaphorical and Aesopian language is much more amenable to various constructions—and distortions. Gramsci, forbidden by the Fascist regime from writing directly on class society and struggle, frequently incorporated the language of the permissible. For Gramsci, "civil society" became an indirect manner of discussing oppressed classes; the "Prince" became a metaphor for the class party; "hegemony" became a euphemism for class domination. In the hands of the revisionists, civil society became synonymous with an amalgamation of classes (exploiters and exploited); the Prince became an eclectic social ensemble; hegemony became an expression of cross-class alliances. Through these "interpretations" the revisionists eviscerated Gramsci's politics based on his analysis of the most momentous event of his lifetime—the formation of the workers' council movement—

and his strategic conception anchored in a "class against class" perspective.[40] The revisionists resurrect the "permeationist" conception of state transformation of Gramsci's arch-enemy, Giolitti—and attribute it to Gramsci. They transform Gramsci's metaphor "war of positions" (used to describe the construction and conquest of working-class institutions by a revolutionary working class party) into a rationale for taking positions in the capitalist-state apparatus—up to and including ministerial advisors in bourgeois regimes. *Violent class confrontations* that were the attributes accompanying Gramsci's concept of "positional warfare" and *independent class organizations* upon which positions of class power were established were eliminated from the revisionist analysis and vocabulary, seeing that they had nothing in common with the march of these apostates through liberal electoral institutions.

Gramsci's politics drew heavily on the experience of the factory councils, and his writings in Ordine Nuovo capture his intransigent rejection of "class compromises" with bourgeois structure, culture, and ideology.[41] In contrast, in the writings of the revisionists, Gramsci emerges as a liberal social historian embracing eclectic and idealistic conceptions of political analysis.

Perhaps the most striking difference between Gramsci and the epigones is in their respective conceptions of political praxis. Gramscian praxis begins from a recognition that the basic parameters of politics and ideological analysis and struggle are anchored in the class structure and that the political and ideological do not operate as disembodied autonomous elements. The strategy and rhetoric of the post-Marxists revolve around the attempt to drive a wedge between discourses and class. The trend began by putting them on the same analytical level and culminated by inverting their causal connections. The revisions and distortions of Gramsci's writing were pivotal to this process. Gramsci's notion of working-class hegemony, originally intended to describe working-class influence over other oppressed classes, in the context of a confrontation with the capitalist state, is relocated into a matrix of multiclass coalition politics rooted in cultural discourses propagated and organized by detachments of intellectuals and electoral politicians.

The starting point for Gramsci's analysis of tactics and strategy is the violent nature and class exclusivity of the state and the subordination of electoral regimes to the rules established by the state. For Gramsci, the pursuit of electoral competition in the parliamentary arena is a tactical issue contingent on the strategic struggles centered in the mass organizations challenging the state. In the revisionist version, Gramsci's distinction between state and regime is conflated, and the relationship between strategic extraparliamentary and tactical electoral moves is inverted. In the hands of the revisionists, the Gramscian notion of *praxis* is divorced from self-organized and autonomous class power and made synonymous with "realism" and "possibilism"—political formulas utilized to rationalize class collaboration. Political institutions stripped of their class matrix are presented as "terrain of action"—institutions without classes for classes without institutions.

Besides those intellectuals who have broken with Marxism (the post-Marxists), there is another group who have attempted to hitch Marxist analysis/concepts/ prescriptions to a variety of non-Marxist and anti-Marxist theoretical frameworks. Purporting to combine neoclassical economic frameworks with Marxism, the self-styled "analytical Marxists" have emptied Marxism of essential theoretical and analytical elements.[42] The common denominator of these hyphenated Marxists is their opposition to revolutionary class politics and efforts to anchor their embrace of liberal-democratic politics and market economics in some sort of normative framework. Hyphenated Marxism is a transitional stopover between classical Marxism and orthodox capitalist political economy. It retains some of the social concerns of the past, repackaged as redistributive justice, while embracing the mechanisms and institutions that undermine it: the price system and the market—divorced from the social relations and the institutions of power through which they operate.

Intellectual untidiness accompanied the juxtaposition of concepts from competing and incompatible systems of thought (and we might add divergent and conflicting class perspectives). The hyphenated Marxists are saddled with the neoclassical reduction of labor to just another "factor of production"—rather than the source of value—and are forced to derive their welfare programs from ethical concerns that have no theoretical status in their economic analysis. By dissociating exploitation from production and redefining it to the sphere of consumption, the hyphenated Marxists have sanctioned capitalist power in order to focus on its distributive functions.[43] But as we see around us today, distribution cannot be dissociated from production: The internationalization and transformation of capital into nonproductive activity undermines the sites and basis for "redistributive politics." Moreover, increasing competitive pressures inherent to the marketplace have turned almost all "distributive liberals and social democrats" into supply-side export promoters.

The abstract individualism—or what C. Wright Mills called abstract empiricism[44]—that characterizes the hyphenated Marxism dissolves social structures and the social divisions of labor around which the real world economy and society are organized into *unreal* "individual" entities which are imputed "choices," "preferences," and "identities" as if there were not preexisting systems of power that determined them.

The Changing Intellectual Pivot

In the past Latin America possessed—in the best of cases—what Gramsci called "organic intellectuals," writers, journalists, and political economists linked directly to political and social struggles against imperialism and capitalism. They were integral parts of trade unions, student movements, and revolutionary parties. Che Guevara, Camilo Torres in Colombia, Luis de la Puente in Peru, Miguel Enriquex in Chile, Roberto Santucho in Argentina, and Julio Castro in Uruguay were a few of the hundreds if not thousands of intellectuals who integrated their intellectual work with the social struggles of their countries. And the consequential organic intellectuals established the norms of behavior for the rest of the intellectual class. For thousands of other intellectuals, the political and personal example of the organic intellectuals served as a measuring rod, which they approximated to a greater or lesser degree. There was a continual "internal" struggle between professional opportunism and political commitments, as Latin American intellectuals strove to make existential choices. Today, this struggle hardly exists—it has been resolved and forgotten among the new breed of research-institute-oriented intellectuals. One of the great ironies of our times is that the Latin American institutional intellectuals have made a fetish of Gramsci— citing and distorting his writings to cover their retreat from Marxism and attack on class politics. The problem now is how best to secure the biggest sum of money from the most accessible outside funding agency.

Today the institutionalized intellectuals are in a Foucaultian sense prisoners of their own narrow professional desires. Their links with the external foundations, international bureaucracies, and research centers dominate a vacuous and vicarious internal political life. In the past, the organic intellectuals struggled with a self-sustaining, self-financing intellectual existence. They lived and suffered the economic cycles of their countries. Today the institutional intellectuals live and work in an externally dependent world, sheltered by payments in hard currency and income derived independently of local economic circumstances. The deep internal horizontal linkages between the organic intellectual and oppressed classes contrasts with the vertical linkages between the institutional intellectual and the external funding agencies and, with the advent of civilian regimes, with the local state and regime.

The period extending from the late 1970s into the 1980s witnessed a major transformation of Latin American intellectuals: a shift from Marxism to liberal-democratic politics, from support of movements of popular power to bourgeois parliamentary institutions, from egalitarianism to social mobility, from collectivism to a very spare "welfare state," from antiimperialism to "interdependence." Structurally, Latin America's intellectuals have shifted from being organic intellectuals connected and dependent on popular movements to institutional intellectuals tied to overseas funding agencies and their intellectual agendas.

Three factors accounted for the shift: (1) Military dictatorships smashed the previous ties between intellectuals and mass struggles—killing many of the organic intellectuals and dispersing the rest; (2) European and North American funding agencies provided a haven and/or financial support; and (3) the remaining intellectuals established institutes that flourished on the basis of external funding. As a result of these linkages at the top and the outside, a new type of intelligentsia with a different political agenda emerged.

A direct connection was established between the institutional integration of the displaced Latin American intellectuals into the liberal/social-democratic welfare state and their increasing consumption of post-Marxist intellectual currents. Upon their return to Latin America, these overseas structural and ideological networks became essential ingredients in the further expansion of new institutes. These networks were crucial because the economic conditions within Latin America in the postmilitary period were highly unfavorable.

The dictatorships directly created a new class of "internationally" oriented intellectuals, ostensible critics of the neoliberal economic model, but just as deeply embedded in dependent relations with overseas networks as their adversaries among the export-oriented and financial elites. This new class has a life- and work style that contrasts sharply with that of preceding generations of organic intellectuals.

The first wave of external funding supported critique of the economic model and publicized human rights' violations of the military dictatorships. The second supported the study of new social movements, while the third bankrolled studies of the democratization process and the debt. The literature produced by this new class of intellectuals formed a general pattern: The studies of the dictatorship focused on its politically repressive feature and not on its economic and military ties to Western European and North American elites. State violence was analyzed in terms of human rights' violations, not as expressions of class domination—as part of the class struggle, as class violence. From these studies the political alternatives that emerged were posed as a conflict between liberal democracy and military dictatorship. The deliberate dissociation of the class structure from state power was justified by the notion that the political sphere was "autonomous" from civil society.

Studies of social movements continued in the same fashion. These studies claimed that the social movements were counterposed to class politics, that the class structure from which they emerged was "heterogeneous," and that the struggles of the social movements were far removed from older ideological politics.[45] The political line in regard to social movements was in the first instance that they should separate themselves from the ideological (radical) political parties. Later, with the rise of the liberal electoral parties, the political line shifted and the movements were described as turning (and/or advised to turn) their attention to the "struggle for democracy." The "autonomy of social movements" was promoted when the researchers sought to separate them from the revolutionary left; "participation in broad democratic fronts" became the formula the researchers promoted when liberal electoral politics came to the fore.

The third phase of funding—on democratization—was the most blatantly ideological: International research teams focused on a set of formulas which justified accommodation with local and foreign military and economic elites as the only "possible" viable option, thus freezing the process of transformation to a transaction between conservative civilians and the military.[46]

The overt consequences of economic dependence manifest themselves at the ideological level, setting the political parameters of intellectual discourse. Hence the importance of retaining a semblance of intellectual autonomy to dissimulate the dependence. Critical research on popular participation, grassroots organization, incomes policies, etc., is essential to foster an image of intellectual autonomy, while the dissociation of these conditions from their imperial-class context further enforces the long-term structural linkages to the external benefactors.

For those institutional intellectuals inside the international foundation circuit have a great deal to lose, but not in the way of any profound commitments to the popular struggle to transform the socioeconomic system. Today's institutional intellectuals look with disdain at the previous organic intellectuals—mere "ideologists"—and look upon themselves as Social Scientists. There is, of course, no such distinction between science and ideology. The institutional ideologists are just as ideologically oriented as their predecessors: Their "science" is harnessed to a world of managed conflict, electoral elites, private markets, and social engineering. They are the ideological watchdogs who have banished the politics of antiimperialism to the netherworld of forgotten languages. They have described their own metamorphosis into intellectual functionaries as the culmination of a scientific revolution that transcends vulgar and parochial ideological preoccupations. The posture of objectivity (the necessary methodology for external acceptance) provides the proper distance from which to observe the struggles as objects to be contracted, managed, and governed.

The problem of intellectual engagement is related to the audience to which each is directed: The institutional intellectual writes for and works within the confines of other institutional intellectuals, their overseas patrons, their international conferences. As political ideologues they establish the boundaries with the liberal political class. The organic intellectuals move in the world of the rank-and-file political activists and militants, with a global vision that challenges the boundaries of the bourgeois liberal marketplace. Their work links local struggles in the mines, banks, and factories, as concrete instances of global imperialist domination. They link social discontent to political struggles against a clearly determined class state.

The ascendancy of the institutional intellectuals has banished the key concepts which illuminated popular struggles. Imperialism, socialism, popular power, and class struggle have disappeared down the memory hole: they are unfashionable. In place of these precise formulations, vacuous notions of "popular participation," disembodied "debt problems," and "social contracts" have surfaced in the conceptual apparatus of the institutional intellectuals. The new language codes of the institutional intellectuals have a double function: They provide the ideological watchdogs with the symbolic signals to evict ideological trespassers, and they legitimate in the intellectuals' own eyes their role as caretakers of the hegemonic ideology of the liberal funding centers. Among institutes engaged in ideological diffusion through popular promotion and training, the negative effects of this style of intellectual work is magnified. In their promotional activity among the popular classes, problem-solving is localized and dissociated from any notion of state power and the construction of an alternative class-based vision of a democratic collectivist society—the original and creative project of the organic intellectuals.

The conceptual and linguistic transformation that accompanies the conversion of organic to institutional intellectuals is manifest in several distinct forms. The politics of language is the language of politics: As striking as what is written and published by the institutes is what is absent. In the present period when the major European and North American banks and corporations are engaged in a massive and sustained extraction of economic surplus, there is not a single externally funded research center in Chile, Argentina, Peru, Colombia, or Uruguay elaborating and deepening our understanding of the theory and practice of imperialist exploitation. Instead, we find the language of evasion, the social science of euphemism: The problem is posed as a balance of payment or "debt problem." The institutional intellectuals engage in an ingenuous and clever abstraction of "debt" from class politics and even more from class struggle. From their vantage point there are only disembodied classless "states" which negotiate with other "states:" the institutional intellectuals have created the metaphysics of postpolitics.

In its broadest sense, the ascendancy of the institutional intellectuals and the decline of the organic intellectuals represent a cultural counterrevolution. It is the world of the intellectual as "inside political advisor"—as manager of political conformity or (in their language) of political consensus. For the repentent ex-radical intellectuals (those who converted from a political to an institutional vocation) the essence of politics is bureaucracy. The axis of politics revolves around narrow institutional interests, developing ties with the chieftans of bureaucratic power centers. In this context, the main intellectual concern is the renovation of formalism and legalism and the marginalization of substantive politics.

There is little relationship between the political options of the institutional intellectuals and the reality of Latin America in the 1980s and early 1990s. Under conditions of absolute and sustained socioeconomic regression, of massive popular misery and growing social discontent, the language and conceptual practice of social and political reconciliation lack substance. They do not reflect objective Latin American realities; they mirror the reconciliation of the intellectual with the ideological parameters of overseas funding agencies. The institutional intellectual entrepreneurs not only know how and where to get abundant external funding, but they also know the dangers involved in posing social alternatives anchored in popular power to the existing decaying liberal democracies. Faced with this dilemma, the most convenient posture to adopt involves claiming that the postdictatorial situation is very difficult and complex—"indeterminant"—and that there are no easy alternatives. This posture allows the institutional intellectuals to continue to receive outside grants while passing over the less-attractive features and policies of their colleagues in the state.

Indeterminacy has become a recurring notion in the "discourses" of the retreating intellectuals. The term itself has been used in several different and contradictory senses. Logically, it calls into question the entire logic of any explanatory model—since all prior assumptions and deductions are subject to the same uncertainty and contingency, leaving us with a universe of facts in constant flux and completely arbitary deductions. This is particularly amusing because some of the exponents of uncertainty have made great efforts to ground their analysis in mathematical models and survey research. It is a peculiar match of translogical mysticism and vulger empiricism.

The ex-leftist intellectuals, having rejected a class analysis of the state and, recognizing the fragility of their regime-focused analytical approach, buy intellectual insurance in case of the bankruptcy of the democratic enterprise by introducing the notion of uncertainty: uncertainty of the transition to democracy based on pacts with the military; uncertainty about the viability of social compromises of workers under capitalism.[47] In place of an analysis of the nonelectoral power centers that shape the parameters of capitalist electoral systems, one finds outcomes contingent on "accidents" and "unpredictability." Uncertainty is largely an artifact of the apostates opting for a method which focuses on the role of individual political choices and calculations in place of the structural/class/institutional interests in shaping the direction and substance of political change. The rules and necessities of capitalist reproduction are clearly not in flux and subject to uncertainty, whatever the vagaries of the marketplace. Nor is the role of the state in upholding those rules—we have yet to find one capitalist state in over 200 years that was uncertain and "indeterminate" about its relationship to capital.

Political and productive systems and class structures are not the sum of individuals or their decisions—even if we assume for a second that all "individual preferences" count the same. (Both the rich and the poor can choose to sleep on the grates of New York City, but only the poor do.) Reality is the reverse of the Robinson Crusoe method: Shifts in individual choices and political calculations reflect the sustained and continuing pressures emanating from stable socioeconomic configurations.[48] The method of focusing on individual decision-making fails to explain the universe in which those decisions are made. By relegating structures and classes into limbo and focusing on the routines of "politics," they build the existing universe of power into their assumptions without explicating the class constraints and determinants in shaping political agendas.

By ignoring long-term, large-scale interests and focusing on idiosyncratic contingencies, the ex-leftists undermine any theoretical position or coherent methodological perspective for understanding political transitions. Disembodied "decision-makers"—the ghosts of power—shape the democratic process without having to confront regional hegemonic powers, international banks, autocratic military chieftains, or local speculators. As one team of writers puts it: "The short-term political calculations we stress here cannot be deduced from or imputed to such structures [macrostructural factors] except perhaps in an act of misguided faith."[49] The big issues of democracy are analyzed best by studying decisions yesterday, today, and maybe tomorrow; the rest is religion, according to this variant of post-Marxism. Clearly, the uncertainty of the authors about the stability of their democracy, the durability of class compromises, and the viability of neoclassical equilibrium models is the tribute that vice pays to virtue. Lurking behind, above, and below are the destabilizing effects of class struggle in its various manifestations: class polarization, interimperial rivalries, ruling-class reversion to dictatorial rulership, etc. But once classes are dismissed and class interests are reduced to the status of an artifact of subjective individual preference, how do you bring the class struggle back into the explanatory model except as a product of every available contingency?

Democracy: With or Without Adjectives

One of the major themes of many of the retreating intellectuals, North and South, is democracy and the process of "democratization," particularly as it unfolded in many parts of the Third World. A good example is the discussion found in the influential multivolume series edited by O'Donnell et. al.—*Transitions from Authoritarianism Rule* (one volume of which is devoted to Latin America). The theoretical and conceptual arguments found in these volumes sum up most of the deficiencies of the current debate. There are at least six major problems with their discussion. The writers (1) conflate the concepts and analyses of state and regime; (2) exaggerate procedural political changes relating to regime behavior and underestimate the importance of authoritarian institutional continuities and the boundaries and rules they impose on the former; (3) ignore the convergence between electoral regimes and the authoritarian state structure; (4) obscure regime and class linkages, their impact on socioeconomic policies, and the subsequent negative impact this has on political freedom for nonelite groups; (5) ignore the centrality of state-class relations in shaping electoral-regime agendas and prospects for democracy through the evasive notion of indeterminancy—which reduces their discussion to little more than a journalistic commentary on political personalities, rules, and events; and (6) simplify the political process by dichotomizing it into the categories of authoritarian and democratic on the basis of formal political procedures, ignoring the complex interplay between repressive practices and structures and electoral rules.

Though it has become fashionable to write about the State, most of the writing is based on a great deal of confusion concerning essential concepts. The state refers to the *permanent* institutions of *government* and the concomitant *ensemble of class relations* which have been embedded in these same institutions. The permanent institutions include those which exercise a *monopoly over the means of coercion* (army, police, judiciary), as well as those that control the *economic levers* of the accumulation process. The "government" refers to those political officials that occupy the *executive* and *legislative* positions and are subject to renewal or replacement. There are various types of government classified along several dimensions. For example, there are civilian or military regimes and elected or self-appointed regimes.

In analyzing the process of political change it is important to recognize the different levels at which transformation takes place in order to determine the scope and direction of policy as well as to be able to adequately characterize the process. For example, in Latin America during the 1980s a number of political changes took place that O'Donnell et al. dubbed a "democratization" process which produced "democratic states." In terms of our conceptual distinctions, however, these political changes have not in the least changed the nature of the *state* but rather have led to changes at the level of *government* or *regime*. The military, police, and judicial officials in the overwhelming majority of cases have remained in place, with the same controls over "security," with the same values and ideologies, and without having been brought to justice for their terrorist behavior. Moreover the same class linkages that defined the state before the political changes continue under the new regimes. The continuities of the basic *state structures* define the *essential nature* of the political system: the *boundaries* and *instrumentalities of social action*. The new political regime exercises its prerogatives—its executive and legislative initiatives—within the framework established by the preexisting configuration of power. This means that any characterization of the process of political change and the political configuration must *include both the continuities of the state* as well as the *changes at the level of the regime*. Moreover, since the state is prior and more basic than the regime in the functioning of the social system, it is the nature of the state which is the "noun" and the regime which is the "adjective" in characterizing the political configuration. For example, in the case of Guatemala the continuities in the state apparatus—organizationally and ideologically intact from the period of terrorist rulership—provide the key to defining the political system, while the change from an appointed military to an elected civilian regime in 1985 provided the modification. Hence the Guatemalan political system could be referred to as an elected-civilian police state. For O'Donnell et al. to discuss democracy without adjectives conflates the different levels of analysis and oversimplifies the state/regime relation.

The accommodation between elected-civilian regimes and the terrorist-military state is based upon converging socioeconomic projects—not circumstances "forced" upon reluctant reform-minded civilians (O'Donnell et al). The civilian regimes in both Argentina and Uruguay elaborated development strategies that were essentially directed toward *integrating the export-oriented growth projects of their predecessors to more "rational management" of the domestic economy and the more effective mobilization of outside economic resources*. Since this economic model was built on supply-side incentives and premised on creating a favorable climate for external funding, it contained the same restrictive domestic income policies that characterized the behavior of the military rulers. Upon taking office the civilians were very aware that their popular "political capital" based on their displacement of the terrorist-military regime would sooner or later begin to dissipate. *In anticipation* of popular protest and in defense of their economic strategy, *the elected-civilian regimes choose to retain their ties to the existing state apparatus.* The *socioeconomic continuities* serve to *bridge the political differences* between the military and civilian, particularly as the former retained the state while the latter were relegated to managing the regime.

The *composition, orientation, and class relations of the state shape the long-term large-scale policies of a political system.* That is why Washington is willing to accept changes in regime (from military to civilian) in order *to preserve the continuity of the state*; conversely, and for the same reason, Washington is adamant in opposing political changes that dismantle the existing state, particularly when the new state is organized to sustain a regime with a nationalist and socialist development project (Cuba, Nicaragua). Washington is willing to sacrifice authoritarian clients such as Marcos, Duvalier, and the violent military rulers in El Salvador and Guatemala, and accept civilians, as long as it can preserve the state apparatus.

There is no question then of discussing electoral-civilian or other kinds of political regimes without referring to the state/class relations upon which they depend. Regimes cannot defend themselves or promote the accumulation process when they act contrary to state interests. This is understood by incoming civilian politicians who proceed to fashion development agendas and political relations adapted to these institutional realities. In many cases the need to "adapt" is very minimal since the civilians *share a common perspective* with the *state elites.* This agreement over policy between the regime and state is obscured by the ideologues of the civilian regime like O'Donnell et al., who promote the notion of "democracy without adjectives"—who attempt to narrow the discussion of the political system to regime changes and the accompanying electoral procedures, without examining the larger historical/structural configuration within which those changes take place.

A major problem in this neoliberal discourse is the marked tendency to dichotomize the political process in terms of the categories of authoritarian and democratic. At several levels this analysis is flawed. First is the fact that the authoritarians are active negotiators and facilitators of the transition. Second, the authoritarians continue to exercise power and control over the instruments of violence. Third, there are issue areas (punishment of military human violators, debt obligations, reform) which are off-limits to the civilian regime. Fourth, in some cases human rights' abuses persist, and even worsen, under the civilian regimes—witness the *massive increases* in killings, torture, and disappearances in Peru under Belaunde and El Salvador under Duarte during the 1980s. Alternately, political terror has become more selective; in Brazil under Sarney, peasant advocates of agrarian reform were prime targets; in Cerezo's Guatemala, political killings at the hands of the armed forces and its death-squad allies became commonplace. The continuation of repressive institutions, policies, and practices expresses the *interpenetration* of electoral-civilian regimes and authoritarian institutions, not their mutual opposition as O'Donnell et al. argue.

Contemporary Latin American history provides numerous examples of elected-civilian regimes presiding over the mass slaughter of civilian noncombatants, in the process refuting the facile equation of these regimes with "democracy" and "democratization"—and concomitant respect for elementary human rights (the security of one's physical state). The tens of thousands of civilian deaths in El Salvador and Peru over the past decade of electoral rule constitute but the *most recent* testimony to the gap between electoral processes and the elementary ingredients of citizenship.

The changes in political regimes have taken place almost totally *divorced* from any profound changes in the totality of society, which O'Donnell et al. argue are necessary and realistic to stabilize democracy.[50] The restructuring and reorganization of society and economy which were completed by the military have become the point of departure for the new civilian regimes and for the elaboration of their socioeconomic policies. In fact, the elected rulers have assumed the burden of securing financial assistance which was unavailable to the military regime to finance the "modernization" of the elitist development model. Moreover, faced with the broad societal delegitimation of the military the civilian regime has assumed the task of absolving the military of all responsibility for unprecedented levels of criminal behavior through quasi- or open amnesties.

What O'Donnell et al. describe as the "democratization process" has the dual character of *reconsolidating authoritarian state power*—both the military institution and accumulation model—while *conceding political space for individual expression* and *limited social mobilization*. The *contradictory* nature of this conjunctural process creates the basis for *deepening the alienation* of those majoritarian social movements which conceived of *democratization* as a *process in which regime transitions would be accompanied by profound change* in the *state apparatus and the accumulation model*. Accepting an electoral system based on the elite export model, O'Donnell et al. attack the class content and program of the labor unions and Left parties, viewing them as destabilizing and lacking in realism. By removing class conflict from politics and obfuscating the role of political structures as apparatuses of bourgeois domination, they fashion an ideology to legitimate the new amalgam of authoritarian state and civilian liberal regime.

The neoliberal concepts of politics propagated by O'Donnell et al.—the focus on the epiphenomena of narrow electoral interests, personalities, and partisan party concerns—emerge in a *transitional period*: in the *aftermath* of the *military terror* and at the *beginning of the revival of mass social movements*. The new civilian regimes capitalize on the temporary mutual impotence: the bourgeois military can no longer directly rule; the mass movements cannot yet project their own political program. In this transitional context, neoliberal theorists delve deeply and ponder seriously about the "durability of democratic institutions," the "intrinsic value of democratic freedom," the "autonomy of the individual." Meanwhile their colleagues in the civilian regime promote "democracy without adjectives" by imposing class-selective austerity programs to pay foreign bankers, promote multinationals to "modernize" the economy, and promulgate amnesties to absolve their military cohabitators of terrorist crimes. The workers and peasants—who fortunately do not read the texts about classless democracy, but feel the painful class effects of their policies—increasingly resort to class action: general strikes in Argentina; permanent confrontation in Brazil and Uruguay; spreading popular insurgency in the Peruvian countryside.

With the reemergence of class politics and the militarization of political life, the proponents of neoliberal doctrines of democracy can be expected to retreat further toward ahistorical notions of political "cycles." What is clear is that the debate that is taking place goes far beyond the confines of academia: today for the Left to be held hostage to a claim of democracy built on the twin pillars of the authoritarian state and supply-side economics is for it to abdicate its role in the emerging class struggles.

Throughout Latin America, powerful mass extraparliamentary sociopolitical movements have emerged as the central axis to any democratization process and beyond, to be prominent actors in the redefinition of the relationship between state and society. The movements have created through their action a new political experience which shapes a new tradition of political practice, one profoundly alien to the postmodernist discourse. We are not in a period of the end of ideology, but in an age of ideology linked to direct popular participation. Class politics has not been replaced by "modernization." It has been reinvigorated and found new sites for struggle, new forms of organization. The practical consequences of the political discourse of the postmodern ideologues have been catastrophic for the populace: The "social contract" formula has allowed liberal electoral regimes to subordinate labor to regressive neoliberal economic strategies (wage freezes, social welfare, cutbacks, price rises, etc.). As a result movement confidence in regime commitments to "equal sacrifice to consolidate democracy" have ebbed and flowed.

In Latin America, the efforts by postmodernist ideologues to patch together a new synthesis of liberalism and democratic socialism on the basis of neoclassical economics, electoral processes, and vague references to the positive role of civil society have come apart as the market has polarized "civil society." Confrontations have occurred between the electoral political class, playing according to the capitalist-democratic rules of the game, and the social movements, playing according to the needs of their impoverished constituents. The deep contradictions between the concentration and centralization of financial and export capital on the one hand, and the declining incomes and increasing precariousness of the working class on the other, have exploded the consensual politics that these ideologues postulated as the realist conception of democratic consolidation and popular advance. They also bear considerable responsibility for the growing disenchantment with the electoral regimes, having defended the subordination of electoral processes to political pacts with the departing military, accepted the debt obligations and the neoliberal export model as the new realism, and thus provoked the deep socioeconomic fissures that agitate Latin American society from bottom to top.

Eastern Europe: Capitalism for the Third World

Today the most striking characteristic of Eastern European and Soviet intellectuals is the *inversion* of their political formulas and the *continuity* of their logic of reasoning. In the past they saw the inevitability of capitalist collapse; today they posit its continuing success. Yesterday they saw socialism resulting from the exhaustion of technicomaterial development under capitalism; today they describe capitalist stability based on the continuity of technical progress. In the past, they described the absolute pauperization of the working class; today they see continuing improvements in living standards. Yesterday they promoted Soviet collectivism as the model for Third World development, based on the power of the Socialist bloc; today they speak of the development of capitalist relations in new states as historically progressive. The same mechanical deductive logic from . . . questionable premises. What makes the Soviet intellectuals' defense of capitalism in the Third World so peculiar is that it occurs at the worst possible moment: with mass hunger in sub-Sahara Africa, with a decade of lost development and mounting debt burdens in Latin America, and with increasing class warfare in some of the newly industrializing countries.

These celebrants of capitalism retain some of their polemical spleen from their Stalinist past—It's either capitalism or barbarism: "Attempts to prevent it (capitalism) where there is no alternative [as in underdeveloped countries] can merely prolong the existing backwardness. Thus the job of the proletarian is to organize, to defend the freedom of the proletarian to struggle, which does not retard the development of capitalism, but accelerates it."[51] This strange new Soviet version of the class struggle could be embroidered on the banners of Thatcher, Reagan, and the International Monetary Fund. It is a short step from the general praise of the magical powers of the marketplace to eulogies for the multinational corporations which might embarrass Lee Iaccoca: "The relatively rapid growth of capitalism in the Third World over the past two-odd decades . . . has been expedited by the economically more powerful and dynamic capitalist system . . . above all, with the emergence of transnational companies as an effective instrument for promoting capitalism in the Third World."[52] The pillage of nature by the multinationals, the mass poverty, and the debt crisis induced by the banks are passed over today in the same glib fashion that in the past Soviet ideologues glossed over the agrarian crisis and the mismanagement that characterized mindless Stalinist collectivism. The failure to recognize internal differentiation within the Third World, the misleading generalizations from aggregate growth data, the incapacity to look at long-term and now-visible adverse consequences of externally funded growth spell trouble not only for Moscow's relations with the Third World, but for all the newly independent states that previously constituted the Soviet Union. The prospects for growth, equity, and democracy are dim indeed if the latter begin to operate under the assumption that dependence on external investors will dynamize their societies.

The doctrinaire liberalism that has taken hold among Soviet intellectuals extends to their discussion of the relationship between capitalism and democracy: private capitalism's progressive role goes beyond providing material prerequisites for socialism. According to one writer, it is during this phase of capitalist development in the Third World that "the basis for bourgeois democracy is laid and a civilian [*sic*] society formed."[53] These scientific observations from the new Soviet intelligentsia must come as revelations to the workers and intellectuals who have suffered (1) fifteen years of dictatorship under the most market-oriented capitalist regime in Chilean history, (2) thirty years of markets and machine guns in South Korea, or (3) forty years of one-party rule in Taiwan. While it is all to the good that Soviet intellectuals revise their traditional ideas on the transition to socialism, their method and theories reflect the same global impressionism and incapacity to deal with autonomous class politics. All the revisionists have done is substituted one regional power bloc for another. The social relations of production—the complex processes of uneven development with a variety of different levels and types of class struggle—get washed out: Stalinist dogma is replaced by liberal dogma.

Western Europe: Marxism for the Ruling Class

From enfant terrible of the revolutionary Left to mainstream policy coach to ruling-class Europe, Andre Gunder Frank is the epitome of the apostate as political realist. With the publication of *The European Challenge* in 1983, Gunder Frank totally abandoned any pretense of class politics and became a publicist for an independent, unified capitalist Europe—as an alternative to U.S. imperialism. His proposals are, of course, unoriginal, having been put forth almost thirty years earlier by Jean Monnet, the father of the European Economic Community. Paradoxically, his defense of a united European capitalism occurs precisely at a time when the latter is increasingly challenging a declining U.S. empire and a rising Japanese imperialism. More particularly, Frank has little or nothing to say about how a unified European capitalism, assuredly under German hegemony, can continue its current dynamic push in the world economy without taking on the characteristics of a revitalized imperial center. Instead, European imperialism is replaced by another Frankism: "the Europeanization of Europe."[54] In Frank's new role as policy coach for (nonclass-defined nonimperial) Europe, the West's increasing domination of Eastern Europe is discussed as "economic and perhaps political cooperation necessary throughout Eastern Europe and the Soviet Union to minimize their own domestic social and political costs of restructuring and transition."[55] This notion of "economic cooperation" between the two Europes leaves out the imperial structures and mechanisms that are exploiting Poland, Hungary, and Yugoslavia through interest payments and unequal exchange. Within Frank's "Europe," he opts for the West German imperial variant over the French, apparently preferring hegemony based on market power over the French nuclear-military version. Frank, having abandoned—at least in relation to Europe—his metropolitan-satellite analysis now argues in the context of interimperial rivalries for a "European policy of its own." Hence, his support for Western European integration and the incorporation of Eastern Europe is largely directed to "strengthen" European imperialism against its competitors.

There are in Frank's current embrace of a regional power, and in his globalist reasoning, similarities to his conception of the contradictions in his earlier radical period. In both instances, he ignores social relations of production and the class basis of exploitation in favor of looking at regions. In the past, he focused on center and periphery, metropole and satellite, and the extraction of "surplus"; in the present, he describes world blocs of capital. The subsuming of class differences in his earlier radical dependency analysis resurfaces in his mainstream imperial "cooperative" framework of the present. It is not surprising that Frank, who now visualizes Europe as an alternative and not as a revived imperial power, looks with favor at those measures taken by the former Communist countries that open them up to European imperial penetration. He welcomes the transition to capitalism and democracy under Deng Xiaoping with the following rather mindless optimism: "China already [*sic*] made enormous strides in the same economic and political reform direction since 1978. Deng Xiaoping managed to install a new reformist leadership at the 1987 party congress."[56] Frank's vision of a demilitarized, unified capitalist Europe, strengthened against the United States and Japan, only leaves out the millions of "European" workers exploited and unemployed, the increasing subordination of the weaker economies to the stronger, and the "new" Europe as a prime exploiter of the Third World. By focusing exclusively on U.S. imperialism, he becomes a useful polemicist for imperialism in his own front yard.

Regis Debray set out earlier than Frank in the same direction and seems to have proceeded further. From his earlier writings supporting guerrilla movements in Latin America, he has become a passionate advocate of the progressive independent French Bomb. Unlike Frank's Eurocentric chauvinism, Debray has a narrower conception of politics—building nationalism in one country. An elegant enterprise on shaky foundations, particularly as the internationalization of capital undermines that particular discourse.

Debray argues that world politics revolves around the central powers—the Third World is a marginal area. And within this big-power universe, Debray is concerned with establishing France's ideological and political identity and place:

a version of a counterrevolution within the counterrevolution. Once again, however, there are certain methological and conceptual similarities between the past and the present. There is the same voluntarist ideological emphasis: in the past, the armed guerrilla foco ignites the masses through will to action; in the present, the same subjective projection of France's independent nuclear force creates its world standing. In both instances, historical and objective, structural conditions are given short shrift. Debray's writings past and present revolve around his attachment to "men of power": Castro in the 1960s, Allende in the 1970s, Mitterand in the 1980s.

Politics is made by individuals, not by classes; ideology and military force shape power, not economic and technical resources. Debray's radical socialist and conservative nationalist phases thus represent two sides of the same elitist conception of politics: the marginalization of autonomous self-organized working class forces and the central importance of ideologically correct heroic leaders. By ignoring the self-organized sociopolitical movements and the centrality of the social relations of exploitation, by focusing on interstate relations (Frank) and elite vanguards (Debray), it is an easy transition to embrace contemporary configurations of bourgeois state power.

Conclusion

The world-wide retreat of the intellectuals is intimately related to the declining power of the working-class movement and the rising power of capital—in the cultural as well as economic sphere. Intellectuals are very sensitive to changes in power. Intellectual shifts between the 1960s and 1980s reflect the changes in the relationship of power. The fundamental paradox of our time, however, is that the tilts in power are not accompanied by the consolidation and expansion of capitalist economic and social systems: the fragility of Western economies, the disintegration of the inner cities, the volatility of the financial markets, the polarization of classes and regions of the world economy, the destruction of the environment all speak to the failure of capitalism to solve any of the basic problems posed by Marxism.

The abandonment of Marxism and the intellectual adaptation to new sources of power thus reveal the profound separation of intellectual "discourse" from historical realities. The escape into the realm of subjectivity and formalism is one aspect of the problem. The structural factor is the deep structural integration of intellectuals into the mainstream academic foundation/professional publication networks that serve as the cultural bridge to established power.

If the retreat of the intellectual is largely a product of shifts in power and if the economic foundations of that power are indeed fragile, we can expect a new cycle of radicalization with the next economic crises and resurgence of popular power. In the East, tensions are already manifest between the workers of Poland and Hungary and the market-oriented liberal intellegentsia. In Latin America, the heyday of post-Marxist adjectiveless democrats has already passed and we enter a period without intellectual political hegemony: of resurgent militarism, guerrilla Maoism, electoral/trade-union–based Marxism, and novel conceptions of decentralized community-based political economy. In North America and Europe, the recent campaigns of the mass media to pronounce the definitive end of socialism and triumph of capitalism may be short-lived as economic recession, urban disintegration, and financial fragility converge with declining incomes toward a major social crisis. If and when an alternative social movement of working people emerges, it is likely that new critical intellectual currents will once again rethink Marxist ideas.

Notes

1. See, for example, Ernesto Laclau and Chantal Mouffe, *Hegemony and Socialist Strategy* (London: Verso, 1985). If one can cut through the gibberish ("the infinite intertextuality of emancipatory discourses in which the plurality of the social takes place"), Laclau's emphasis on "collective wills," amorphous social groupings, and disembodied democracy is a throwback to his earlier Peronist intellectual formation. In both instances, crude national/populist formulations paper over antagonistic class interests.

2. John Roemer, *A General Theory of Exploitation and Class* (Cambridge: Harvard University Press, 1982); John Elster, *An Introduction to Marx* (Cambridge: Cambridge University Press, 1986); John Roemer, *Analytical Marxism* (Cambridge: Cambridge University Press, 1986); Adam Przeworski, "Marxism and Rational Choice," *Politics and Society*, Vol. 14, No. 4, 1985, pp. 379–410; Adam Przeworski, "Class Production and Politics: A Reply to Burawoy," *Socialist Review*, Vol. 19, No. 2, April–June 1989, pp. 87–111; Guillermo O'Donnell, et al., *Transitions From Authoritarian Rule*, Vol. 1–4 (Baltimore: Johns Hopkins University Press, 1986).

3. On state autonomy, see Theda Skocpol, *States and Social Revolution* (Cambridge: Cambridge University Press, 1979). On the autonomous role of "discourses," see Laclau and Mouffe, *Hegemony and Socialist Strategy*. For the distributionist argument, see Roemer, *A General Theory of Exploitation and Class*.

4. The argument is spelled out in greater detail in James Petras, "The World Market: Battleground for the 1990's," *Journal of Contemporary Asia*, Vol. 20, No. 2 1990, pp. 145–176.

5. Barry Bluestone and Bennett Harrison, *The Great U-Turn* (New York: Basic Books, 1988).

6. Ibid.

7. See Przeworski, "Class, Production and Politics: A Reply to Burawoy," pp. 87–111.

8. Ibid.

9. See *The General Council of the First International: Minutes*, 2 vol., 1864–1866, 1866–1868 (Moscow: Progress Publishers, 1974).

10. Laclau's attack on what he calls the class reductionism of Marxism is a blatant illustration of the distortions and caricatures of the complex analysis of class, ideology, and political action found in the texts and practices of the classical Marxists. One wonders if Laclau, Przeworski, et al. could possibly have read Trotsky's *History of the Russion Revolution* or *1905*, or Lenin's *The Development of Capitalism in Russia*, before they began to engage in the reductionist "labeling" game.

11. Polemical and uninformed critiques of Lenin's political theory can be found in the U.S. journal *Socialist Review*, which has, ironically, uncritically accepted the Stalinist version dubbed "Leninism" as the real thing. What is surprising is the narrow scope of the intellectual debates in this "democratic socialist" publication.

12. See Hal Draper, *Marx's Theory of Revolution* (New York: Monthly Review Press, 1976).

13. See Samuel Bowles and Herbert Gintis, *Democracy and Capitalism: Property, Community and the Contradictions of Modern Social Thought* (New York: Basic Books, 1986); Martin Carnoy, *State and Political Theory* (Princeton: Princeton University Press, 1984); Derek Shearer, *Economic Democracy: The Challenge of the 1980's* (White Plains: M.E. Sharpe, 1980) and *A New Social Contract: The Economy and Government after Reagan* (New York: Harper and Row, 1983).

14. Skocpol deepens and multiplies the confusion on the state/regime distinction in "Bringing the State Back In: Strategies of Analysis in Current Research," in Peter B. Evans et al., eds., *Bringing the State Back In* (New York: Cambridge University Press, 1987), pp. 3–43.

15. Skocpol, *States and Social Revolutions*; O'Donnell et al., *Transitions From Authoritarian Rule*.

16. See Elster, *An Introduction to Marx*; Roemer, *A General Theory of Exploitation and Class*.

17. An excellent discussion of the centrality of social relations of production is found in Kim Moody, *An Injury to All* (London: Verso, 1989).

18. Laclau and Mouffe, *Hegemony and Socialist Strategy*.

19. The practitioners of the "analytical Marxist" approach are the object of this critique.

20. Leon Trotsky, *In Defense of Marxism* (New York: Pathfinder Press, 1990).

21. Alan Wald, *New York Intellectuals* (Chapel Hill: University of North Carolina Press, 1987).

22. Isaac Deutscher, *Russia in Transition* (New York: Hamish Hamilton, 1957), pp. 223–236.

23. James Petras, "Berkeley and the New Conservative Backlash," *New Left Review*, No. 31, May–June 1965, pp. 58–64.

24. For an excellent critique of the retreat from political economy to language studies,

see Perry Anderson, *Considerations on Western Marxism* (London: New Left Books, 1976).

25. See John Tagliabue, "Polish Cabinet Nominees Pledge Market Economy," *New York Times*, September 9 1989, p. 3.

26. For a clear statement of the subordination of the trade unions to the neoliberal party-state in Spain see the interview with Ludolfo Parmio, "Ni Los Sindicatos ni Los Partidos Seran Como Antes," *La Ciudad Futura*, No. 6, August 1987, pp. 30–31. On the retreat of Spanish intellectuals, see "El PCE Convertido en Cantero de Cuadros para El Poder Socialista," *El Independiente*, August 19, 1986, p. 7.

27. See Juan Carlos Portantiero, "Gramsci en clave latinoamericana," and Jose Arico, "Gramsci y El Jacobinismo Argentino," in *La Ciudad Futura*.

28. O'Donnell et al., *Transitions from Authoritarian Rule*.

29. Samuel Bowles et al., *Beyond the Wasteland: A Democratic Alternative to Economic Decline* (Garden City: Anchor/Doubleday, 1983).

30. Roemer, *Analytical Marxism*.

31. Skocpol, *States and Social Revolutions*. For a fine, critical analysis, see Steven Vieux, "Containing the Class Struggle: Skocpol on Revolution," *Studies in Political Economy*, No. 27, Autumn 1988, pp. 87–111.

32. Przeworski, "Class, Production and Politics: A Reply to Burawoy," pp. 87–111.

33. See Moody, *An Injury to All*.

34. See Perry Anderson's discussion of Bobbio, "The Affinities of Norberto Bobbio," *New Left Review*, No. 70, July/August 1988, pp. 3–36, for a fine critical analysis of this position.

35. Roemer, *Analytical Marxism*.

36. It is interesting to compare David Truman's "interest group" conception of politics, with its multiple determinations and fragmentation of class into social grouping, with Przeworski's conception of electoral coalition politics and subclass theorizing. See David Truman, *The Governmental Process, Political Interests and Public Opinion* (New York: Alfred Knopf, 1951).

37. Compare Nelson Polsby's behavioral conception of interest in his *Community Power and Political Theory: A Future Look at Problems of Inference and Evidence* (New Haven: Yale University Press, 1980) with Przeworski's subjective imputation of class in his *Capitalism and Social Democracy* (Cambridge: Cambridge University Press, 1985), p. 66.

38. Przeworski, "Class, Production and Politics: A Reply to Burawoy," pp. 87–111. Buroway, who otherwise has raised some important criticisms of the analytical school, shares in some of the same theoretical pitfalls as his erstwhile adversaries. He underestimates the role of force in establishing the parameters for consent and the class nature of the state in establishing the rules in which "hegemonic" processes function, and betrays a narrow-focus empiricism in conceptualizing the labor/capital relation as a nonzero sum, thus undercutting his own theoretical basis for understanding class conflict located in production. See Michael Burawoy, "Marxism without

Micro-Foundations," *Socialist Review*, Vol. 19, No. 2, April–June 1989, pp. 53–86.

39. See Portantiero, "Gramsci en Clave Latinoamericana," and Arico, "Gramsci y El Jacobinismo Argentino."

40. See Antonio Gramsci, *Selections from Political Writings 1910–1920* (New York: International Publishers, 1977); see especially part II, "L'Ordine Nuovo and the Factory Councils," pp. 65–126.

41. Perry Anderson, "The Antinomies of Antonio Gramsci," in *New Left Review* No. 100, November 1976–January 1977 pp. 5–80. Also see Norman Geras, *Literature of Revolution* (London: Verso, 1986); and Ellen Wood, *The Retreat from Class* (London: Verso, 1986).

42. See Michael Liebovitz, "Is Analytical Marxism Marxism," *Science and Society*, Vol. 52, No. 2, Summer 1985, pp. 191–214.

43. Ibid.

44. C. Wright Mills, *The Sociological Imagination* (New York: Grove Press, 1961).

45. Eugenio Tironi, "Marginalidad, Movimientos Sociales y Democracia," *Proposici-ónes*, No. 14, pp. 9–23; Elizabeth Jelin, "Los ausentes: Movimientos Sociales y Participación Democrática Restringida," in Fernando Calderon and Marco dos Santos, *Los Conflictos por la Constitución de un Nuevo Orden* (Buenos Aires: Clacso, 1987).

46. See O'Donnell et al., *Transitions from Authoritarian Rule*.

47. Ibid.

48. For an excellent critique of the Crusoian metaphor, see Steve Hymer, "Robinson Crusoe and the Secret of Primitive Accumulation," *Monthly Review*, Vol. 23, No. 4, Sept. 1971, pp. 11–36.

49. O'Donnell et al., *Transitions from Authoritarian Rule: Tentative Conclusions about Uncertain Democracies*, Vol. 4, p. 5.

50. See Arthur McEwan's critique of O'Donnell in "Transitions from Authoritarian Rule," *Latin American Perspectives*, Vol. 15, No. 3, Summer 1988, pp. 115–130.

51. Typical of the new Soviet thinking is Dr. Alexici Kiva, who heads the Sector of the Working Class and Communist Movement at the U.S.S.R. Academy of Sciences, Institute of Oriental Studies. The quotes are drawn from his influential article, "Developing Countries, Socialism, Capitalism," *International Affairs*, March 1989, p. 61.

52. Ibid., p. 62.

53. Ibid., p. 63.

54. Andre Gunder Frank, "World Debt, the European Challenge and 1992," *Economic and Political Weekly*, April 29, 1989, p. 916.

55. Ibid., p. 916.

56. Ibid., p. 915. One month after Frank's article hailing Deng's great accomplishments was published, the government was butchering thousands in the streets of Beijing.

Conclusion

8

Democratic Regimes, Terrorist States, and Western Political Amnesia in Latin America

Introduction

A great gap has developed between the West's moral concerns for human rights in Latin America during the 1970s and its indifference to everyday violations in the 1980s and 1990s. The victims have disappeared from the consciousness of U.S. and European political leaders and their publics as if time erases the nature and existence of crime. What accounts for this political amnesia? The dead have not been resurrected; the state criminals are known; their crimes have been documented. In Latin America exhaustive investigations and detailed reports have been published . . . and nothing has happened.

The disappearance of moral indignation is due, in large part, to the emergence of civilian electoral regimes in Latin America embedded in authoritarian state structures. In the eyes of Western politicians, the existence of these electoral regimes has served as an alibi, a pretext to overlook past and present human rights' violations, political disappearances, yesterday, today, and tomorrow. They have joined with the elites in Latin America in imposing and then celebrating "reconciliation" between victims and executioners—as if the issue of justice can be forgotten and viable democracies can be constituted on the mass anonymous graves of the victims.

Political amnesia and the celebration of "reconciliation" is not only morally repugnant but creates conditions for the destabilization of democracy and the return of authoritarian politics—whether of the military or civilian variety. The immunity granted the military and police means that they feel free to repeat their crimes without fear of retribution. But judgment and condemnation of past crimes will put them on notice that future violations of human rights will be punished, thus acting as a deterrent, protecting democracy against its enemies.

Today Western complicity in the opportunist cohabitation of electoralists and the military may facilitate elections in the short run, but in the near future, particularly given the deepening socioeconomic crises, it is likely that forces within the authoritarian state will once again seize power and assault civil society.

To understand why the politics of "reconciliation" between electoralists and the military in Latin America undermine democracy it is important to recover the recent past and subject it to critical analysis. Several key issues need to be discussed: (1) the political context of original crimes perpetrated by the state in the 1960s and 1970s—who were the targets and what were the political consequences, particularly for civil society? (2) the nature of the transition from military dictatorship to civilian/military cohabitation, and the role of the laws granting immunity and amnesty to the repressive authorities; and (3) the continuities of economic policy and state structures under the civilian regimes, and the consequent reemergence of state terrorism under the electoral facade. Examining these issues provides important insights into the origins of the moral and political crises that affect both the Western and Latin American political conscience.

From State Terror to Civilian/Military Electoral Pacts

During the 1950s and 1960s civic organizations, social movements, neighborhood organizations, peasant and trade unions, and ethnic and gender associations flourished throughout Latin America. A powerful network of popular democratic associations emerged in civil society, even as, at the national level, regimes alternated between electoral and military authoritarian elites. In the latter half of the 1960s and 1970s these democratic movements began to coalesce and challenge the elite political class and their military guardians for control over the public sphere. As the conflict between the free associations in civil society and the traditional capitalist state deepened, the military intervened. The unprecedented levels of state terror unleashed by the neoliberal military regimes were directly related to the scope and breadth of the social movements: The deeper and more extensive these movements were in civil society, the more extended and savage was the state repression. The objective of the mass torture and disappearances was to disarticulate the movements and their activist leaderships. The purpose of the terror was to destroy the theory and practice of building democracy from the bottom up, from civil society to the state.

The struggle against immunity and amnesty thus is not purely moral, but an effort to recover the theory and practice of democracy from below. The recovery begins by bringing to trial the state subversives of that democracy and reconstructing the democratic experience, thus liberating contemporary civil society from the fear of the past and offering it an example for the future. A democracy created from civil society and deriving its "rules of the game" from its institutions stands a far better chance of consolidation than an electoral regime based on, and allied with, the authoritarian military and state institutions continuing from the terrorist period. The first weakness of Latin American democracy today is based, in part, on the disarticulation of civil society by the military, the assassination of civic activists, and the decimation of civil organizations.

The second source of weakness of democratic consolidation in Latin America was the decision of the electoral political class to accept the idea of a pact with the authoritarian institutions. Under the terms of this pact, the civilians agreed to share power with the military, accept the new elite export model, and grant amnesty to those state officials guilty of crimes against humanity. In those cases where immunity was not granted immediately, the presence and power of the military in the new regime of "cohabitation" virtually assured the same result in a later period. The impunity laws of the electoral regimes allowed for the continuity of the same individuals, institutions and ideology responsible for the prior state terrorism. And, following a relatively short hiatus, these institutions have once again begun to practice the repressive policies of the past: In Central America this has taken the form of increasing disappearances of social activists and even members of the electoral regimes; in Brazil, the active repression of strikes and labor unions; in Argentina, an expanded role for the intelligence agencies and secret political police. Immunity has reproduced the institutional conditions for a return of authoritarian politics—today under an electoral facade, tomorrow under a totalitarian military state.

In the economic realm the new electoral regimes have perpetuated and even deepened the elite export model: They have followed the brutal anti–working-class politics of the International Monetary Fund/World Bank (cutting wages, increasing prices, etc.) and maintained payments on the foreign debt at the cost of massive hunger and malnutrition while simultaneously promoting the interests of a narrow class of Latin transnational capitalists with links to the overseas banks and markets. In response to this elite economic strategy, socioeconomic and political movements in civil society have reemerged to defend the interests of the wage-and-salaried majority. The laws granting immunity and amnesty to the repressive forces are a threat to the rebirth of civil society: They stand as a warning from the past that further demands for social justice can evoke retribution from the state.

By bringing together the military institutions and the economic model of the past, the electoral regimes have created the conditions for a new round of conflict between authoritarian state institutions and democratic forces in civil society. This confrontation is not between "democracy" and "extremists," as the apologists of the electoral regimes would have it, but between a democracy growing in civil society and a corrupt and opportunist political class subject to the rules and power of the authoritarian state.

Amnesty and immunity are both symbol and substance of the capitulation of the electoral regime to the visible power of the nonelected, nonrepresentative powers in the military and economic spheres. Earlier in the transition from military to electoral politics there was an apparent consensus among both the political class and the human rights movements in civil society to cleanse the state of torturers, assassins, and kidnappers. This was the basis for the broad democratic struggle against the dictatorships. In retrospect, however, it is clear that the consensus was viewed differently by the electoral political class and the human rights movement. The former regarded it as a tactical agreement to secure bargaining positions with the military, to be discarded once having secured acceptance by the authoritarian regime. The latter, on the other hand, viewed the agreement as a strategic one in which political office was a means (not an end) to democratizing the state.

At the theoretical level, this led to divergent conceptions of democracy: for the politicos what was essential was the establishment of rules and procedures for "honest elections"—not the transformation of the authoritarian economic and state institutions that defined the boundaries ("rules of the game") of the electoral process. For the human rights movement it was the reverse: the transformation of the state (through the prosecution of the state terrorists) and the ideology and recruitment of state personnel became the prior basis for fulfilling the majoritarian promise of democracy.

For a time, the electoral class has been able to deceive and/or manipulate public opinion through a limited number of trials (Argentina); study commissions that published reports that were never acted upon (Peru, Argentina, and Bolivia) or allowed only for the naming of the victims—not the military torturers and assassins (Chile); and agreements to indemnify the victims (Chile) or vague promises to consider the issue (Argentina). In Brazil, Central America, and Paraguay no official investigations were undertaken. In the cases of Guatemala and El Salvador, the elected Christian Democratic regimes did not even undertake token gestures toward examining the past—only promising to stop new repressive acts (and failing miserably at that).

More recently, the shallow commitment of the electoral politicians to the victims of military regimes has become manifest. In Argentina, the only country where terrorist generals were tried, convicted, and incarcerated for crimes against humanity, the current civilian regime has seen fit to reverse the earlier guilty verdicts. In late December 1990, President Menem pardoned the remaining senior military officials, including former armed forces' commanders Jorge Videla and Roberto Viola, for their role in the "Dirty War" of 1976–1983, which led to the disappearances and killings of at least 9,000 civilians. When tens of thousands of people took to the streets to protest this decision to grant immunity to mass murderers, the government's moral bankruptcy reached new heights: Menem denounced the demonstrations as "an expression of total savagery."[1]

In March 1991, the Aylwin government in Chile released the *Report of the Commission for Truth and Conciliation*, which exhaustively documented the responsibility of members of the Pinochet armed forces and secret police (DINA) for widespread disappearances, tortures, murders, and other atrocities against the civilian population between 1973 and 1990. The report was particularly damning of their behavior during the early period of military rule, virtually accusing the generals of orchestrating a species of low-level genocide: There was a "pattern of previous planning and central coordination . . . a will to exterminate a category of people—those deemed to have a high degree of political dangerousness."[2]

Aylwin's reluctance to act on the report in any substantial way was evidenced by his refusal to demand Pinochet's resignation as army commander, even after the latter had personally denounced the report before an assembly of 1,500 army officers. Aylwin rationalized his failure to confront the ex-president on the absurd grounds that he "has discovered in . . . Pinochet a new constitutionalist vocation."[3] Senior Catholic Church officials and local human rights organizations accused the government of capitulating to military pressure and seeking to shelve any further investigation of the terrorist Pinochet state.[4]

The electoral regimes in Argentina and Chile release, or refuse to prosecute, military officials because in their scheme of things, accommodating the demands of the armed forces takes precedence over justice for the latter's victims. Meanwhile, the sounds of concern emanating from the West have been deafening. The actions of neither Menem nor Aylwin evoked an outcry in Washington, Bonn, London, or other leading capitals.

Today, however, under conditions of immunity from prosecution, serious human rights' violations—torture, disappearances, summary executions—are on the rise throughout Latin America. In Columbia at least five people a day are victims of state political violence; in Peru more than half the country is under de facto military rule; in Guatemala scores of peasants and Indians "disappear" after military assaults on their villages every month; in El Salvador, the assassination of trade-union leaders and church people and the murder of urban and rural social activists are a feature of the political landscape; in Argentina, massive police assaults on peaceful demonstrators, military attacks on hunger rioters, and selective kidnappings are becoming commonplace. The law of impunity has become a policy tool that conservative, Christian, and social-democratic electoral regimes can use to secure the collaboration of the military in putting down legitimate protest against their economic and social policies. The experience is clear: The less a regime did to punish state terrorists in the past, the greater the likelihood that their human rights offenses will be repeated in the future.

Indisputably, the reconstruction of civil society has led to a profound divergence between the popular movements and the electoral regimes, not only in the conception and practice of democracy, but also regarding the more specific question of who decides policy. Except in Uruguay, where a referendum on amnesty was organized by the progressive forces, the issue of armed forces' immunity has been decided behind the backs of the people through agreements and "deals" between the political elite and the authoritarian military forces. In essence, through threats and military uprisings, through pressure and blackmail, the elected officials were forced to accept the boundaries of political action defined by nonelected officials using antidemocratic measures. Even in the case of Uruguay, the most telling argument used by the proponents of impunity to convince the voters was the possibility of a new military coup, the fragility of democracy, the threat of a return of terror: A sector of the political class became the medium for the threats and blackmail of the military. This intimidation of voters was almost certainly a major contributory factor in the electoral victory of the immunity forces.

Electoral systems in which major economic and political decisions, like impunity, are made through the threats and pressures of nonrepresentative, nonelective authoritarian elites cannot be referred to as pluralistic democracies or, as some have suggested, "restricted democracies." Rather, they are regimes, defined by the state institutions which establish the rules and boundaries of political action.

Conclusion

There is a grave danger that impunity laws, the politics of "reconciliation," and the preservation of authoritarian institutions, personnel, and ideology from the previous period have become an invitation for the return of the practices of mass state terrorism in Latin America once again. Those officials who have been absolved of past crimes are free to commit new homicides in the 1990s. Indeed, there are numerous cases where the civilian regimes have not only forgiven but also promoted them to higher positions in the military, police, and other state coercive institutions. The secret police and intelligence agencies responsible for disappearances and torture under the dictatorships have been in some instances renamed, merely facilitating their ability to commit new crimes under complicit democracies.

Senior civilian regime officials in Argentina have gone beyond support for impunity laws and have praised the military for its role in the Dirty War; President Menem has proceeded even further, encouraging direct military involvement in internal political conflicts. Similar experiences have occurred in Brazil and Central America where elected "presidents" have praised the armed forces for their role in repressing "subversion." The civilian regimes have come full circle: from rising to power on the backs of the popular movements in opposition to the torturers, to dependency on the military and rewriting a falsified history of past repression.

The irony of history, however, is that the civilian electoral regimes are creating their own grave diggers: by legitimating and extending the military's role in society and politics, by making them indispensable to the continuation of their rule, *they* become expendable. When the electoral regimes have lost their political usefulness in securing the legitimacy of the police and military, when they no longer can secure big loans from the US and Europe, when the economic and social crisis gets out of control, the military, with the support of the economic elites, will discard the electoral regime easily and quickly and proceed to a new round of mass disappearances and terror—easily, because the civilian regime have already increased the role of the coercive institutions, legitimized their status in the state, and allowed human rights' violations to weaken the democratic social movements in civil society.

The warning signals are already there in Argentina, Brazil, Peru, and Central

America. The military, acting with impunity, is playing an increasing role in defining the "security agenda": disappearances, killings, and torture are on the increase. This rise in state terrorism has accompanied the ascendancy of "free market" electoralists in these same countries, whose austerity measures are pushing the people's endurance to the limit, provoking strikes, protests and inevitable state violence.

Unlike the 1970s, the West has failed to respond. While celebrating the demise of Stalinist police states in Eastern Europe, it conveniently overlooks or apologizes for the continuing and deepening gross violations of human rights in Latin America's "free-market" states. The political leadership and mass media in the United States and Europe confuse democracy, which is rooted in a strong civil society and the rule of law, with the hemisphere's current electoral regimes, which cohabitat with state terrorists. Through foreign aid, loans, and diplomatic praise they have sustained governments like those in Guatemala and El Salvador, which have "disappeared" thousands of unarmed citizens.

The issue of crimes of state must once again become a high priority on the Western political agenda, particularly in those parts of Latin America where Western powers exercise influence or hegemony. Before selective crimes of today become the massive crimes of tomorrow and history repeats itself, Europeans and North Americans concerned with the stabilization of democracy must reopen the book on those in the state apparatus who have committed crimes because they are in many instances the same ones committing the crimes in the present. It is not yet too late. Even today, fifty years after the Holocaust, Nazi war criminals are brought to justice under the correct slogan of "Never again!" There are no calls for a reconciliation with the terrorists of that era. The same should hold for the Latin American state terrorists of the 1970s and 1980s. They should be put on trial in order that civil society can be allowed to act freely—to confront the economic crisis and resolve it without the threat of military interference.

The consolidation of Latin American democracy depends on vindication for the victims of state terrorism. This is both a moral and a political imperative. Those who forget the crimes of the past are doomed to repeat them in the future. The conscience of the West can and should recover the best traditions of the antifascist, anticolonial, and solidarity struggles of the recent past and speak to the literal life-and-death issues of freedom and democracy, in favor of civil society, against the rising tide of irrationalism and "free-market" terrorism.

Notes

1. Quoted in "Argentine Leader on Shaky Grounds," *Washington Report on the Hemisphere*, February 6, 1991, p. 6.

2. Quoted in "Stability Threatened by Guzman Murder," *Latin American Monitor: Southern Cone*, April 1991, p. 884. According to a study issued almost simultaneously by the Catholic Church, the report actually understated by at least 450 the number of

civilians assassinated by the Pinochet regime. See "Supreme Court Bashes Rettig," *Latin American Weekly Report*, May 30, 1991, p. 3.

3. "Army Dismisses the Rettig Report," *Latin American Weekly Report*, April 18, 1991, p. 2.

4. See "Anti-Terrorism Puts Aylwin in a Bind," *Latin American Weekly Report*, May 16, 1991, p. 10.

9

Global Transformations and the Future of Socialism in Latin America

Introduction

Five world-historic facts condition the discussion of socialism and democracy in Latin America today:

1. The collapse of the capitalist "free-market" growth model in Latin America, evidenced by a decade of regressive socioeconomic indicators (what is universally referred to as the "lost decade"), chronic crises, and no relief in sight for the Nineties.

2. The disintegration of the Stalinist model in Eastern Europe and the Soviet Union, and the emergence of a new class of neoliberal political rulers oriented toward Western capitalist integration.

3. The intensification of U.S.-Japanese-German competition for global supremacy and the increasing primacy of economic resources over military and ideological in shaping hegemonic outcomes.

4. The decline of U.S. industrial power and the increase of its ideological influence, creating a gap between its capacity to displace ideological adversaries and its economic incapacity to sustain new client regimes.

5. The end of the "Cold War" (European bloc warfare) accompanied by the nonsymmetrical withdrawal of hegemonic forces. Increasing Soviet isolationism, then internal disintegration, is accompanied by intensified U.S. and European interventionism, opening a new round of class and national conflicts, within the Eastern bloc and between the West and the Third World.

These world-historic changes present a new set of challenges for the Latin American Left, a need to rethink traditional political formulas and to cast the discussion of socialism and democracy in a new context. The new world-historic situation contains constraints and opportunities that need to be analyzed and evaluated as a prior condition to any pronouncements about the demise or advance of socialism. Moreover, these global factors need to be analyzed in the context of the profound class and political changes which have occurred in Latin America over the past twenty years and in light of the new hegemonic strategies which Washington has practiced over the past decade. The relation between the world-historic facts, sociopolitical changes, U.S. strategy, and problems of socialism and democracy in Latin America is a vast subject which can only be treated in a telegraphic fashion in this chapter.

World-Historic Facts

The failure of "free-market" capitalism in Latin America is as significant a fact in contemporary world history as the collapse of the Stalinist regimes in Eastern Europe. Only the latter has been highlighted in the world-wide capitalist media for obvious reasons. Nevertheless, the socioeconomic crises of Latin American capitalism are even more profound by any reasonable indicator: declining living standards, economic stagnation, astronomical rates of inflations, capital flight, unsupportable debt/export ratios, massive immigration, etc. If the crises and political changes in Eastern Europe are increasing the scope of Western capitalist influence, the crises in Latin America raise at a minimum serious questions about the future of capitalism and, at a maximum, have created the groundwork for the emergence of anticapitalist political regimes. At the political level, the crises of Latin American capitalism have continued and deepened, despite changes in political regimes, from military to electoral, from U.S.-backed "free-market" conservatives to Second International social democrats. This is not a crisis of the "superstructure." Nor is it a question of particular economic policies. Nationalizations or privatizations, open or regulated economies, debt payments or debt ceilings, devaluations and austerity programs, new currencies or rotating economic ministers, all have failed to stem capitalism's downward drift. If anything, the "purer" the capitalist market policies (the less regulation, restrictions on capital flows), the deeper and more profound the crises, i.e., the greater the flight of capital, the pillage of domestic resources, the capital movement into speculative sectors, as the Argentine example strikingly illustrates. Objectively, the Latin American Left has never confronted a socioeconomic situation on a continent-wide basis as "ripe" for socialist solutions as the present. The complex and difficult problem of analyzing the gap between objective conditions will be discussed later.

The disintegration of the Stalinist model in Eastern Europe and the Soviet Union, and the ascendancy of capitalist politicians, is a major historical triumph of Western imperialism but can have a potentially strategic positive value for the Socialist movement in Latin America. For those on the Latin American Left, including the revolutionary states, which received economic, ideological, and logistic aid, these changes will certainly increase their vulnerability to Western capitalist pressures. More important, the changes will probably heighten Eastern Europe's dependency and subordination to Western investors and markets, lessening its commercial ties to the Third World. Furthermore, the shift in Western Europe toward financing the exploitation of the Eastern markets and labor will limit the funds available to Latin American social democrats.

Nonetheless, several counterpoints need to be stressed. East Europe and the newly independent states of the former Soviet Union will continue to depend on export markets and imports from Latin America, even if easy credits may become less available. Second, the austerity and "free-market" policies currently pursued in Poland and Hungary are destroying longstanding social-welfare programs without stimulating growth. Sooner or later, they will provoke a new round of class and national conflicts, and the political rulers have very fragile organized support. So, the triumphs of the West may be ephemeral. More significantly, the Stalinist model was a negative factor shaping the political practices of the Latin American Left, undermining its capacity to build dynamic democratic grassroots organizations. Moreover, class-conscious workers and intellectuals were not enamored of the choice between hunger liberalism or police-state welfarism. The demise of Stalinism is a strategic asset because it opens up the perspective of building an alternative model of socialism, reflecting the deep democratic and solidarity practices found in the domestic Latin social movements.

The intensification of U.S.-Japanese-German competition for hegemony reflects the decay of the U.S. monopoly of global power of the past half-century. The implications of global hegemonic competition for the Left in Latin America are contradictory. On the one hand, it potentially opens up new markets, trading partners, and opportunities to "play off" one hegemon against another. On the other hand, the combined action of the hegemons has been a major factor in the perpetuation of the debt pillage of Latin America. The tendency of the competing hegemons is to "specialize" in different regions: Japan in Asia, the United States in the Western hemisphere, Germany in Europe (East/Central/West/South). The growth and diversification of Japanese and German investment and markets may provide some added leverage and political breathing space for progressive Latin American regimes. However, in regions considered strategic and with regimes deemed adversaries by the U.S. (Central America, Nicaragua), Europe and Japan have refrained from jumping in to replace U.S. economic ties. If and when the competition deepens into open trade wars, the Latin American Left could increase its bargaining position much more so than it has up to now.

One of the great paradoxes of our time has been the increasing ideological influence of the United States at a time of declining economic power. This reflects the growing dualism of the U.S. state: the overdevelopment of its mass media state and military apparatuses and the relative decline of its productive, industrial, and commercial structure. The result has been the increasing tendency of U.S. policy to focus on destroying or undermining rival political and economic movements and regimes without being able to finance and promote dynamic alternatives. The classic case is postinvasion Grenada with its fifty-percent unemployment.

The ascendancy of Reagan-Bush promoted "free-market" economic dogma throughout Western and Eastern Europe and in many parts of the Third World is paradigmatic. The same is true of the successful diffusion of the U.S. mass media's message and entertainment. The diffusion of the economic doctrines of unrestricted capitalism at the top and mindless mass distractions at the bottom has contributed to weakening the appeals of the welfare programs of the Left and spawned the growth of right-wing "image" politics and mass-media-created political leaders (Collor in Brazil, Belmont in Lima, etc.). The cultural and mass-media influence of the United States has been effective because it resonates with the needs of the local ruling and governing classes: U.S. cultural products transform critical publics into malleable masses for both.

Nevertheless, the ideological influence of the United States is not solely dependent on the "fit" with local ruling-class interests; it depends on the degree to which counterhegemonic movements have emerged and created autonomous spheres of political action. The globalization of U.S. cultural influence is increasingly transparent, even as it is omnipresent. Ideological influence which is not sustained by economic growth deteriorates over time, particularly where the Left is able to focus on the gap between the ideological imagery and economic realities. The strategic opportunity for the Latin American Left is found precisely in this historical gap between U.S. ideological hegemony and its economic decline and incapacity to sustain dominance.

The decline of the Cold War—namely, East-West bloc conflict—has been accompanied by nonreciprocal withdrawal of hegemonic forces. While Soviet and allied forces withdrew from Afghanistan, Cambodia, and Angola, the United States intensified its involvement with the Pol Pot–led forces in Cambodia, the Afghan tribalists, and Savimbi and National Union for the Total Independence of Angola (UNITA) in Angola; invaded Panama; extended Special Forces bases in Peru and Bolivia; and intervened massively before and during the Nicaraguan elections. The decline and withdrawal of Soviet influence in the Third World was not reciprocated by the West. On the contrary, it encouraged aggressive expansion of West Europe in the East, while revitalizing the weakening hegemonic drives in Washington. Global nuclear disarmament agreements between Gorbachev and the West may lessen nuclear threats in the North. However, increased Western interventionism in the Third World and, in particular in Latin America, means a new round of antiimperialist and class warfare. Those sectors of the Left oriented toward nationalist and class politics are better situated to intervene in this situation than the proponents of interdependence and social pacts. The Left which based its analysis and practices on "global bloc" alliances will become increasingly irrelevant. In summary, the end of the Cold War will intensify U.S. intervention in Latin America, disorient the bloc-based traditional Left, undermine reformers who envision a world without blocs as a world of peace and development, and provide increasing space and opportunities for the "nationally" anchored antiimperialist and class-struggle–oriented Left.

These "world-historic facts" that define the new configurations of global power do not impact directly on Latin America and shape the conditions of struggle for socialism. They are mediated by the state, class structure, and the global linkages of Latin American political and social forces.

Transformations in the Latin American Political and Social Structure

The ultimate impact of these contradictory world-historical changes depends on the relative strengths and weaknesses of the conflicting sociopolitical forces in Latin America, even as they shape the conditions under which they operate. The problem of analyzing the interrelationship between global changes and Latin American sociopolitical structures is complicated by the ongoing structural transformations which have occurred in Latin America over the past two decades. The problem for socialists is to take account of these structural transformations and their external ramifications and link them to an effective strategy.

A number of structural changes form the terrain for Latin American political and economic strategy. The first and most striking factor defining the Latin American social economy is the ascendancy of Latin American transnational capitalists and their associated entourage. From top to bottom of the class structure, in varying degrees of importance, Latin America has moved toward an accumulation model controlled and directed by national investors, speculators, traders, and exporters linked to international banks, markets, and finance. Interrelated at the top, Latin transnational capitalists are followed by a middle state which includes overseas dollar depositors, petty speculators, paid-in-dollars professionals and externally funded intellectuals, and, at the bottom, low-income families linked to the dollar economy through overseas remittances. Interfacing with this formal socioeconomic configuration is the dynamic illicit economy—drugs, speculation, money laundering—which is linked to the export economy and which has vertical ties throughout the social system. Both the formal and informal economies are products and promoters of the increasingly "deregulated" economy which has found political expression in the rise of right-wing "free-market" politicians and the conversion of populists (Menem) and social democrats (Carlos Andres Perez) to the same.

The main instrument of U.S. ideological influence and the principal factor generating the socioeconomic crises in Latin America is the ascendancy of the Latin American transnational capitalists and the politicians who shape economic strategies to fit their needs ("export strategies," austerity programs, debt equity swaps). If the socioeconomic crisis is generated by the unregulated economy, the extension and linkage of numerous subaltern groups operating in the unregulated market to the transnational capitalists at the top block a political solution. Insofar as the Left has to gain control over the levers of economic power, it must deal decisively with the network of capitalists who form the "transnational networks." Socialist or progressive regimes beholden to the transnationalist capitalists will be subject to the pressures and blackmail exercised by those around whom the accumulation model is organized. Latin America's transition from national to transnational capital did not follow the U.S. or European patterns or have the same consequences. Latin American capital's transition from "national" to "transnational" included not a broadening but a pillaging of the local market. It did not lead to technologically upgrading the local industry but rather to the transfer of industrial profits to finance. The deregulation of the economy led to early inflows and later massive outflows of capital. Socialism has the difficult task of uprooting the model, it cannot socialize what is not in its national sphere of power; it cannot harness the existing model to a welfare program: the class incompatibilities are too strong and the possibilities for Latin transnational capital to escape are too easy for it to accept state regulation.

The second change in the social structure is related to the first. The deregulation of the economy and the massive "informalization" of labor mean that the whole social-welfare and labor-protective legislative fabric created over the past century has been severely eroded. The working class has and has not been undermined. The massive growth of temporary labor, the multiple workplace locations, and the combined wage and nonwage payments have brought forth a labor category that is a cross between the wage-laboring class and the self-employed. These working people (pueblo trabajador) are essential, pivotal protagonists of any vital social movement for social transformation. They are the object of the depredations of the deregulated market (inflation, employment insecurity, rising prices) and the subject in the "informal market" (of buying and selling goods). Their insertion in the political process creates a new context for the organization of socialist politics in two interrelated locations—the factory and the marketplace. Socialists must devise strategies that take account of the market, imposing constraints on trade earnings without letting the market run rampant, thus increasing the costs for wage earners. New economic linkages (a parallel economy) between the working people, both in their formal and informal positions, are a necessary prior condition to political power. The parallel economy becomes the basis for unifying the heterogeneous working people in a common political organization for state power.

The third structural change has been the routinization of state terror and the continuity of the institutions of state terror before, during, and after the inauguration of electoral regimes in Latin America. The advent and prolonged crises of unregulated capitalism have been accompanied by the increasing role of the repressive state and the diminished role of the political regime. The permanent political institutions of the state have increasingly defined the "rules of the political game" and limited the scope of legislative actions by opposition politicians and parties. The *cyclical* pattern of *regime change* (military and electoral regimes) is accompanied by the *continuity* of the underlying *state structures*. The gap between bourgeois control over the state and decreasing hegemony over civil society has been filled by the increasing resort to state terror. The combined impact of deepening economic crises and expanding state terror on popular consciousness is problematical. The responses are manifold: Some blame the political class and seek "apolitical politicians" of the Right; some engage in defensive actions (general strikes) or heightened left-wing militant political activity; yet others withdraw from politics into crime and "informal" activity. The Left confronts a difficult situation between the objective socioeconomic conditions favoring its socialist project and the increasingly restrictive political conditions limiting its capacity to mobilize its constituencies. State repression has proven to have contradictory effects on exploited groups. Among the politicized and organized, repression hardens their commitments against the state or the external aggressor. Among the unorganized and less politicized, the violence is blamed on those who propose change and the tendency is to embrace elite authorities for immediate relief from violence.

The fourth and final change in Latin America and, perhaps, the most significant is the massive growth of democracy in the grassroots social movements. The alternative to the authoritarianism of Stalinist socialism and the depredations of the "free-market" electoral regimes is found in the proliferation and organization of sociopolitical movements. The movements have brought into common organization the members of the heterogeneous labor force in their neighborhood associations. They have provided a political structure in which working people are directly represented and can articulate their grievances. They have created the solidarity networks to sustain survival against the market. They have organized struggles when their representatives in the political class have been unable to deliver the promised changes. The growth and proliferation of civic, neighborhood, and workplace sociopolitical movements reflects the rising political capacities of the working people and their capacity to resist the state and exist as an alternative to the current forms of political representation.

If the transnational class at the top represents the most significant obstacle to a socialist transformation, the growth of social movements at the bottom represents the most formidable force for transforming society. Practically every major change in Latin America over the past thirty years—agrarian reforms, toppling of military regimes, social revolutions—was initiated or consummated by sociopolitical movements. The 26 of July Movement in Cuba, FSLN in Nicaragua, the industrial councils in Allende's Chile, and the agrarian reform in Peru during the 1960s were all products of movement politics. The phenomenon of the relationship between sociopolitical movements and other political formations is problematical, as is the relationship of movement to transformations of the state. But it is obvious that in Latin America the "movement" form has been the most effective structure for mobilizing and expressing the energy, enthusiasm, and intelligence of the working people. The debate about socialism and democracy must draw its negative lessons from the European Stalinist experience and its positive lessons from the practices of the ongoing Latin American sociopolitical movements.

Changing U.S. Strategy

Fundamental to pursuing a socialist strategy in Latin America in the 1990s is an understanding of Washington's political strategy based on the distinction between changes in regime and state. For U.S. strategists, political regimes represent transitory interests based on shifting political alliances anchored in elected or nonelected civilian or military officials. On the other hand, states represent strategic interests of hegemony, economy, and security and are located in the permanent institutions—the military, police, judiciary, central bank, and other "nonelected" economic bodies. Washington's alliances with state institutions are long-term, with regimes transitory.

This framework, based on the regime/state distinction, has served to guide (and explain) U.S. policy toward political change in Latin America. Washington has followed a three-pronged approach.

1. Support for regime changes when existing clients have lost power, legitimacy, and/or are threatened by mass popular movements in order to preserve the state. This policy is evident in the negotiated transition from military to electoral regimes throughout Latin America in the 1980s, which left unscathed the existing state institutions supporting U.S. strategic interests. Washington has described the cohabitation of electoral regimes and authoritarian state power as the democratization process.

2. Opposition to movements proposing to change state institutions, along with political regimes. Throughout Latin America during the 1980s, Washington promoted, financed, and assisted efforts to isolate, repress, or electorally defeat sociopolitical movements whose conception of democratization included the transformation of the state. Throughout Central America, Washington financed the repression of political parties and organizations seeking state change, while supporting Christian Democratic electoral politicians willing to collaborate with strategic state clients. A similar pattern occurred in South America: Washington distinguished between antiregime and antisystemic (state) electoralists, favoring the former and opposing the latter.

3. Promotion of state change against revolutionary state adversaries. This is best exemplified in U.S. strategy toward Nicaragua, where Washington organized and financed a military counterrevolutionary army and an electoral force to dismantle the popular-revolutionary state. The Reagan-

Bush administrations combined military violence to destroy the economy and organized an electoral force to capitalize on the internal discontent. The U.S. policy of military/economic destabilization and elections
was tried some two decades earlier in Cuba but was blocked by Castro's
refusal to allow an electoral opposition. In this approach, military and
economic aggression and social dislocation are the precondition for
supporting elections.

Washington follows a clear class-analysis approach to political change and
democracy. Political strategy is based on supporting proponents of electoral
regime change in capitalist states and advocates of state change (armed mercenaries and electoralists) in noncapitalist states. While U.S. and European propagandists and their foundation-funded intellectuals talk of "democracy without adjectives," the operational behavior of Washington strategists is guided by the criteria
of hegemonic interests.

In this context, Washington has used electoral processes against democracy.
By supporting the juxtaposition of electoral regimes and authoritarian states,
U.S. policy-makers have perpetuated massive violations of human rights in El
Salvador, Guatemala, and Honduras. They have also utilized the existence of
electoral regimes cohabitating with elitist export-based economic institutions to
perpetuate debt payments, IMF austerity programs, and multinational buyouts of
national productive enterprises. The electoral strategy has provided Washington
with an ideology to pursue the politics of the new authoritarianism—to harness
a section of the political class to the new export model, the repressive state, and
the international bankers.

Socialists in Latin America have failed, in many cases, to come to terms with
this new electoral strategy. They have considered the electoral process in itself
a partial, progressive stage, opening up space for a more complete democratization. This "quantitative" approach ("more" or "less" democracy based on access
to an electoral arena and correct voting procedures on election day) is based on
a mistaken focus on the process of regime change as the key to the democratization
process. This approach overlooks the more basic institutional constraints and the
broader inhibiting political context in which the electoral politics is embedded.
The continuation of state institutions in the political sphere and the centrality of
transnational Latin capitalists in the economic ultimately define the authoritarian
and socially regressive nature of the process. Electoral processes are determined
to be democratic by socialists when they open the prospects for transforming the
state and the elite export model, not when they are conditioned by the perpetuation
of the latter.

The prominence of nonelective state institutions and economic power (including the United States) in establishing the "political rules of the game," the
boundaries of acceptable legislation, means that the emerging electoral regime
must pursue policies that demobilize popular movements, formulate development

strategies oriented toward the Latin transnational capitalists and foreign bankers, and recognize the power and prerogatives of the military, police, and judiciary powers. As a result, under these constraints, electoral regimes have weakened the democratic component in Latin political life. If we use the term "democratic" to connote something more than electoral procedures—such as majoritarian presence and influence in civil society, the influence of popular needs in state budgetary allocations, responsiveness of public officials to popular pressures and demands, a decrease in nonelected internal and external elite control of the national economy—it is evident that the "democratic" component in Latin American public life has deteriorated over the past decade of electoral regimes. The electoral regimes have attempted to demobilize social movements and concentrate decisions in the hands of nonelected decision-makers, including overseas bankers and IMF officials. They have reduced budget allocations for public health and education to unprecedented levels. They have increased the role of the repressive state institutions in civil society.

Electoral regimes have not created conditions for democratic advance: They have deepened the division between authoritarian bourgeois state and civil society, creating the conditions for the reversion to nonelectoral regimes when and if popular discontent exceeds existing state boundaries.

United States policy has been and continues to favor the cohabitation of electoral politics and authoritarian state because it facilitates securing congressional financing of imperial clients. The challenge for the Latin American Left is to redefine the terrain for democracy. This requires a broader conception that moves beyond electoral competition over regime change and political procedures, to a reconceptualization of democratization that focuses on state transformations and the restructuring of the economic model based on the dominant Latin American transnational capitalist class.

Latin American socialists can learn from, as well as provide lessons to, the anti-Stalinist movements in East Europe. First, they can learn that bureaucratic collectivism and police states stifle popular initiatives and block the development of the productive forces. Second, they can learn that fundamental transformations require going beyond overthrowing repressive regimes, toward changes in the state apparatus and relations with former hegemonic powers. (It is interesting to contrast how the Western countries define the democratization process in Eastern Europe and Latin America: favoring wholesale state purges in one and limited regime changes in the other.) On the other hand, the Eastern European anti-Stalinists could learn from Latin American socialists the devastating socioeconomic problems that result from the application of "free-market" policies: unemployment, massive inequalities, debt, dependency, and repressive politics.

Conclusion

The dual crises, Stalinism in the East and "free-market" capitalism in Latin America, are parts of the restructuring of the world political economy. These crises suggest that movements for democracy and socially directed economies are relevant socialist responses. Western propagandists who claim to find a relationship between democracy and "free markets" are obviously economic illiterates when it comes to reading the Latin American experience. "Free-market" economic structures, elites, and policies have been the solvent dissolving democratic institutions and practices of Latin American society, eroding national productive enterprises, facilitating the flight of capital, and disintegrating the stability of working-people's households. Socialism today must be in the first instance authentically conservative: It must conserve or restore the national market, reconstruct public enterprises, stabilize household incomes, and defend traditional working-class values against the dogmatic market extremists who have uprooted households and fragmented the labor force. Socialist regimes cannot confront the world market through the existing configuration of state/private transnational capitalists and operate through their circuits. They must restructure the export economy and strengthen the national market, and the domestic productive forces and classes, at the expense of the transnational capitalists. A change in regime must be accompanied by a transformation of the state. Situations where regimes and states are based on incompatible class interests lead to a political impasse in the short run and to the overthrow of the regime by the state in the middle run. Most likely to avoid this outcome the regime sacrifices its social base to reach accommodation with the state.

Socialist regimes need to avoid engaging in electoral competition with imperial-backed opposition on the political terrain devised by its enemies. They must avoid the trap of being subject to the "pincer" operation, pressured militarily and economically from the outside and electorally attacked from the inside. Socialist regimes must see elections as the products of peace and economic reconstruction—not conditions for achieving those ends. The electoral interlocutors of a democratic socialist regime should include only those political forces that accept the basic principles of national sovereignty—and reject those parties that are the political arm of mercenary imperial-funded surrogates. These are the political reflections derived from the Sandanista electoral experience.

The decline in U.S. economic power and the spread of its ideological influence in Latin America mean that socialists have to deepen the cultural/intellectual struggle. They should focus on Washington's economic incapability to sustain its electoral clients and implement the former's vision of the good society.

Recent world-historical transformations are mediated through the structural changes taking place in Latin America and the renewed efforts of U.S. policymakers to reassert hegemony. Latin American socialists initially must unmask and confront the electoral-military strategy based on the new transnational social forces that have emerged over the past twenty years. Breaking the stranglehold of U.S. imperial domination means displacing the power of the transnational Latin American networks (capital, state, intelligentsia) through which hegemony is exercised. Socialists have to reconstruct Latin America's distinct political/economic space from below in order to address themselves to the "world-historic" transformation occurring in the global economy—the growing intercapitalist rivalries, the ascendancy of market hegemony (Japan and Germany) over military/ideological imperialism (United States).

The tasks and opportunities facing Latin American socialists are formidable: the economic crisis of capitalism is both a strength and a weakness. It creates mass disaffection and deprives the economy of resources. Apart from the democratic Left, there are, however, no other political forces on the horizon capable of meeting the daily needs of people—reconstructing stable everyday existence, recreating a national economy, and transforming the social relations of production. It is this combination of turning inward and downward in order to turn outward and upward that defines part of the socialist project. Conserving or reconstructing the solidarity and stability in work, household, and community of working people in a context of a basic transformation of social power defines contemporary socialism in Latin America as both profoundly conservative and radically transformative. Against the ravages of the unrestrained market it must conserve the solidarity of labor and household economy. It must reconstruct a new political regime and state rooted in the democratic traditions and practices of the social movements' developing socialist and democratic programs.

World-historical changes and transformations in Latin American society have a contradictory impact on the socialist Left in Latin America. Some of the changes reinforce the enemies of socialism and others create opportunities for advance. Whether the positive opportunities opened by these transformations can be turned to advantage and heighten the presence and autonomy of the Left will depend upon the creative capacity of the Left to develop strategies and programs that link its struggles to the burgeoning democratic movements.

Index